Fromm

P O R T A B L E

New York City

by Cheryl Farr Leas
with research assistance from Nathaniel R. Leas

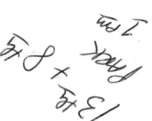

Macmillan • USA

ABOUT THE AUTHOR

Cheryl Farr Leas was a senior editor at Macmillan Travel before embarking on a freelance writing career. She also authors *Frommer's New York City from $80 a Day* and *The Complete Idiot's Travel Guide to Hawaii*; and contributes to numerous other publications. When she's not traveling, Cheryl is at home in Park Slope, Brooklyn.

MACMILLAN TRAVEL

A Pearson Education Macmillan Company

1633 Broadway
New York, NY 10019

Find us online at **www.frommers.com.**

Copyright © 2000 by Ahsuog, Inc.
Maps copyright © by Ahsuog, Inc.

MACMILLAN is a registered trademark of Macmillan, Inc.
FROMMER'S is a registered trademark of Arthur Frommer.
Used under license.

ISBN 0-02-863448-9
ISSN 1520-555X

Editor: Lisa Renaud
Production Editor: Robyn Burnett
Photo Editor: Richard Fox
Design by Michele Laseau
Staff Cartographers: John Decamillas and Roberta Stockwell
Photo Editor: Richard Fox
Page Creation by Natalie Hollifield, Marie Kristine Parial-Leonardo, Carl Pierce

SPECIAL SALES

Bulk purchases (10+ copies) of Frommer's and selected Macmillan travel guides are available to corporations, organizations, mail-order catalogs, institutions, and charities at special discounts, and can be customized to suit individual needs. For more information write to Special Sales, Macmillan General Reference, 1633 Broadway, New York, NY 10019.

Manufactured in the United States of America

5 4 3 2 1

Contents

List of Maps

AN INVITATION TO THE READER

In researching this book, we discovered many wonderful places—hotels, restaurants, shops, and more. Please tell us about them so we can share the information with your fellow travelers in upcoming editions. If you were disappointed with a recommendation, we'd love to know that, too. Please write to:

Frommer's Portable New York City 2000
Macmillan Travel
1633 Broadway
New York, NY 10019

AN ADDITIONAL NOTE

Please be advised that travel information is subject to change at any time—and this is especially true of prices. We therefore suggest that you write or call ahead for confirmation when making your travel plans. The authors, editors, and publisher cannot be held responsible for the experiences of readers while traveling. Your safety is important to us, however, so we encourage you to stay alert and be aware of your surroundings. Keep a close eye on cameras, purses, and wallets, all favorite targets of thieves and pickpockets.

WHAT THE SYMBOLS MEAN
✪ Frommer's Favorites

Our favorite places and experiences—outstanding for quality, value, or both.

The following abbreviations are used for credit cards:

AE	American Express	EURO	Eurocard
CB	Carte Blanche	JCB	Japan Credit Bank
DC	Diners Club	MC	MasterCard
DISC	Discover	V	Visa
ER	enRoute		

FIND FROMMER'S ONLINE

Arthur Frommer's Budget Travel (www.frommers.com) offers more than 6,000 pages of up-to-the-minute travel information—including the latest bargains and candid, personal articles updated daily by Arthur Frommer himself. No other Web site offers such comprehensive and timely coverage of the world of travel.

Planning Your Trip to New York City

*I*n the pages that follow, you'll find everything you need to know to handle the practical details of planning your trip to the Big Apple.

Note that there's no need to rent a car for your visit to New York. Driving is a nightmare and parking is ridiculously expensive (or near-to-impossible in some neighborhoods). It's much easier to get around using public transportation and taxis. If you're going to visit Aunt Erma on Long Island or you have some other need to travel beyond the five boroughs, call one of the major car-rental companies, such as **Hertz** (☎ **800/654-3131**; www.hertz.com), **National** (☎ **800/227-7368**; www.nationalcar.com), or **Avis** (☎ **800/230-4898**; www.avis.com), all of which have airport and multiple Manhattan locations.

1 Visitor Information

For information before you leave home, your best source (besides this book, of course) is the **New York Convention & Visitors Bureau** (NYCVB). You can call the bureau's 24-hour hotline at ☎ **800/NYC-VISIT** or 212/397-8222 to order a **Big Apple Visitors Kit**, detailing hotels, restaurants, theaters, attractions, events, and more. The bureau also has a terrific website at **www.nycvisit.com**. To speak to a travel counselor who can answer specific questions, call ☎ **212/484-1222** Monday through Friday from 9am to 5pm EST (multilingual counselors are available). If you prefer to write for information, send your request to the NYCVB at 810 Seventh Ave., New York, NY 10019.

For visitor center and information desk locations once you arrive, see "Orientation" in chapter 2.

FOR BRITISH VISITORS In late 1998, an **NYCVB Visitor Information Center** opened in London at 33–34 Carnaby St (☎ **0171/437-8300**). The new center offers a wealth of information and free one-on-one travel-planning assistance to New

York-bound travelers. It's open Monday through Friday from 10am to 4pm.

SITE SEEING: THE BIG APPLE ON THE WEB

The NYCVB's **www.nycvisit.com** is a terrific online resource offering tons of information on the city, from trip-planning basics to tips on where to take the kids. But there's much more to be learned from the web than the official line:

- **www.newyork.sidewalk.com** The Microsoft-backed **Sidewalk** is an excellent source for up-to-the-minute information on what's happening in the city. Be patient, because Sidewalk can be a bit slow to download at times, and it may take wading through a few pages to get where you want.

- **www.newyork.citysearch.com** Done in cooperation with the *Daily News* and *Time Out* magazine, **Citysearch** is much more well organized than Sidewalk, with the home page directly linking you wherever you want to go, and much quicker to load. The listings are as comprehensive as Sidewalk's, sometimes more so, but new stuff almost always hits Sidewalk first. I suggest checking them both out—that's what I do!

- **www.nytoday.com** Set up in an easy-access daily calendar format, this *New York Times* site is an expanded version of the paper's coverage. You'll find even more events listings and critics' reviews in this electronic version, including museum schedules and sports events, plus the *Times'* definitive restaurant reviews.

2 When to Go

Summer or winter, rain or shine, there's always great stuff going on in New York City, so there's no real "best" time to go.

If money is your biggest concern, you might want to visit in winter, between the first of the year and early April. Sure, the weather can suck, but hotels are suffering from the post-holiday blues, and rooms often go for a relative song.

Spring and fall are the busiest, and most expensive, seasons after holiday time. From April to June and September to November, temperatures are mild and pleasant, and the light is beautiful! Don't expect hotels to be handing you deals, but you may be able to negotiate a decent rate.

New York's spit-shined image means that the city is drawing more families these days, and they usually visit in the summer. Still, the prospect of heat and humidity keeps some people away, making

June, July, and the first half of August a generally cheaper time to visit than later in the year, and very good hotel deals are often available.

At Christmas, all bets are off—expect to pay top dollar for everything. But Thanksgiving can be a great time to come: It's a little-known secret that most hotels away from the Thanksgiving Day Parade route have empty rooms, and they're usually willing to make great deals to fill them.

NEW YORK CITY CALENDAR OF EVENTS

As with any schedule of events, the following information is always subject to change. Call the venue or the city's visitors bureau at ☎ **212/484-1222** (Mon–Fri 9am–5pm EST), or go to **www. nycvisit.com/cgi/calendar.html** for the latest details on these or other events taking place within the span of your trip.

January

• **New York National Boat Show.** Slip on your docksiders and head to the **Jacob K. Javits Convention Center** for the 90th edition, which promises a leviathan fleet of boats and marine products from the world's leading manufacturers. Call ☎ **212/ 922-1212.** January 8–16.

February

• **Chinese New Year.** Every year Chinatown rings in its own New Year (based on a lunar calendar) with two weeks of celebrations, including parades with dragon and lion dancers and vivid costumes of all kinds. The year 2000 (4698 in the Chinese designation) is the Year of the Dragon, and the Chinese New Year falls on February 5. Call the NYCVB hotline at ☎ **212/484-1222** or the Chinese Center at 212/373-1800.

✪ **Westminster Kennel Club Dog Show.** The ultimate purebred pooch fest. Some 30,000 dog fanciers from the world over congregate at **Madison Square Garden** for the "World Series of Dogdom." Call ☎ **800/455-3647** for information. Tickets become available after January 1 through **Ticketmaster** (☎ **212/ 307-7171** or 212/307-1212; www.ticketmaster.com). February 14–15.

March

• **St. Patrick's Day Parade.** More than 150,000 marchers join in the world's largest civilian parade, as Fifth Avenue from 44th to 86th streets rings with the sounds of bands and bagpipes. The parade usually starts at 11am, but go extra-early if you want a good spot. Wear green and insist you're Irish if anyone asks—you are, at least for today. Call ☎ 212/484-1222. March 17.

- **Ringling Bros. and Barnum & Bailey Circus.** The circus comes to town in grand style as elephants and bears and other performing animals parade down the city streets from the railroad at Twelfth Avenue and 34th Street to **Madison Square Garden** early on the morning before the first performance (usually well before daybreak). Call ☎ 212/465-6741 for this year's dates, or **Ticketmaster** (☎ 212/307-7171 or 212/307-1212; www. ticketmaster.com) for tickets. Usually late March to early April.

April

- **The Easter Parade.** This isn't a traditional parade, per se: There are no marching bands, no baton twirlers, no protesters. Once upon a time, New York's gentry came out to show off their tasteful but discreet toppings. Today, it's more about flamboyant exhibitionism, with hats and costumes that get more outrageous every year—and anybody can join right in for free. The parade generally runs Easter Sunday from about 10:30am to 3pm. Call ☎ 212/484-1222.

May

- ✪ **Fleet Week.** About 10,000 Navy and Coast Guard personnel are "at liberty" in New York at the end of May. Usually from 1 to 4pm daily, you can visit the ships and aircraft carriers as they dock in at the piers on the west side of Manhattan, and watch some dramatic exhibitions by the U.S. Marines. But even if you don't take in any of the events, you'll know it's Fleet Week, since those 10,000 sailors invade midtown in their starched white uniforms. It's simply wonderful—just like *On the Town* come to life. Call the **Intrepid Sea-Air-Space Museum** at ☎ 212/245-2533, or visit **www.uss-intrepid.com.** Late May.

June

- **Lesbian and Gay Pride Week and March.** Fifth Avenue goes wild as the gay/lesbian community celebrates the Stonewall Riot of June 27, 1969—which for many marks the beginning of the gay liberation movement—with bands, marching groups, floats, and plenty of panache. The parade starts on upper Fifth around 52nd Street and continues into the Village, where a street festival and a waterfront dance party with fireworks cap the day. Call ☎ 212/807-7433. Mid- to late June.

- ✪ **Shakespeare in the Park.** The Delacorte Theater in **Central Park** is the setting for first-rate free performances under the stars.

Be prepared to line up hours in advance for tickets; you're allowed to get two. Call ☎ 212/539-8750 or 212/539-8500, or point your web browser to **www.publictheater.org**. June through August.

❂ **Restaurant Week.** Dine for only $20 at some of New York's finest restaurants. Participating places vary each year, so watch for the full-page ads in the *New York Times* and other publications, or call ahead to the visitors bureau, since they usually have a list of who's participating by mid- or late May. *Reserve instantly*. One week in late June; some restaurants extend their offers through summer to Labor Day.

• **JVC Jazz Festival.** The biggest names in jazz play sites like **Avery Fisher Hall, Carnegie Hall, the Beacon Theater**, and **Town Hall;** free concerts at **Bryant Park** may also be in this year's mix. Call ☎ **212/501-1390,** or visit **www.jvc-america.com/jazz**. Late June to early July.

July

❂ **Independence Day Harbor Festival and Fourth of July Fireworks Spectacular.** Start the day amid the patriotic crowds at the Great July Fourth Festival in Lower Manhattan, watch the tall ships sail up the Hudson River in the afternoon, and then catch Macy's great fireworks extravaganza (one of the country's most fantastic) over the East River (the best vantage point is from the FDR Drive, which closes to traffic several hours before sunset). Call ☎ **212/484-1222,** or Macy's Special Events at 212/494-2922. July 4.

• **Lincoln Center Festival 2000.** This festival celebrates the best of the performing arts from all over the world—theater, ballet, contemporary dance, opera, even puppet and media-based art. Schedules are usually available in mid-March, and tickets go on sale in late May or early June. Call ☎ **212/546-2656,** or visit **www.lincolncenter.org**. July.

August

• **Lincoln Center Out-of-Doors.** Schedules for this series of free alfresco music and dance performances are available in July. Call ☎ **212/875-5108,** or visit **www.lincolncenter.org**. August to September.

• **New York Fringe Festival.** Held in a variety of tiny Lower East Side venues for a mainly hipster crowd, this ten-day arts festival presents alternative as well as traditional theater, musicals, dance, comedy, and all manner of performance art, including new media. The quality can vary wildly and some performances really push the envelope, but you'd be surprised at how many shows are actually *good*. Call ☎ **888/FRINGENYC** or 212/307-0229, or point your web browser to **www.fringenyc.org**. Mid- to late August.

☼ **U.S. Open Tennis Championships.** The final Grand Slam event of the tennis season is held at the slick new facilities at **Flushing Meadows Park** in Queens. Tickets go on sale in May, and the event sells out far in advance. You can usually scalp tickets outside the complex (an illegal practice, of course). The last few matches of the tournament are most expensive, but you'll see a lot more tennis early on, when your ticket allows you to wander the outside courts and view several different matches. Call ☎ **718/760-6200** or Telecharge at ☎ **800/524-8440** for tickets as far in advance as possible; visit **www.usopen.org** for additional information. Two weeks surrounding Labor Day.

• **Harlem Week.** The world's largest black and Hispanic cultural festival actually spans about two weeks. Expect a whole slate of music, from gospel to hip hop, and lots of other festivities. Call ☎ 212/862-7200 or 212/484-1222 for this year's schedule of events and locations. Mid-August.

September

☼ **Wigstock.** Come see Lady Bunny, Hedda Lettuce, Lypsinka, and even RuPaul—plus hundreds of other fabulous drag queens—strut their stuff. The crowd is usually wilder than the stage acts. Wigstock outgrew its original East Village location, Tompkins Square Park, and has been held on the pier at 11th Street on the Hudson River in recent years, but another move could be in the offing. For information, point your web browser to **www.wigstock.nu** or call ☎ **800/494-TIXS** or the Lesbian and Gay Community Services Center at ☎ 212/620-7310. Labor Day weekend.

• **Broadway on Broadway.** This free afternoon show features the songs and casts from virtually every Broadway production performing on a stage erected in the middle of **Times Square.** Call ☎ 212/768-1500. Early or mid-September.

• **Feast of San Gennaro.** An atmospheric Little Italy street fair honoring the patron saint of Naples, with great food, traditional music, carnival rides, games, and vendors set up along Mulberry Street north of Canal Street. Usually mid-September.

• **New York Film Festival.** Legendary hits *Pulp Fiction* and *Mean Streets* both had their U.S. premieres at the Film Society of

Lincoln Center's two-week festival, a major stop on the film fest circuit. Screenings are held in various **Lincoln Center** venues throughout the days of the festival; advance tickets are a good bet always, and a necessity for certain events (especially evening and weekend screenings). Call ☎ **212/875-5610**, or point your web browser to **www.filmlinc.com**. Two weeks from late September to early October (Sept 24–Oct 10 in 1999, Sept 22–Oct 9 in 2000).

• **BAM Next Wave Festival.** One of the city's most important cultural events takes place at the **Brooklyn Academy of Music.** The months-long festival showcases experimental new dance, theater, and music works by both renowned and lesser-known international artists. Recent celebrated performances have included Astor Piazzolla's *Maria de Buenos Aires*, the 25th anniversary of the Kronos Quartet, and choreographer Bill T. Jones's *We Set Out Early . . . Visibility Was Poor.* Call ☎ **718/636-4100** or visit **www.bam.org.** September through December.

October

• **Ice-Skating.** Show off your skating style at the diminutive **Rockefeller Center** rink (☎ **212/332-7654**), open from mid-October to mid-March (you'll skate under the magnificent Christmas tree for the month of December), or at the larger **Wollman Rink** in Central Park, at 59th Street and Sixth Avenue (☎ **212/396-1010**), which usually closes in early April, depending on the weather.

✪ **Feast of St. Francis.** Animals from goldfish to elephants are blessed as thousands of Homo sapiens look on at the **Cathedral of St. John the Divine.** A magical experience; pets, of course, are welcome. A festive fair follows the blessing. Buy tickets well in advance. Call ☎ **212/316-7540** or visit **www.stjohndivine.org.** Early October.

✪ **Greenwich Village Halloween Parade.** This is Halloween at its most outrageous, with drag queens and assorted other flamboyant types parading through the village in wildly creative costumes. The parade route has changed over the years, but most recently it has started after sunset at Spring Street and marched up Sixth Avenue to 23rd Street or Union Square. Check the papers for the exact route so you can watch—or participate, if you have the threads and the imagination. October 31.

November

✪ **New York City Marathon.** Some 25,000 hopefuls from around the world participate in the largest U.S. marathon, and at least a million fans will cheer them on as they follow a route that touches on all five New York boroughs and finishes at Central Park. Call ☎ **212/860-4455**, or point your web browser to **www.nyrrc.org**. November 7 in 1999; call for the 2000 date (most likely to be November 4 or 11).

- **Radio City Music Hall Christmas Spectacular.** A rather gaudy extravaganza starring the Radio City Rockettes and a cast that includes live animals, but lots of fun nonetheless. For information, call ☎ **212/247-4777** or visit **www.radiocity.com**; buy tickets at the box office or via Ticketmaster's **Radio City Hotline** (☎ **212/307-1000**). Mid-November to early January.

❂ **Macy's Thanksgiving Day Parade.** The procession from Central Park West and 77th Street down Broadway to Herald Square at 34th Street continues to be a national tradition. Huge hot-air balloons in the forms of Rocky and Bullwinkle, Snoopy, Underdog, the Pink Panther, Bart Simpson, and other cartoon favorites are the best part of the fun. The night before, you can usually see the big blow-up on Central Park West at 79th Street; call in advance to see if it will be open to the public again this year. Call ☎ **212/494-5432** or 212/494-2922. November 25 in 1999, November 23 in 2000.

❂ **Big Apple Circus.** New York City's homegrown, not-for-profit circus is a favorite with children and the young at heart. A tent is pitched in **Damrosch Park** at **Lincoln Center.** Tickets available starting in early October. Call ☎ **212/268-2500.** November to January.

- **The Nutcracker.** Tchaikovsky's holiday favorite is performed by the New York City Ballet at **Lincoln Center.** Tickets are usually available starting in early October. Call ☎ **212/870-5570,** or point your web browser to **www.nycballet.org.** Late November through early January.

December

❂ **Lighting of the Rockefeller Center Christmas Tree.** The annual lighting ceremony is accompanied by an ice-skating show, singing, entertainment, and a huge crowd. The tree stays lit around the clock until after the new year. Call ☎ **212/632-3975.** Early December.

❂ **Holiday Trimmings.** Stroll down festive Fifth Avenue, and you'll see doormen dressed as wooden soldiers at **FAO Schwarz,** a 27-foot sparkling snowflake floating over the intersection outside **Tiffany's,** the **Cartier** building ribboned and bowed in red, wreaths warming the necks of the **New York Public Library's** lions, and fanciful figurines in the windows of **Saks Fifth Avenue** and **Lord & Taylor.** Throughout December.

✪ **New Year's Eve.** The biggest party of them all happens in **Times Square,** where hundreds of thousands of raucous revelers count down in unison the year's final seconds until the new lighted ball drops at midnight at 1 Times Square. Call ☎ **212/354-0003** or 212/484-1222. December 31.

3 Tips for Travelers with Special Needs

FOR FAMILIES

Many hotels have babysitting services or will provide you with lists of reliable sitters. If this doesn't pan out, there's the **Baby Sitters' Guild** (☎ 212/682-0227) or the **Frances Stewart Agency** (☎ **212/439-9222**). The sitters are licensed, insured, and bonded, and can even take your child on outings.

FOR TRAVELERS WITH DISABILITIES

Hospital Audiences, Inc. (☎ **888/424-4685,** Mon–Fri 9am–5pm), provides details about accessibility at cultural institutions, hotels, restaurants, and transportation as well as cultural events adapted for people with disabilities. Trained staff members answer specific questions based on your particular needs and the dates of your trip. This nonprofit organization also publishes the **Access for All** guidebook, available by sending a $5 check to **Hospital Audiences, Inc.,** 220 W. 42nd St., 13th floor, New York, NY 10036 (☎ **212/ 575-7676;** TTY 212/575-7673; www.hospitalaudiences.org).

Another terrific source is **Big Apple Greeter** (☎ **212/669-8159;** TTY: 212/669-8273; www.bigapplegreeter.org). All of their employees are extremely well-versed on accessibility issues. They can provide a resource list of agencies that serve the city's disabled community, and sometimes have special discounts available to theater and music performances. Big Apple Greeter even offers one-to-one tours that pair volunteers with disabled visitors; reserve at least one week ahead.

GETTING AROUND   Gray Line Air Shuttle (☎ **800/ 451-0455** or 212/315-3006) operates minibuses with lifts from JFK, La Guardia, and Newark airports to midtown hotels by reservation; be sure to arrange pick-up three or four days in advance.

Taxis are required to carry people who have folding wheelchairs and Seeing Eye or hearing-ear dogs. However, don't be surprised if they don't run each other down trying to get to you; even though you shouldn't have to, you may have to wait a bit for a friendly (or fare-desperate) driver to come along.

Public buses are an inexpensive and easy way to get around New York. All buses' back doors are supposed to be equipped with wheelchair lifts (though the city has had complaints that not all are in working order). Buses also "kneel," lowering their front steps for people who have difficulty boarding. Passengers with disabilities pay half-price fares (75¢). The **subway** isn't yet fully wheelchair accessible, but some stations are. Call the **Accessable Line** at ☎ **718/596-8585** (daily 6am–9pm) for bus and subway transit info, or point your web browser to **www.mta.nyc.ny.us/nyct.**

FOR SENIOR TRAVELERS

One of the benefits of age is that travel often costs less. New York subway and bus fares are half price (75¢) for people 65 and older. Many museums and sights (and some theaters and performance halls) offer discounted entrance and tickets to seniors, so don't be shy about asking. Always bring an ID card, especially if you've kept your youthful glow.

Members of the **American Association of Retired Persons (AARP)**, 601 E St. NW, Washington, DC 20049 (☎ **800/424-3410** or 202/434-2277; www.aarp.org), get discounts not only on hotels but on airfares and car rentals, too. If you're not already a member, do yourself a favor and join.

FOR GAY & LESBIAN TRAVELERS

If you want help planning your trip to New York, the **International Gay & Lesbian Travel Association (IGLTA)** (☎ **800/448-8550** or 954/776-2626; fax 954/776-3303; www.iglta.org) can link you up with the appropriate gay-friendly service organization or tour specialist. Members are kept informed of gay and gay-friendly hoteliers, tour operators, and airline and cruise-line representatives.

The **Lesbian and Gay Community Services Center** is at 1 Little W. 12th Street, between Ninth Avenue and Hudson Street, one block south of West 13th Street (☎ **212/620-7310;** www.gaycenter.org), and is open daily 9am to 10:30pm. (This is its temporary home for about two years while its headquarters at 208 W. 13th St. is being renovated.) You can call to request the Community Calendar of Events that lists happenings like lectures, dances, concerts, readings, and films.

Another good source for lesbian and gay events during your visit is **Homo Xtra (HX)**, a weekly magazine you can pick up in appropriate bars, clubs, and stores throughout town. Lesbians now have their own version, **HX for Her.** Both mags have information online at **www.hx.com.** In addition, the weekly **Time Out New York** boasts a terrific gay and lesbian section.

4 Getting There

BY PLANE

Three major airports serve New York City: **John F. Kennedy International Airport** (JFK) in Queens, about 15 miles (or one hour's driving time) from midtown Manhattan; **LaGuardia Airport** also in Queens, about 8 miles (or 30 minutes) from midtown; and **Newark International Airport** in nearby New Jersey, about 16 miles (or 45 minutes) from midtown. Online information on all three airports is available at **www.panynj.gov.**

Almost every major domestic carrier serves at least one of these airports; most serve two or all three. Among them are: **America West** (☎ 800/235-9292; www.americawest.com), **American** (☎ 800/433-7300; www.americanair.com), **Continental** (☎ 800/525-0280 or 800/523-3273; www.flycontinental.com), **Delta** (☎ 800/221-1212; www.delta-air.com), **Northwest** (☎ 800/225-2525; www.nwa.com), **TWA** (☎ 800/221-2000; www.twa.com), **US Airways** (☎ 800/428-4322; www.usairways.com), and **United** (☎ 800/241-6522; www.ual.com). Most major international carriers also serve New York.

These smaller, sometimes struggling airlines may offer lower fares, but don't expect the same kind of service you get from the majors: **Frontier AirTran** (☎ 800/AIRTRAN; www.airtran.com), **Spirit Airlines** (☎ 800/772-7117; www.spiritair.com), **Midway** (☎ 800/446-4392; www.midwayair.com), **Midwest Express** (☎ 800/452-2022; www.midwestexpress.com), **Tower Air** (☎ 800/34-TOWER or 718/553-8500; www.towerair.com), **ATA** (☎ 800/I-FLY-ATA; www.ata.com), **SunJet International** (☎ 800/4-SUNJET; www.sunjet.com), and **Sun Country** (☎ 800/752-1218; www.suncountry.com). The nation's leading discount airline, **Southwest** (☎ 800/435-9792; www.iflyswa.com), flies into Islip's MacArthur Airport on Long Island, 40 miles east of Manhattan.

TRANSPORTATION TO & FROM THE NEW YORK AREA AIRPORTS

For complete transportation information for all three airports (JFK, La Guardia, and Newark), call **Air-Ride** (☎ 800/247-7433); it

Money-Saving Package Deals

Before you start your search for the lowest airfare, you may want to consider booking your flight as part of a travel package.

Package tours are not the same as escorted tours. They are simply a way to buy airfare and accommodations (and sometimes extras like sightseeing tours and hard-to-get theater tickets) at the same time. For visiting New York, a package can be a smart way to go. In many cases, a package that includes airfare, hotel, and transportation to and from the airport will cost you less than your hotel bill alone had you booked it yourself. That's because packages are sold in bulk to tour operators, who then resell them to the public at a cost that drastically undercuts standard rates. Packages, however, vary widely. Some offer the same hotels for lower prices. Some offer a better class of hotels than others. Some offer the same hotels for lower prices. With some packagers, your choice of accommodations and travel days may be limited. Which package is right for you depends entirely on what you want.

The best place to start your search for a package deal is the travel section of your local Sunday newspaper. Also check the ads in the back of national travel magazines like *Travel & Leisure*, *National Geographic Traveler*, and *Condé Nast Traveler*.

One of the biggest packagers in the Northeast, **Liberty Travel** (☎ **888/271-1584**; www.libertytravel.com) boasts a full-page ad in many Sunday papers. You won't get much in the way of service, but you will get a good deal. They offer great-value 2- to

gives recorded details on bus and shuttle companies and private car services registered with the New York and New Jersey Port Authority.

On the arrivals level at each airport, the Port Authority also has Ground Transportation Information counters where you can get information and book on all manner of transport. Most transportation companies also have courtesy phones near the baggage-claim area.

Your best bet is to stay away from the MTA when traveling to and from the airport. You might save a few dollars, but subways and buses that currently serve the airports involve multiple transfers and staircases up and down which you must drag your luggage. On some subways you'd be traveling through undesirable neighborhoods. Spare yourself the drama.

7-night New York packages that usually include such freebies as a Circle Line cruise and discounts at Planet Hollywood, plus lots of good hotels to choose from.

The major airlines offering good-value packages to New York include **Continental Airlines Vacations** (☎ 800/634-5555; www.coolvacations.com); **Delta Vacations** (☎ 800/872-7786; www.deltavacations.com); **United Vacations** (☎ 800/328-6877; www.unitedvacations.com); **US Airways Vacations** (☎ 800/455-0123; www.usairwaysvacations.com); **American Airlines Vacations** (☎ 800/321-2121; aav3. aavacations.com); and **Northwest WorldVacations** (☎ 800/800-1504; www.nwa.com/vacpkg).

For one-stop shopping on the web, go to **www.vacationpackager.com**, a search engine that will link you to many different package-tour operators offering New York City vacations, often with a company profile summarizing the company's basic booking and cancellation terms.

In New York, many **hotels** also offer package deals, especially for weekend stays. Some of the best deals in town are those that include theater tickets, sometimes for otherwise sold-out shows like *The Lion King.* (Most aren't air/land combos, however; you'll have to book your airfare separately.) I've included tips on hotels that regularly offer them in chapter 3, but always ask about available packages when you call any hotel.

TAXIS Taxis are available at designated taxi stands outside the terminals, with uniformed dispatchers on hand during peak hours (follow the **Ground Transportation** or **Taxi** signs). There may be a long line, but it generally moves pretty quickly. Fares, whether fixed or metered, do not include bridge and tunnel tolls ($3.50 to $4) or a tip for the cabbie (15% to 20% is customary). They do include all passengers in the cab and luggage—never pay more than the metered or flat rate, except for tolls and a tip (from 8pm to 6am a 50¢ surcharge also applies on New York yellow cabs). Taxis have a four-passenger limit. For more on taxis, see "Getting Around" in chapter 2.

- **From JFK:** At press time, the flat rate of $30 to and from Manhattan (plus any tolls and tip) was in place. The meter will not be turned on and the surcharge will not be added.

- **From La Guardia.** $20 to $25, metered.
- **From Newark.** The dispatcher for New Jersey taxis gives you a slip of paper with a flat rate ranging from $30 to $45 (toll and tip extra, depending on where you're going in Manhattan. The yellow-cab fare from Manhattan to Newark is the meter amount plus $10 and rolls (about $40 to $50, perhaps a few dollars more with tip).

PRIVATE CAR & LIMOUSINE SERVICES Private car and limo companies provide convenient 24-hour door-to-door airport transfers. Call at least 24 hours in advance (even earlier on holidays), and a driver will meet you near baggage claim or at your hotel for a return trip. Prices can vary slightly, but expect to pay around the same as you would for a taxi if you request a basic sedan and have only one stop; toll and tip policies are the same. (Note that car services are not subject to the flat-rate rule that taxis have for rides to and from JFK.) Ask when booking what the fare will be and if you can use your credit card to pay for the ride so there are no surprises at drop-off time. There may be waiting charges tacked on if the driver has to wait an excessive amount of time for your plane to land when picking you up, but the dispatcher will usually check on your flight beforehand to get an accurate landing time.

I've had the best luck with **Carmel** (☎ **800/922-7635** or 212/666-6666); **Executive Town Car & Limousines** (☎ **800/716-2799** or 516/538-8551), which also serves New Jersey and Connecticut; and **Allstate** (☎ **800/453-4099** or 212/741-7440). All have good cars, responsive dispatchers, and polite drivers.

PRIVATE BUSES & SHUTTLES Gray Line Air Shuttle (☎ 800/451-0455 or 212/315-3006; www.graylinenewyork.com) vans depart JFK, La Guardia, and Newark every 20 minutes between 7am and 11:30pm. They will drop you off at most hotels between 23rd and 63rd streets in Manhattan, or Port Authority (34th Street and Seventh Avenue) or Grand Central (42nd Street and Park Avenue) terminals. No reservation is required; just go to the ground-transportation desk or use the courtesy phone in the baggage-claim area and ask for Gray Line. You must call a day in advance to arrange a hotel pickup. The one-way fare to and from JFK is $19, to and from La Guardia is $16, and to and from Newark is $19, but you can save a few bucks by pre-paying your round-trip at the airport.

The familiar blue vans of **Super Shuttle** (☎ **800/258-3826** or 718/482-9703; www.supershuttle.com/nyc.htm) serve all three area airports, providing door-to-door service to Manhattan and points on Long Island every 15 to 30 minutes around the clock. As with Gray Line, you don't need to reserve your airport-to-Manhattan ride; just go to the ground-transportation desk or use the courtesy phone in the baggage-claim area and ask for Super Shuttle. Hotel pickups for your return trip require 24 to 48 hours' advance booking. One-way fares are $15 to and from JFK, $14 to and from LaGuardia, and $17 to and from Newark.

New York Airport Service (☎ **718/706-9658**) buses travel from JFK and La Guardia to the **Port Authority Bus Terminal** (42nd Street and Eighth Avenue), **Penn Station** (34th Street and Seventh Avenue), **Grand Central Terminal** (Park Avenue between 41st and 42nd streets), or your **midtown hotel,** plus the **Jamaica LIRR Station in Queens,** where you can pick up a train for Long Island. Follow the **Ground Transportation** signs to the curbside pickup or look for the uniformed agent. Buses depart the airport every 20 to 70 minutes (depending on your departure point and destination) between 6:30am and midnight. Buses to JFK and La Guardia depart the Port Authority and Grand Central Terminal on the Park Avenue side every 15 to 30 minutes, depending on the time of day and the day of the week. To request direct shuttle service from your hotel, call at least 24 hours in advance. One-way fare for JFK is $13, and $10 to and from La Guardia; children under 12 ride free with a parent.

Olympia Trails (☎ **888/662-7700** or 212/964-6233; www.olympiabus.com) provides frequent service from Newark Airport to four Manhattan locations: the **World Trade Center** (on West Street, next to the Marriott World Trade Center Hotel), **Penn Station** (the pickup point is the northwest corner of 34th Street and Eighth Avenue and the drop-off point the southwest corner), the **Port Authority Bus Terminal** (on 42nd Street between Eighth and Ninth avenues), and **Grand Central Terminal** (41st Street between Park and Lexington). Passengers to and from the Grand Central Terminal location can connect to Olympia's midtown shuttle vans, which service most hotels between 30th and 65th streets. From the above departure points in Manhattan, service runs every 15 to 30 minutes depending on your pickup point; call for exact schedule. The one-way fare is $10, or $15 if you connect to the hotel shuttle.

BY TRAIN

Amtrak (☎ **800/USA-RAIL;** www.amtrak.com) runs frequent service to Penn Station (Seventh Avenue between 31st and 33rd streets). To get the best rates, book early (as much as six months in advance) and travel on weekends.

BY BUS

Greyhound (☎ **800/231-2222**) buses arrive at the **Port Authority Terminal** (Eighth Avenue between 40th and 42nd streets). I don't suggest taking the bus, because the ride is long and uncomfortable, and fares are usually no cheaper than the much quicker and more comfortable train.

BY CAR

From the **New Jersey Turnpike** (I-95) and points west, there are three Hudson River crossings into the city's west side: the **Holland Tunnel** (lower Manhattan), the **Lincoln Tunnel** (midtown), and the **George Washington Bridge** (upper Manhattan).

From **upstate New York,** take the **New York State Thruway** (I-87), which becomes the **Major Deegan Expressway** (I-87) through the Bronx. For the east side, continue to the Triborough Bridge and then down the FDR Drive. For the west side, take the Cross Bronx Expressway (I-95) to the Henry Hudson Parkway (9A) or the Saw Mill River Parkway to the Henry Hudson Parkway south.

From **New England,** the **New England Thruway** (I-95) connects with the **Bruckner Expressway** (I-278), which leads to the Triborough Bridge and the FDR on the east side. For the west side, take the Bruckner to the Cross Bronx Expressway (I-95) to the Henry Hudson Parkway south.

5 For Foreign Visitors

ENTRY REQUIREMENTS

The following requirements may have changed somewhat by the time you plan your trip. Check at any U.S. embassy or consulate for current information and requirements, or plug into the U.S. State Department's website at **http://travel.state.gov.** Go to **http:// travel.state.gov/visa_services.html** for the latest entry requirements, while **http://travel.state.gov/links.html** will provide you with contact information for U.S. embassies and consulates worldwide.

VISAS The U.S. State Department has a Visa Waiver Pilot Program allowing citizens of certain countries to enter the United States without a visa for stays of up to 90 days.

At press time, this visa waiver program applied to citizens of these countries: Andorra, Argentina, Australia, Austria, Belgium, Brunei, Denmark, Finland, France, Germany, Iceland, Ireland, Italy, Japan, Liechtenstein, Luxembourg, Monaco, the Netherlands, New Zealand, Norway, San Marino, Slovenia, Spain, Sweden, Switzerland, and the United Kingdom. Citizens of these countries need only a valid passport and a round-trip air or cruise ticket in their possession upon arrival.

Canadian citizens may enter the United States without visas; they need only proof of residence.

Citizens of all other countries must have: (1) a valid passport that expires at least six months later than the scheduled end of their visit to the United States; and (2) a tourist visa, which may be obtained without charge from any U.S. consulate.

Obtaining a Visa To obtain a visa, you must submit a completed application form (either in person or by mail) with a $1^1/_2$-inch-square photo, and must demonstrate binding ties to a residence abroad. Usually you can obtain a visa at once or within 24 hours, but it may take longer during the summer rush from June through August. If you cannot go in person, contact the nearest U.S. embassy or consulate for directions on applying by mail. Your travel agent or airline office may also be able to provide you with visa applications and instructions. The U.S. consulate or embassy that issues your visa will determine if you will be issued a multiple- or single-entry visa and any restrictions regarding the length of your stay.

British subjects can obtain up-to-date passport and visa information by calling the **U.S. Embassy Visa Information Line (☎ 0891/ 200-290)** or the **London Passport Office (☎ 0990/210-410)** for recorded information).

MEDICAL REQUIREMENTS Unless you're arriving from an area known to be suffering from an epidemic (particularly cholera or yellow fever), inoculations or vaccinations are not required for entry into the United States. If you have a disease that requires treatment with narcotics or syringe-administered medications, carry a valid signed prescription from your physician to allay any suspicions that you may be smuggling narcotics (a serious offense that carries severe penalties in the U.S.).

For up-to-the-minute information concerning HIV-positive travelers, contact the Center for Disease Control's **National Center for HIV** (☎ **404/332-4559;** www.hivatis.org) or the **Gay Men's Health Crisis** (☎ **212/367-1000;** www.gmhc.org).

DRIVER'S LICENSES   Foreign driver's licenses are mostly recognized in the U.S., although you may want to get an international driver's license if your home license is not written in English.

MONEY

The U.S. monetary system is simple: The most common bills (all ugly, all green) are the $1 (colloquially, a "buck"), $5, $10, and $20 denominations. There are also $2 bills (seldom encountered), $50 bills, and $100 bills (the last two are usually not welcome as payment for small purchases). Note that a newly redesigned $100 and $50 bill were introduced in 1996, and a redesigned $20 bill in 1998. Expect to see redesigned $10 and $5 notes in the year 2000. Despite rumors to the contrary, the old-style bills are still legal tender.

There are six denominations of coins: 1¢ (1 cent, or a penny); 5¢ (5 cents, or a nickel); 10¢ (10 cents, or a dime); 25¢ (25 cents, or a quarter); 50¢ (50 cents, or a half dollar); and the rare $1 piece. A new gold $1 piece will be introduced by the year 2000.

The "foreign-exchange bureaus" so common in Europe are rare even at airports in the United States, and nonexistent outside major cities. You'll find them in New York's prime tourist areas like Times Square, but expect to get extorted on the exchange rate. **American Express** (☎ **800/AXP-TRIP;** www. americanexpress. com) has many offices throughout the city, including at the New York Hilton, 1335 Sixth Ave., at 53rd Street (☎ 212/664-7798); the New York Marriott Marquis, 1535 Broadway, in the 8th floor lobby (☎ 212/575-6580); on the mezzanine level at Macy's Herald Square, 34th Street and Broadway (☎ 212/695-8075); and 65 Broadway, between Exchange Place and Rector Street (☎ 212/493-6500). **Thomas Cook Currency Services** (☎ **212/753-0132;** www.thomascook.com) has locations at JFK Airport; 1590 Broadway, at 48th Street (☎ 212/265-6049); 317 Madison Ave., at 42nd Street (☎ 212/883-0040); and 511 Madison Ave., at 53rd St. (☎ 212/753-2398).

2

Getting to Know
New York City

*T*his chapter gives you an insider's take on Manhattan's most distinctive neighborhoods and streets, tells you how to get around town, and serves as a handy reference to everything from personal safety to libraries and liquor.

1 Orientation

VISITOR INFORMATION
INFORMATION OFFICES

The **Times Square Visitors Center,** 1560 Broadway, between 46th and 47th streets (where Broadway meets Seventh Avenue), across from the TKTS booth (☎ **212/768-1560;** www.timessquarebid.org), is the city's top info stop. It features a helpful information desk offering loads of citywide information. There's also a tour desk selling tickets for Gray Line bus tours and Circle Line boat tours; a Metropolitan Transportation Authority (MTA) desk staffed to sell MetroCard fare cards, provide maps, and answer all of your questions on the transit system; a Broadway Ticket Center selling full-price show tickets; ATMs and currency exchange machines; computer terminals with free Internet access courtesy of Yahoo!; an international newsstand; and more. It's open daily from 8am to 8pm.

The **NYCVB Visitor Information Center** is at 810 Seventh Ave., between 52nd and 53rd streets. In addition to loads of information on attractions and a multilingual information counselor on hand to answer questions, the center also has interactive terminals that provide free touch-screen access to visitor information via Citysearch and sell advance tickets to major attractions. There's also an ATM and a bank of phones that connect you directly with American Express card member services. The center is open Monday through Friday from 8:30am to 5:30pm, and Saturday and Sunday from 9am to 5pm. For over-the-phone assistance, call ☎ **212/484-1222** weekdays from 9am to 5pm.

PUBLICATIONS

For comprehensive listings of films, concerts, performances, sporting events, museum and gallery exhibits, street fairs, and special events, the following publications are your best bets:

- **The New York Times (www.nytimes.com)** features terrific arts and entertainment coverage, particularly in the two-part Friday "Weekend" section and the Sunday "Arts & Leisure" section.
- **Time Out New York (www.timeoutny.citysearch.com)** is my favorite weekly magazine. *TONY* features excellent coverage in all categories, and it's attractive, well organized, and easy to use. A new issue hits newsstands every Thursday.
- The free weekly Village Voice (www.villagevoice.com), the city's legendary alterna-paper, is available late Tuesday downtown and early Wednesday in the rest of the city. The arts and entertaiment coverage couldn't be more extensive, but I find the paper a bit unwieldy to navigate, and the exposé tone of its features can be tiresome.

Other useful weeklies include the glossy **New York** magazine (**www.newyorkmag.com**), whose "Cue" section is a selective guide to city arts and entertainment; and **The New Yorker,** which features an artsy "Goings On About Town" section at the front of the magazine.

CITY LAYOUT

Open a map and you'll see the city is comprised of five boroughs: **Manhattan;** the **Bronx; Queens; Brooklyn;** and **Staten Island.** But it is Manhattan, the long finger-shaped island pointing southwest off the mainland, that most visitors think of when they envision New York. Despite the fact that it's the city's smallest borough ($13^1/_2$ miles long, $2^1/_4$ miles wide, 22 square miles), Manhattan contains the city's most famous attractions, buildings, and cultural institutions.

In most of Manhattan, finding your way around is a snap because of the logical, well-executed grid system by which the streets are numbered. If you can discern uptown and downtown, and East Side and West Side, you can find your way around pretty easily.

Avenues run north and south (uptown and downtown). Most are numbered. **Fifth Avenue** divides the East Side from the West Side of town, and serves as the eastern border of Central Park north of 59th Street. **First Avenue** is all the way east and **Twelfth Avenue**

Orientation Tips

When you're giving a taxi driver an address, always specify the cross streets. New Yorkers, even most cab drivers, probably wouldn't know where to find 994 Second Ave., but they do know where to find 51st and Second. The exact number is given only as a further precision.

is all the way west. The three most important unnumbered avenues on the East Side you should know are between Third and Fifth Avenues: **Madison** (east of Fifth), **Park** (east of Madison), and **Lexington** (east of Park, just west of Third). Important unnumbered avenues on the West Side are **Avenue of the Americas,** which all New Yorkers call Sixth Avenue; **Central Park West,** which is what Eighth Avenue north of 59th Street is called as it borders Central Park on the west; **Columbus Avenue,** which is what Ninth Avenue is called north of 59th Street; and **Amsterdam Avenue,** or Tenth Avenue north of 59th.

Broadway is the exception to the rule—the only major avenue that doesn't run uptown–downtown. It cuts a diagonal path across the island, from the northwest tip down to the southeast corner. As it crosses most major avenues, it creates **squares** (Times Square, Herald Square, Madison Square, and Union Square, for example).

Streets run east–west (crosstown) and are numbered consecutively as they proceed uptown from Houston Street. So to go uptown, simply walk north of, or to a higher-numbered street, than where you are. Downtown is south of (or a lower-numbered street than) your current location. Traffic generally runs east on even-numbered streets and west on odd-numbered streets, with a few exceptions, like the major east–west thoroughfares—**14th, 23rd, 34th, 42nd, 57th, 72nd, 79th, 86th,** and so on—which have two-way traffic.

As I've already mentioned, Fifth Avenue is the dividing line between the **East Side** and **West Side** of town (except below Washington Square, where Broadway serves that function). On the East Side of Fifth Avenue, streets are numbered with the distinction East, on the West Side of that avenue they are numbered West. East 51st Street, for example, begins at Fifth Avenue and runs to the East River, and West 51st Street begins at Fifth Avenue and runs to the Hudson River.

Unfortunately, these rules don't apply to neighborhoods in Lower Manhattan, south of 14th Street—like Wall Street, Chinatown,

SoHo, TriBeCa, the Village—since they sprang up before engineers devised this brilliant grid scheme. A good map is essential when exploring these areas.

MANHATTAN'S NEIGHBORHOODS IN BRIEF

DOWNTOWN

Lower Manhattan: South Street Seaport & the Financial District   Lower Manhattan constitutes everything south of Chambers Street. Battery Park (point of departure for the Statue of Liberty and Ellis Island) is on the very south tip of Manhattan Island, while historic South Street Seaport lies a bit north on the east coast (just south of the Brooklyn Bridge). The rest of the area is considered the Financial District, which is anchored by the World Financial Center, the World Trade Center, and Battery Park City to the west and Wall Street running crosstown to the south. Most of the streets are narrow concrete canyons, with Broadway serving as the main uptown–downtown artery.

Just about all of the major subway lines converge here before they either end or head to Brooklyn (the Sixth Avenue B, D, F, Q line being the chief exception).

During the week this neighborhood is the heart of capitalism and city politics, and the sidewalks are crowded with the business-suit set. It's fun to be here at the height of the hustle and bustle, between 8am and 6pm on weekdays.

TriBeCa   Bordered by the Hudson River to the west, the area north of Chambers Street, west of Broadway, and south of Canal Street is the *Tri*angle *Be*low *Ca*nal Street, or TriBeCa. Since the 1980s, as SoHo became saturated with chic, the spillover has been quietly transforming TriBeCa into one of the city's hippest residential neighborhoods, where celebrities and families quietly coexist in cast-iron warehouses converted into spacious, expensive loft apartments. Still, historic sidestreets evoke a bygone, more human-scaled New York, as do a few hold-out businesses and old-world pubs.

The main uptown-downtown drag is West Broadway (two blocks to the west of Broadway), and the main subway line is the 1/9, which stops at Franklin in the heart of the 'hood. Take your map; the streets are a maze.

Chinatown   The former marshlands northeast of City Hall and below Canal Street, from Broadway to the Bowery, are where Chinese immigrants were forced in the 1870s. This booming neighborhood is

Manhattan Neighborhoods

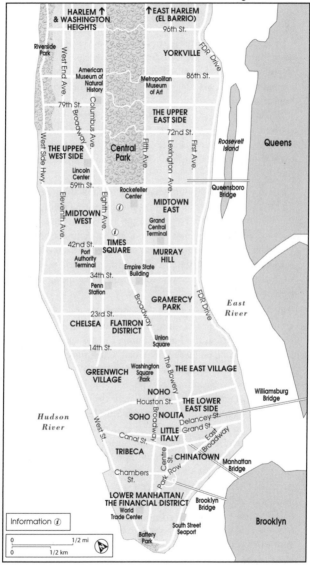

HARLEM ↑
& WASHINGTON
HEIGHTS

↑EAST HARLEM
(EL BARRIO)
96th St.

Riverside
Park

FDR Drive

YORKVILLE

West End Ave.

American
Museum of
Natural
History

Metropolitan
Museum
of Art

86th St.

79th St.

Broadway

Columbus Ave.

THE UPPER
EAST SIDE

72nd St.

THE UPPER
WEST SIDE

West Side Hwy.

Central
Park

Fifth Ave.

Lexington Ave.

First Ave.

Roosevelt
Island

Queens

Lincoln
Center
59th St.

Rockefeller
Center

Eleventh Ave.

Eighth Ave.

ⓘ

MIDTOWN
EAST

Queensboro
Bridge

MIDTOWN
WEST

ⓘ

Grand
Central
Terminal

42nd St.
Port
Authority
Terminal

TIMES
SQUARE

MURRAY
HILL

Empire State
Building

34th St.
Penn
Station

Broadway

GRAMERCY
PARK

FDR Drive

East
River

23rd St.

CHELSEA

FLATIRON
DISTRICT

Union
Square

14th St.

GREENWICH
VILLAGE

Washington
Square
Park

The Bowery

THE EAST VILLAGE

NOHO
Houston St.

Williamsburg
Bridge

SOHO

Broadway

NOLITA

THE LOWER
EAST SIDE

Delancey St.

West St.

LITTLE
ITALY

Grand St.

East Broadway

Canal St.

TRIBECA

Hudson
River

Chambers
St.

Park Centre St.

Park Row

CHINATOWN

Manhattan
Bridge

LOWER MANHATTAN/
THE FINANCIAL DISTRICT
World
Trade Center

Brooklyn
Bridge

Brooklyn

Information ⓘ

Battery
Park

South Street
Seaport

0   1/2 mi
0   1/2 km

Ⓝ

23

now a conglomeration of Asian populations. As such, it offers tasty cheap eats and exotic shops offering strange foods, herbs, and souvenirs. The area is also home to sweatshops, however, and doesn't have quite the quaint character you'd find in San Francisco. Still, it's a blast to walk down Canal Street, peering into the myriad electronics and luggage stores and watching crabs cut loose from their handlers at the exotic fish markets.

The Grand Street (B, D, Q) and Canal Street (J, M, Z, N, R, 6) stations will get you to the heart of the action. The streets are crowded during the day and empty out after around 9pm; they remain quite safe, but the neighborhood is more enjoyable during the bustle.

Little Italy   Nearby is Little Italy, just as ethnic if not quite so vibrant, and compelling for its own culinary treats. Traditionally the area east of Broadway between Houston and Canal streets, the community is shrinking today, due to the encroachment of thriving Chinatown. It's now limited mainly to Mulberry Street, where you'll find most restaurants, and just a few offshoots. Walk up Mulberry from the Grand Street Station, or east from the Spring Street station on the no. 6 line.

The Lower East Side   Of all the successive waves of immigrants and refugees who passed through here from the mid-19th century to the 1920s, it was the Eastern European Jews who left the most lasting impression on the neighborhood, which runs between Houston and Canal streets, and east of the Bowery.

Drugs and crime ultimately supplanted the immigrant communities, dragging the Lower East Side into the gutter until recently. While it has been gentrifying nicely over the last few years, the area can still be very dicey in spots. There are some remnants of what was once the largest Jewish population in America along Orchard Street, where you'll find great bargain hunting in its many fabric and clothing stores. The trendy set can be found mostly along Ludlow Street, north of Delancey, with the biggest concentration of action being just south of Houston.

This area is not well served by the subway system, so your best bet is to take the F train to Second Avenue and walk east on Houston; when you see Katz's Deli, you'll know you've arrived.

SoHo & NoLiTa   No relation to the London neighborhood of the same name, **SoHo** got its moniker as an abbreviation of "South of Houston Street" (pronounced HOUSE-ton). This super-fashionable neighborhood extends down to Canal Street, between Sixth Avenue to the west and Lafayette Street (one block east of Broadway) to the east.

An industrial zone during the 19th century, SoHo is now a prime example of urban gentrification and a major New York attraction thanks to its impeccably restored cast-iron buildings, influential arts scene, fashionable restaurants, and stylish boutiques. On weekends, the cobbled streets are crowded with gallery goers and shoppers, with the prime action between Broadway and Sullivan Street north of Grand Street.

The neighborhood is easily accessible by subway: Take the B, D, F, or Q train to the Broadway–Lafayette stop; the N, R to the Prince Street Station; or the C, E to Spring Street.

In recent years SoHo has been crawling its way east, taking over Mott and Mulberry streets—and white-hot Elizabeth Street in particular—north of Kenmare Street, an area now known as **NoLiTa** for its *No*rth of *Li*ttle *Ita*ly location. NoLiTa is becoming increasingly well known for its hot shopping prospects. The 6 to Spring Street will get you closest by subway, but it's just a short walk east from SoHo proper.

The East Village   The East Village, which extends between 14th Street and Houston Street, from Broadway east to First Avenue and beyond to Avenues A, B, C, and D, is where the city's real Bohemia has gone. It's a fascinating mix of affordable ethnic and trendy restaurants, upstart clothing designers and kitschy boutiques, punk-rock clubs (yep, still) and folk cafes, all of which give the neighborhood a youthful vibe. The gentrification that has swept the city has made a huge impact on this neighborhood, but there's still a seedy element that some of you won't find appealing.

Unless you're traveling along 14th Street (the L Line will drop you off at Third and First avenues), your best bet is to take the N, R to 8th Street or the 6 to Astor Place and walk east. Always stay alert in the East Village. The landscape changes from one block to the next, especially the farther east you go. Venture only with care into Alphabet City (avenues A, B, C, and D).

Greenwich Village   Tree-lined streets crisscross and wind, each block revealing yet another row of Greek Revival town houses, a well-preserved Federal-style house, or a peaceful courtyard or square. This is "the Village," from Broadway west to the Hudson River, bordered by Houston Street to the south and 14th Street to the north. It defies Manhattan's orderly grid system with streets that predate it, virtually every one choc-a-block with activity, and unless

you live here it may be impossible to master the lay of the land—
so be sure to have a map on hand as you explore.

The Village changes faces depending on what block you're on.
Some of the highest-priced real estate in the city runs along lower
Fifth Avenue, which dead-ends at Washington Square Park. Serpen-
tine Bleecker Street stretches through most of the neighborhood,
and is emblematic of the area's historical bent. The tolerant,
anything-goes attitude in the Village has fostered a large gay community, which is still largely in evidence around Christopher Street
and Sheridan Square. The streets west of Seventh Avenue, an area
known as the West Village, boast a more relaxed vibe and some of
the city's most charming and historic brownstones. Three colleges
(New York University, Parsons School of Design, and the New
School for Social Research) keep the area thinking young—hence
the popularity of Eighth Street, lined with shops selling cheap, hip
clothes to bridge-and-tunnel kids and the college crowd.

The Seventh Avenue line (1, 2, 3, 9) is the area's main subway
artery, while the West 4th Street stop (where the A, C, E lines meet
the B, D, F, Q lines), serves as its central hub.

MIDTOWN

Chelsea   This neighborhood is coming on strong of late as a hip
address, especially for the gay community. A low-rise composite of
town houses, tenements, lofts, and factories, Chelsea comprises
roughly the area west of Sixth Avenue from 14th to 30th streets. Its
main arteries are Seventh and Eighth avenues, and it's primarily
served by the C, E and 1, 9 subway lines.

The Chelsea Piers sports complex to the far west and a host of
shops, well-priced bistros, and thriving bars along the main drags
have contributed to the area's rebirth. You'll find a number of very
popular flea markets set up in parking lots along Sixth Avenue, between 24th and 27th streets, on the weekends. The cutting edge of
today's New York art scene is on far West 22nd Street, the city's
newest "gallery row."

The Flatiron District, Union Square & Gramercy Park   These
adjoining and at places overlapping neighborhoods are some of the
city's most appealing.

The **Flatiron District** lies south of 23rd Street to 14th Street,
between Broadway and Sixth Avenue, and centers around the historic Flatiron Building on 23rd (so named for its triangular shape)
and Park Avenue South, which has become a sophisticated new

Restaurant Row. Below 23rd Street along Sixth Avenue, mass-market discounters like Filene's Basement and Bed Bath & Beyond have moved in. The shopping gets classier on Fifth Avenue and along Broadway, the city's home-furnishings alley.

Union Square is the hub of the entire area; the N, R, 4, 5, 6, and L trains stop here, making it easy to reach from most other city neighborhoods. Union Square has experienced a major renaissance in the last decade. It's perhaps best known as the setting for New York's premier greenmarket every Monday, Wednesday, Friday, and Saturday.

From about 16th to 23rd streets, east from Park Avenue South to about Second Avenue, is the leafy, largely residential district known as **Gramercy Park.**

Times Square & Midtown West   Midtown West, the vast area from 34th to 59th streets west of Fifth Avenue to the Hudson River, is New York's tourism central, where you'll find the bright lights and bustle that draw people from all over the world.

The 1, 2, 3, 9 subway line serves the massive neon station at the heart of Times Square, at 42nd Street between Broadway and Seventh Avenue, while the B, D, F, Q line runs up Sixth Avenue to Rockefeller Center. The N, R line cuts diagonally across the neighborhood, following the path of Broadway before heading up Seventh Avenue at 42nd Street. The A, C, E line serves the west side, running along Eighth Avenue.

If you know New York but haven't been here in a few years, you'll be quite surprised by the "new" Times Square. Longtime New Yorkers like to kvetch nostalgic about the glory days of the old peep-show-and-porn-shop Times Square that this cleaned-up, Disney-fied one supplanted, but the truth is that it's a hugely successful regentrification. Most of the great Broadway theaters light up the streets just off Times Square.

Midtown East & Murray Hill   Midtown East, the area including Fifth Avenue and everything east from 34th to 59th streets, is the more upscale side of the midtown map. This side of town is short of subway trains, served primarily by the Lexington Avenue 4, 5, 6 line.

Midtown East is where you'll find the city's finest collection of grand hotels, mostly along Lexington Avenue and near the park at the top of Fifth. The stretch of Fifth Avenue from Saks at 49th Street extending to FAO Schwarz at 59th is home to the city's most high-profile haute shopping.

Claiming the territory east from Madison Avenue, **Murray Hill** begins somewhere north of 23rd Street (the line between it and Gramercy Park is fuzzy), and is most clearly recognizable north of 34th Street to 42nd Street. This is largely a quiet residential neighborhood, most notable for its handful of good budget and mid-priced hotels.

UPTOWN

The Upper West Side   North of 59th Street and encompassing everything west of Central Park, the Upper West Side contains Lincoln Center, arguably the world's premier performing-arts venue; the American Museum of Natural History, whose renovated Dinosaur Halls garner justifiably rave reviews; and a number of mid-priced hotels whose larger-than-midtown rooms and nice residental location make them particularly good bets for families. Unlike the more stratified Upper East Side, the Upper West Side is home to an egalitarian mix of middle-class yuppiedom, laid-back wealth, and ethnic families who were here before the gentrification. Two major subway lines service the area: the 1, 2, 3, 9 line runs up Broadway, while the B and C trains run up glamorous Central Park West.

The Upper East Side   North of 59th Street and east of Central Park is some of the most expensive residential real estate in the city—and probably the world. This is New York at its most gentrified: Walk along Fifth and Park avenues, especially between 60th and 80th streets, and you're sure to encounter some of the wizened WASPs and Chanel-suited socialites that make up the most rarefied of the city's population. Madison Avenue to 79th Street is the monied crowd's main shopping strip, so bring your platinum card. The main attraction of this neighborhood is Museum Mile, the stretch of Fifth Avenue fronting Central Park that's home to no fewer than ten terrific cultural institutions, anchored by the mind-boggling Metropolitan Museum of Art. The Upper East Side is served solely by the Lexington Avenue subway line (4, 5, 6 trains).

Harlem   Harlem is really two areas. Harlem proper stretches from river to river, beginning at 125th Street on the West Side and 96th Street on the East Side. Spanish Harlem (El Barrio), an enclave east of Fifth Avenue, runs between East 100th and East 125th streets. Parts of Harlem are benefiting from the same kinds of revitalization that has swept so much of the city, with national-brand retailers moving in and visitors arriving to tour historic sites related to the Golden Age of African-American culture. By all means, come see

Harlem—it's one of the city's most vital and historic neighborhoods. But your best bet is to take a guided tour (see chapter 5). Sights tend to be far apart, and neighborhoods change quickly. Don't wander thoughtlessly through Harlem, especially at night.

2   Getting Around

Frankly, Manhattan's transportation systems are a marvel. It's simply miraculous that so many people can gather on this little island and move around it. For the most part, you can get where you're going pretty quickly and easily using some combination of subways, buses, cabs, and walking.

Forget driving yourself around the city. It's not worth the headache. If you do arrive in New York City by car, park it in a garage (expect to pay in the neighborhood of $20 to $30 per day) and leave it there for the duration of your stay.

As you walk around the city, **never take your walking cues from the locals.** Wait for walk signals, and always use crosswalks—don't cross in the middle of the block, or you could quickly end up with a jaywalking ticket (or worse—as a flattened statistic). And **always pay attention to the traffic flow.** Walk as if you're driving, staying to the right. Pay attention to what's happening in the street, even if you have the right of way. At intersections, keep an eye out for drivers or bicyclists who don't yield, turn without looking, or think a yellow traffic light means "Hurry up!" as you cross.

BY SUBWAY

The much-maligned subway system is actually the best way to travel around New York, especially during rush hours. The subway runs 24 hours a day, seven days a week.

PAYING YOUR WAY   The subway fare is $1.50 (half-price for seniors and those with disabilities), and children under 44 inches tall ride free (up to three per adult). **Tokens** still exist (for now), but most people pay fares these days with the **MetroCard,** a magnetically encoded card that debits the fare when swiped through the turnstile, or the farebox on any city bus. Once you're in the system, you can transfer freely to any subway line that you can reach without exiting your station. MetroCards—not tokens—also allow you **free transfers** between the bus and subway within a two-hour period.

The MetroCard can be purchased in a few different configurations:

Pay-Per-Ride MetroCards, which can be used for up to four people by swiping up to four times (bring the whole family). Every time you put $15 on your Pay-Per-Ride MetroCard, it's automatically credited 10%—that's one free ride for every $15.

Unlimited-Use MetroCards, which can't be used for more than one person at a time or more frequently than 18-minute intervals, are available in three values: the **daily Fun Pass,** which allows you a day's worth of unlimited subway and bus rides for $4; the **7-Day MetroCard,** for $17; and the **30-Day MetroCard,** for $63. These MetroCards cannot be renewed; you throw it out once it's been used up and buy a new one. Note that Fun Passes cannot be purchased at token booths—you can buy them only from a MetroCard merchant or at a station that has a MetroCard vending machine.

If you have any MetroCard questions, ask the token booth clerk or call ☎ **212/METROCARD.** (You can also call this number to locate a Metrocard vendor selling the Fun Pass near you.)

USING THE SYSTEM   The subway system basically mimics the lay of the land above ground, with most lines in Manhattan running north and south, like the avenues, and a few lines east and west, like the streets.

Lines have assigned colors on subway maps and trains—red for the 1, 2, 3, 9 line; green for 4, 5, 6 trains; and so on—but nobody ever refers to them by color. Always refer to them by number or letter when asking questions. Within Manhattan, the distinction between different numbered trains that share the same line is usually that some are express and others local. Express trains often skip about three stops for each one that they make; express stops are indicated on subway maps with a white (rather than solid) circle. Regular stops usually come about nine blocks apart.

Directions are almost always indicated using "Uptown" (northbound) and "Downtown" (southbound), so be sure to know what direction you want to head in. The outsides of some subway entrances are marked UPTOWN ONLY or DOWNTOWN ONLY; read carefully, as it's easy to head in the wrong direction. Once you're on the platform, check the signs overhead to make sure that the train you're waiting for will be traveling in the right direction. If you do make a mistake, it's a good idea to wait for an express station, like 14th Street or 42nd Street, so you can get off and change for the other direction without paying again.

For **subway safety tips,** see "Playing It Safe" later in this chapter.

For More Bus & Subway Information

For additional transit information, call the **MTA/New York City Transit's Travel Information Center** at ☎ **718/330-1234.** Extensive automated information is available at this number 24 hours a day, and travel agents are on hand to answer your questions and provide directions daily from 6am to 9pm. For online information, point your web browser to **www.mta.nyc.ny.us.**

To request system maps or the *Token Trips Travel Guide* brochure, which gives subway and bus travel directions to more than 120 popular sites, call the **Customer Assistance Line** at ☎ **718/330-3322** (Mon–Fri 9am–5pm). For transit info for disabled riders, call the **Accessable Line** at ☎ **718/596-8585** (daily 6am–9pm).

You can get bus and subway maps and additional transit information at most tourist information centers (see "Visitor Information" earlier in this chapter). Maps are sometimes available in subway stations (ask at the token booth), but rarely on buses.

BY BUS

Less expensive than taxis and more pleasant than subways, buses are a good transportation option. Their very big drawback: They can get stuck in traffic, sometimes making it quicker to walk. They also stop every couple of blocks, rather than the eight or nine blocks that local subway traverse between stops. So for long distances, the subway is your best bet; but for short distances or traveling crosstown, try the bus.

PAYING YOUR WAY   Like the subway fare, the **bus fare** is $1.50, half-price for seniors and riders with disabilities, free for children under 44 inches (up to three per adult). The fare is payable with a **MetroCard, token** (for now, anyway), or **exact change.** Bus drivers don't make change, and fare boxes don't accept dollar bills or pennies. You can't purchase MetroCards or tokens on the bus, so you'll have to have them before you board; for details, see "Paying Your Way" under "By Subway" above.

If you pay with a MetroCard, you can freely transfer to another bus or to the subway for up to two hours. If you use a token, you must request a **free transfer** slip that allows you to change to an intersecting bus route only (legal transfer points are listed on the transfer paper) within one hour of issue. Transfer slips cannot be used to enter the subway.

Taxi-Hailing Tips

- When you're waiting on the street for an available taxi, look at the medallion light on the top of the coming cabs. If the light is out, the taxi is in use. When the center part (the number) is lit, the taxi is available—this is when you raise your hand to flag the cab. If all the lights are on, the driver is off duty.
- A taxi can't take more than four people, so expect to split up if your group is larger.

USING THE SYSTEM   You can't flag a city bus down—you have to meet it at a bus stop. **Bus stops** are located every two or three blocks on the right-side corner of the street (facing the direction of traffic flow). They're marked by a curb painted yellow and a blue-and-white sign with a bus emblem and the route number or numbers. Guide-A-Ride boxes at most stops display a route map and a hysterically optimistic schedule.

Every major avenue has its own **bus route.** They run either north or south. Additionally, **crosstown buses** run along all major east-west-bound streets. Some bus routes, however, are erratic: The M104, for example, starts at the East River, then turns at Eighth Avenue and goes up Broadway. The buses of the Fifth Avenue line go up Madison or Sixth and follow various routes around the city. Most routes operate 24 hours a day, but service is infrequent at night.

To make sure the bus you're boarding goes where you're going, check the maps on the bus signs, get your hands on a route map, or **just ask.** The drivers are helpful, as long as you don't hold up the line too long.

BY TAXI

If you don't want to deal with the hustle and bustle of public transportation, finding an address that might be a few blocks from the subway station, or sharing your ride with $3^1/2$ million other people, then take a taxi. Cabs can be hailed on any street and will take you right to your destination.

Official New York City taxis are yellow, with the rates printed on the door and a light with a medallion number on the roof. You can hail a taxi on any street. *Never* accept a ride from any other car except an official city yellow cab (private livery cars are not allowed to pick up fares on the street).

The base fare on entering the cab is $2 (a surcharge of 50¢ is added from 8pm to 6am). The cost is 30¢ for every $1/5$ mile or 20¢ per minute in stopped or very slow-moving traffic (or for waiting time). There's no extra charge for each passenger or for luggage. However, you must pay bridge or tunnel tolls. A 15% to 20% tip is customary.

The TLC has posted a **Taxi Rider's Bill of Rights** sticker in every cab. Drivers are required by law to take you anywhere in the five boroughs, to Nassau or Westchester counties, or to Newark Airport. They are supposed to know how to get you to any address in Manhattan, and all major points in the outer boroughs. They are also required to provide air conditioning and turn off the radio on demand, and they cannot smoke while you're in the cab. They are also required to be polite.

You are allowed to dictate the route taken. It's a good idea to look at a map before you get in a taxi. Taxi drivers have been known to jack up the fare on visitors who don't know better by taking a circuitous route between point A and point B. On the other hand, listen to drivers who propose an alternate route. A knowledgeable driver will know how to get you to your destination quickly and efficiently.

Always make sure the meter is turned on at the start of the ride. You'll see the red LED read-out register the initial $2 and start calculating the fare as you go. I've witnessed a good number of unscrupulous drivers buzzing unsuspecting visitors around the city with the meter off, and then overcharging them at drop-off time.

Always ask for the receipt—it comes in handy if you need to make a complaint or have left something in a cab. In fact, it's a good idea to make a mental note of the driver's four-digit medallion number (usually posted on the divider between the front and back seats) just in case you need it later. You probably won't, but it's a good idea to play it safe.

For driver complaints and lost property, call the 24-hour Consumer Hotline at ☎ **212/NYC-TAXI.** For further taxi information, point your web browser to **www.ci.nyc.ny.us/taxi**.

3 Playing It Safe

New York has experienced a dramatic drop in crime and is generally safe these days, especially in the neighborhoods visitors are prone to frequent. Still, it's important to take precautions. Visitors should remain vigilant, as swindlers and criminals are expert at spotting newcomers who appear disoriented or vulnerable.

Men should carry their wallets in their front pockets. Cross camera and purse straps over one shoulder, across your front, and under the other arm. Never hang a purse on the back of a chair or on a hook in a bathroom stall; keep it in your lap or between your feet with one foot through a strap and up against the purse itself. Avoid carrying large amounts of cash. Skip the flashy jewelry and keep valuables out of sight when you're on the street.

Panhandlers are seldom dangerous but should be ignored (more aggressive pleas should firmly be answered, "Not today"). I hate to be cynical, but experience teaches that if a stranger walks up to you on the street with a long sob story ("I live in the suburbs and was just attacked and don't have the money to get home") it should be ignored—it's a scam. Walk away and don't feel bad. Be wary of an individual who "accidentally" falls in front of you or causes some other commotion, because he or she may be working with someone else who will take your wallet when you try to help. And remember: You *will* lose if you place a bet on a sidewalk card game or shell game.

When using the **subway,** don't wait for trains near the edge of the platform or on extreme ends of a station. During non-rush hours, wait for the train in view of the token booth clerk or under the yellow DURING OFF HOURS TRAINS STOP HERE signs, and ride in the train operator's or conductor's car (usually in the center of the train; you'll see his or her head stick out when the doors open). Choose crowded cars over empty ones—there's safety in numbers. Splurge on a cab after about 10 or 11pm—it's money well spent to avoid a long wait on a deserted platform. Or take the bus.

The Top Safety Tips: Trust your instincts, because they're usually right. You'll rarely be hassled, but it's always best to walk with a sense of purpose and self-confidence, and don't stop in the middle of the sidewalk to pull out and peruse your map. There's a good police presence on the street, so don't be afraid to stop an officer, or even a friendly looking New Yorker (trust me—you can tell), if you need help getting your bearings.

Anywhere in the city, if you find yourself on a deserted street that feels unsafe, it probably is; leave as quickly as possible. If you do find yourself accosted by someone with or without a weapon, remember to keep your anger in check and that the most reasonable response (maddening though it may be) is not to resist.

FAST FACTS: New York City

American Express   Travel service offices are at many Manhattan locations, including the New York Hilton, 1335 Sixth Ave., at 53rd Street (☎ 212/664-7798); at Macy's Herald Square, 34th Street and Broadway (☎ 212/695-8075); and 65 Broadway, between Exchange Place and Rector Street (☎ 212/493-6500). Call ☎ **800/AXP-TRIP** or visit **www.americanexpress.com** for other city locations or general information.

Area Codes   From late 1998, there'll be four area codes in the city: two in Manhattan, **212** and **646,** and two in the outer boroughs, **718** and (new in fall 1999) **347.** At press time, dialing procedures for local calls hadn't been determined. Before making a call, check for instructions in a phone book or on a phone booth or dial 0 and ask the operator. It may always be necessary to dial 11 digits (1, the area code, and the number), even when making a call within the same 212 or 646 or 718 area codes.

Emergencies   Dial ☎ **911** for fire, police, and ambulance. The **Poison Control Center** is at ☎ **212/764-7667** or 212/340-4494.

Fire   Dial ☎ **911.**

Hospitals   **Downtown:** New York Downtown Hospital, 170 William St., at Beekman Street (☎ **212/312-5000**); St. Vincent's Hospital, Seventh Avenue and 11th Street (☎ **212/604-7000**); and Beth Israel Medical Center, First Avenue and 16th Street (☎ **212/420-2000**). **Midtown:** Bellevue Hospital Center, 462 First Avenue and 27th Street (☎ **212/562-4141;** New York University Medical Center, 560 First Avenue and 33rd Street (☎ **212/263-7300**); and Roosevelt Hospital Center, Tenth Avenue and 59th Street (☎ **212/523-4000**). **Upper West Side:** St. Luke's Hospital Center, Amsterdam Avenue and 114th Street (☎ **212/523-4000**). **Upper East Side:** New York Hospital's Emergency Pavilion, York Avenue and 70th Street (☎ **212/746-5050**), and Lenox Hill Hospital, 77th Street between Park and Lexington avenues (☎ **212/434-2000**). Don't forget your insurance card.

Internet Centers   The **Times Square Visitors Center,** 1560 Broadway, between 46th and 47th streets (☎ **212/768-1560**), has computer terminals with free Internet access courtesy of Yahoo!. The **Internet Cafe,** 82 E. 3rd St., between First and Second avenues in the East Village (☎ **212/614-0747;** www.bigmagic.com), offers direct Internet access at $10 per hour.

Cybercafe, 273 Lafayette St., at Prince Street in SoHo (☎ **212/ 334-5140;** www.cyber-cafe.com), is more expensive at $12.80 an hour, but their T1 connectivity gives you much speedier access.

Liquor Laws   The minimum legal age to purchase and consume alcoholic beverages in New York is 21. Liquor and wine are sold only in licensed stores, which are closed on Sundays, holidays, and election days while the polls are open. Beer can be purchased in grocery stores and delis 24 hours a day, except Sundays before noon.

Pharmacies   There are two 24-hour pharmacies, both branches of **Duane Reade:** at Broadway and 57th Street (☎ **212/541-9708**) and at Third Avenue and 74th Street (☎ **212/744-2668**).

Police   Dial ☎ **911** in an emergency; otherwise, call ☎ **212/ 374-5000** for the number of the nearest precinct.

Post Office   The main New York City post office is on 421 Eighth Ave., between 31st and 33rd streets and is open 24 hours a day (☎ **212/967-8585**). Call ☎ **800/275-8777** to locate the nearest branch office.

Smoking   Smoking is prohibited on all public transportation, in the lobbies of hotels and office buildings, in taxis, and in most shops. Smoking also may be restricted or not permitted in restaurants; for more on this, see chapter 6.

Taxes   **Sales tax** is 8.25% on meals, most goods, and some services. **Hotel tax** is 13.25% plus $2 per room per night (including sales tax). **Parking garage tax** is 18.25%.

Telephone Information   Dial ☎ **411.**

Weather   For the current temperature and next day's forecast, call ☎ **212/976-1212.** If you want to know how to pack before you arrive, point your web browser to **www.cnn.com/weather** or **www.weather.com** for the four- or five-day forecast.

3

Accommodations

*A*s you're probably well aware, New York is more popular than it's been in decades. On one hand, that's terrific: It's a reflection of how well the city's doing, and how well it's projecting that positive image to the rest of the world. This popularity makes the city feel vital and self-assured; you can practically feel the excitement and energy as you walk down the street.

Now the downside: Occupancy rates are higher than they've been since the pre-war years, and rates have responded accordingly. Average room rates are now hovering around $195, higher than ever before in the city's history. With rates at these levels, accommodations are likely to be the biggest financial commitment of your trip. Choose carefully.

That doesn't mean that there aren't a few bargains out there—so even if money is tight, don't give up yet. In the pages that follow, I'll tell you about some truly wonderful places to stay that won't break your bank account. But when deciding what you're willing to afford vs. what you're willing to put up with, keep in mind that this is the land of $200-a-night Holiday Inns and HoJos—so if you only want to spend 100 bucks a night, you're going to have to put up with some inconveniences. For instance, you may have to stay in a residential district rather than your first-choice neighborhood. Or you may have to give up New York's rarest asset: space. Don't be surprised if your room isn't much bigger than the bed that's in it. For the best bargains in town, you'll have to get used to the idea of sharing a bath—if you're willing to do so, you can get a lot of bang for your buck.

ON THE LISTINGS IN THIS CHAPTER The rates quoted in the listings below are the **rack rates**—the maximum rates that a hotel charges for rooms. I've used these rack rates to divide the hotels into four price categories, ranging from "Very Expensive" to "Inexpensive," for easy reference.

But rack rates are only guidelines. Hardly anybody pays these prices. In the listings below, I tried to give you an idea of the kind of deals that may be available at particular hotels: which ones have the best discounted packages, which ones offer AAA and other discounts, which ones allow kids to stay with Mom and Dad for free, and so on. But there's no way of knowing what the offers will be when you're booking, so **always ask for the lowest-priced package available,** and don't be afraid to bargain. Pick a few hotels to call, and shop around so you're satisfied in the end that you're getting the best deal possible.

Many **features** come standard in most hotel rooms these days. If you stay in a hotel listed under the "Very Expensive" or "Expensive" categories below, you can assume that your room will have an alarm clock, hair dryer, an in-room safe, an iron and ironing board, and voice mail and dataport on the telephone unless I've otherwise noted. But in hotels listed under "Moderate" and "Inexpensive" these features aren't a given, so I've explicitly noted what's included.

RESERVATION SERVICES   These outfits usually work as consolidators, often garnering special deals that range from 10 to 50% off rack rates. You'll often do better by dealing directly with a hotel, but it's worth checking with a reservation service for comparison shopping. Here are a few of the more reputable providers: The **Hotel Reservations Network** (☎ 800/846-7666; www.newyorkhotel.com) charges no fee for booking your hotel, and can save you up to 65% on the cost of your room at 140 city hotels ranging from budget to deluxe. **Microsoft Expedia (www.expedia.com)** features an online "Travel Agent" that will also direct you to affordable lodgings. **Hotel ConXions** (☎ **800/522-9991** or 212/840-8686; www.hotelconxions.com) may be able to save you up to 40% off rack rates and, because they have guaranteed room blocks in select properties, can often get you into a hotel that's otherwise sold out.

1 The Financial District

To locate this hotel, see the "Lower Manhattan, TriBeCa & Chinatown" map in chapter 4.

EXPENSIVE

The Millenium Hilton. 55 Church St. (btw. Fulton and Dey sts.), New York, NY 10017. ☎ **800/835-2220** or 212/693-2001. Fax 212/571-2316. www.hilton.com. 561 units. A/C MINIBAR TV TEL. $300–$350 double, $400 junior suite, $700–$1,550 suite. Rates drop to $120–$199 double on weekends, depending on season; continental breakfast usually included in weekend rates. Corporate, senior, and other promotions may also be available. Extra person $30. Children under 18 stay free in parents' room. AE, CB, DC, DISC, JCB, MC, V. Valet parking $35. Subway: 1, 9, N, R to Cortlandt St.; C, E to World Trade Center.

This Mobil four-star, AAA four-diamond hotel is the top choice in the Financial District for bulls and bears. Facing the World Trade Center but reaching only halfway up the 58-story tinted-glass monolith, it's great for vacationers, too—especially on weekends, when it becomes one of the best values in town. This area goes from bustling to near-desolate on weekends, but multiple subway lines are nearby, ready to whisk you uptown in no time.

The rooms are light and bright on every floor, but the views become more and more glorious as you go up. The accommodations are extremely comfortable, with excellent platform beds fitted with cushioned quilts, firm mattresses, and down pillows. Other appealing in-room features include well-designed built-ins that maximize work and storage space; big bathrooms with lots of counter space; two-line phones; fax/printer/copiers; and cushy bathrobes. I saw some wear in the wood furnishings in some rooms, but everything else was in beautiful shape.

Dining/Diversions: Two American restaurants—one upscale, one casual—serve just-fine-but-nothing-special fare; there's also a comfortable bar.

Amenities: Business center with conference room, well-equipped fitness center with a great pool and a dry sauna, concierge, 24-hour room service, twice-daily maid service, express checkout, complimentary car service to midtown, gift shop and newsstand. Secretarial services available; lots of meeting space.

2 TriBeCa

To locate this hotel, see the "Lower Manhattan, TriBeCa & Chinatown Dining" map in chapter 4.

INEXPENSIVE

✪ **Cosmopolitan Hotel–Tribeca.** 95 W. Broadway (at Warren St., 1 blk. south of Chambers St.), New York, NY, 10007. ☎ **888/895-9400** or 212/566-1900. Fax 212/566-6909. www.cosmohotel.com. 104 units. A/C TV TEL. $99–$139 double. AE, CB, DC, JCB, MC, V. Parking $20 (with validation) 1 blk. away. Subway: 1, 2, 3, 9, A, C, E to Chambers St.

Hiding behind a plain-vanilla Tribeca awning is the best hotel deal in Manhattan for budget travelers who don't want to sacrifice the luxury of a private bathroom to save. Every room comes with its own small but spotless bath, telephone with dataport, air conditioning, satellite TV, alarm, and ceiling fan, all for as little as 99 bucks a night. Everything is strictly budget, but nice: The modern IKEAish furniture includes an armoire (a few rooms have a dresser and hanging rack instead) and a work desk; for a few extra bucks, you can have a loveseat, too. Beds are comfy, and sheets and towels are better quality than in many more expensive hotels. Rooms are small but make the most of the limited space, and the whole place is pristine. The two-level mini-lofts have lots of character, but expect to duck on the second level: Downstairs is the bath, TV, closet, desk, and club chair, while upstairs is a low-ceilinged bedroom with a second TV and phone. The neighborhood is safe, hip, and subway-convenient; the Financial District is just a walk away. There's no room service, but a range of great restaurants, from budget to deluxe, will deliver. All services are kept at a bare minimum to keep costs down, so you must be a low-maintenance guest to be happy here. If you are, this place is a smokin' deal.

3 SoHo

To locate these hotels, see the "The East Village & SoHo Area" map in chapter 4.

VERY EXPENSIVE

The Mercer. 99 Prince St. (at Mercer St.), New York, NY 10012. ☎ **888/ 918-6060** or 212/966-6060. Fax 212/965-3838. www.themercer.com. 75 units. A/C MINIBAR TV TEL. $350–$400 double, $430–$450 studio, from $875 suite. AE, DC, MC, V. Parking $26 nearby. Subway: N, R to Prince St.

André Balazs, owner of L.A.'s chic Chateau Marmont, opened the Mercer in April 1997, and the beautiful people have been keeping the place booked ever since. The lobby feels like a postmodern library lounge, with design books lining the shelves and a hip staff scurrying about in Isaac Mizrahi finery. Word is that the hotel is more service-oriented than competitors like the Royalton, but I found its ultra-cool, almost frosty air a little offputting. Even the entrance, guarded by heavy curtains, feels almost uninviting.

The high-ceilinged guest rooms, by French designer Christian Liaigre, are more welcoming, with simple, clean-lined furnishings in beautiful African wenge wood (the material of the moment in design circles). The linens are gorgeous textured cottons. There's comfortable seating and a large work table in every room that easily can double as a dining table. The austerely beautiful tile-and-marble baths have a steel cart for storage and oversized shower stalls (request a tub when booking if you want one). Nice extras include ceiling fans, VCRs and video games, stereos with CD players, minibars stocked with goodies from Dean & Deluca, and free local phone calls.

Dining/Diversions: Mercer Kitchen is the downtown domain of superstar chef Jean-Georges Vongerichten, of JoJo, Vong, and Jean Georges. The experimental French/Asian fusion cuisine is good, but not quite good enough for what they're charging. Still, it's about as hip as a scene gets these days. On the lobby level is Mercer Cafe, serving breakfast, lunch, and cocktails.

Amenities: Concierge, 24-hour room service, valet service, free access to nearby David Barton Gym, meeting rooms.

✪ **Soho Grand Hotel.** 310 W. Broadway (btw. Grand and Canal sts.), New York, NY 10013. ☎ **800/965-3000** or 212/965-3000. Fax 212/965-3200. www.sohogrand.com. 373 units. A/C MINIBAR TV TEL. $334–$414 double; penthouse suite prices available upon request. AE, CB, DC, DISC, EURO, JCB, MC, V. Valet parking $30. Pets welcomed. Subway: A, C, E, 1, 9, N, R to Canal St.

New in 1996, this stop-off for the image-conscious was the first hotel to open in SoHo in more than a century. Built from the ground up, the hotel was designed as a modern ode to the neighborhood's cast-iron past; the result is a Industrial Age–meets–21st century environment that will probably have a longer shelf life than wholly modern rivals like the Mercer and W New York. Here, they got the mix right: the self-conscious modern design that overwhelms at the Mercer is toned down and warmed up with a '90s affinity for natural textures and materials, but without the contrivance that reigns at W.

The guest rooms boast retro-reproduction furnishings with an Asian slant, including desks that resemble artists' drafting tables and end tables that look like sculptors' stands. The natural colors are warm and soothing, William Morris fabrics abound, and there's beautiful lighting throughout (including Edison bulbs in the public spaces). The beds are fitted with Frette linens, cushioned naugahyde headboards, and gorgeous coverlets. Decked out in ceramic subway tile, the baths are beautiful but simple. In-room conveniences include full-length mirrors, VCRs and stereos with CD players, double-paned windows that open, two-line phones with free local calls, and your very own goldfish in a bowl—courtesy of owner Hartz Mountain, of course.

Dining/Diversions: Awarded two stars by *The New York Times,* Canal House serves sophisticated New England-style tavern fare; the macaroni and cheese (made with three-year-aged cheddar) is excellent. The Grand Bar is a clubby retro-hip bar that's so popular the action often spills out into the lobby's living room-like "salon." On street level is Caviarteria, a wonderful caviar-and-champagne bar.

Amenities: Fitness center, concierge, 24-hour room service (including a menu for your pooch or kitty), valet service, newspaper delivery, express checkout, conference room. Butler's pantry with complimentary coffee, tea, and hot chocolate on every floor. On street level is Privé, a chic salon.

4   Greenwich Village

To locate this hotel, see the "Greenwich Village" map in chapter 4.

INEXPENSIVE

✪ **Larchmont Hotel.** 27 W. 11th St. (btw. Fifth and Sixth aves.), New York, NY 10011. ☎ **212/989-9333.** Fax 212/989-9496. www.citysearch.com/nyc/larchmonthotel. 55 units (none with private bathroom). A/C TV TEL. $60–$70 single; $85–$99 double. Children under 13 stay free in parents' room. Rates include continental breakfast. AE, CB, DC, DISC, MC, V. Parking $20 nearby. Subway: 4, 5, 6, N, R, L to Union Square; A, C, E, B, D, F, Q to West 4th St. (use 8th St. exit); F to 14th St.

Excellently located on a beautiful tree-lined block in a quiet residential part of the village, this European-style hotel is simply a gem. If you're willing to put up with the inconvenience of shared bathrooms, you can't do better for the money. The entire place has a wonderful air of warmth and sophistication; the butter-yellow lobby even *smells* good. Each bright guest room is tastefully done in rattan and outfitted with a writing desk, a wash basin, a mini-library of books, an alarm clock, and a few extras that you normally have to pay a lot more for, such as cotton bathrobes and ceiling fans. Every floor has two shared baths and a small, simple kitchen. The management is constantly renovating, so everything feels clean and fresh. Free continental breakfast, including fresh-baked goods every morning, is the crowning touch that makes the Larchmont an unbeatable deal. And with some of the city's best shopping, dining, and sightseeing, plus your choice of subway lines, just a walk away, you couldn't be better situated. As you might expect, the hotel is always full, so book *well* in advance (the management suggests six to seven weeks' lead time).

5   The Flatiron District

INEXPENSIVE

Gershwin Hotel. 7 E. 27th St. (btw. Fifth and Madison aves.), New York, NY 10016. ☎ **212/545-8000.** Fax 212/684-5546. www.gershwinhotel.com. 94 doubles, 31 4-person dorms. TV TEL (in doubles only). $109–$139 double, $119–$149 triple, $129–$159 quad, depending on season; $22 per person in dorm. Check website for seasonal deals. AE, MC, V. Parking $20 nearby. Subway: N, R, 6 to 28th St.

If you see glowing horns protruding from a lipstick-red facade, you're in the right place. This budget-conscious, youth-oriented hotel caters to up-and-coming artistic types with its bold modern art collection and wild style. The lobby is a colorful, post-modern cartoon of kitschy furniture and pop art by Lichtenstein, Warhol, de Koonig, and lesser names. The standard rooms are clean and saved from the budget doldrums by bright colors, Picasso-style wall murals, Starck-ish takes on motel furnishings, and more modern art. All have private bathrooms; none of the bathrooms are bad, but try to nab yourself one of the cute, colorful new ones. The cheapest accommodations are four- and eight-bedded dorms: just basic rooms with IKEA bunk beds sharing a bath, but better than a hostel, especially if you're traveling with a group and can claim one as your own.

One of the best things about the Gershwin is its great, Factory-esque vibe, sort of like an artsy frat or sorority house. The hotel is more service-oriented than you usually see at this price level, and there's always something going on, whether it's live comedy or jazz in the beer and wine bar, a barbecue on the rooftop garden, or an opening at the hotel's own art gallery. Air conditioning was also in the planning stage, but make sure before you book an August stay.

6 Chelsea

MODERATE

Hotel Chelsea. 222 W. 23rd St. (btw. Seventh and Eighth aves.), New York, NY 10011. ☎ **212/243-3700.** Fax 212/675-5531. www.hotelchelsea.com. 400 units, 100 available to travelers (most with private bathroom). A/C (in most rooms) TV TEL. $150–$285 double or junior suite, from $300 suite. AE, JCB, MC, V. Valet parking $18. Subway: 1, 9, C, E to 23rd St.

If you're looking for predictable comforts, book a room next door at the Chelsea Savoy. But if it's Warhol's New York you're here to discover—or Sarah Bernhardt's or Eugene O'Neill's or Lenny Bruce's—the Hotel Chelsea is the only place to stay. Arthur Miller penned *After the Fall* in the Chelsea's welcoming arms; William Burroughs moved in to work on *Naked Lunch*; and in a defining moment of punk history, Sid Vicious killed screechy girlfriend Nancy Spungen here. No other hotel boasts so much genuine atmosphere. Currently, most of the 400 rooms are inhabited by long-term residents of the creative bent, so the Bohemian spirit and sense of community are as strong as ever.

A designated landmark, the 1884 redbrick Victorian boasts graceful cast-iron balconies and a bustling lobby filled with museum-quality works by prominent current and former residents. A recent

Midtown Accommodations & Dining

Accommodations

The Algonquin
The Avalon
Belvedere Hotel
Broadway Inn
Chelsea Savoy Hotel
Clarion Hotel Fifth Avenue
Comfort Inn Midtown
Crowne Plaza Manhattan
Doubletree Guest Suites
Four Seasons Hotel
   New York
Gershwin Hotel
The Gorham
Hotel Chelsea
Hotel Edison
Hotel Metro
Hotel Wolcott
Millennium Broadway &
   the Premier
Morgans
New York Marriott Marquis
The Peninsula–New York
Quality Hotel & Suites
   Midtown
The Royalton
The Sherry-Netherland
The Time
The Waldorf-Astoria &
   Waldorf Towers
The Wyndham

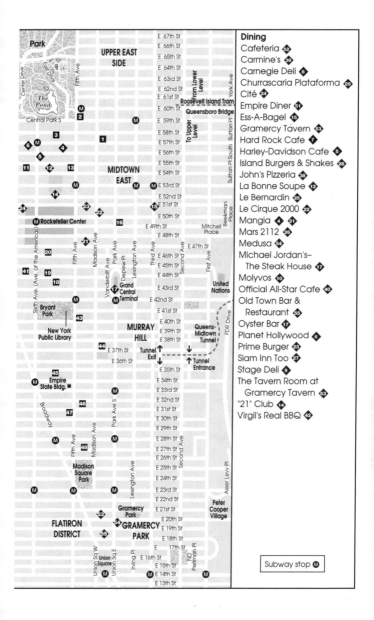

Dining

Cafeteria 52
Carmine's 39
Carnegie Deli 8
Churrascaria Plataforma 29
Cité 24
Empire Diner 51
Ess-A-Bagel 15
Gramercy Tavern 53
Hard Rock Cafe 7
Harley-Davidson Cafe 5
Island Burgers & Shakes 28
John's Pizzeria 48
La Bonne Soupe 12
Le Bernardin 25
Le Cirque 2000 22
Mangia 4 21
Mars 2112 26
Medusa 54
Michael Jordan's–
  The Steak House 17
Molyvos 10
Official All-Star Cafe 40
Old Town Bar &
  Restaurant 55
Oyster Bar 17
Planet Hollywood 6
Prime Burger 23
Siam Inn Too 27
Stage Deli 9
The Tavern Room at
  Gramercy Tavern 53
"21" Club 14
Virgil's Real BBQ 42

Subway stop Ⓜ

45

renovation has taken the seediness out of the allure—these days, the hotel is looking very nice. It's still very quirky, mind you, and not for everybody: Most of the individually decorated rooms and suites have air-conditioning, and they tell me that all rooms have TVs and telephones now, but otherwise it's a crapshoot. The accommodations tend to be sparsely furnished, but they're almost universally large and virtually soundproof. I loved no. 520, a pretty purple-painted junior suite with two double beds, a ceiling fan, sofa, and a pantry kitchenette. Everything is clean, but don't expect new. The hotel is service-oriented, but in an appropriately fluid way: There's no room or valet service, but the bellmen will be happy to deliver takeout to your room or run your dirty clothes to the cleaners.

INEXPENSIVE

✪ **Chelsea Savoy Hotel.** 204 W. 23rd St. (at Seventh Ave.), New York, NY 10011. ☎ **212/929-9353.** Fax 212/741-6309. www.citysearch.com/nyc/chelseasavoy. 90 units. A/C TV TEL. $99–$115 single, $125–$155 double, $155–$185 quad. Children under 13 stay free in parents' room. Rates include continental breakfast. AE, MC, V. Parking $16 nearby. Subway: 1, 9 to 23rd St.

This two-year-old hotel is our top choice in Chelsea, a neighborhood abloom with art galleries and restaurants but formerly devoid of nice, affordable hotels. The six-story Savoy was built from the ground up, so it isn't subject to the eccentricities of the mostly older hotels in this price range: The hallways are attractive and wide, the elevators are swift and silent, and the generic but cheery rooms are good-sized and have big closets and roomy, immaculate baths with tons of counter space. Creature comforts abound: The rooms boast mattresses, furniture, textiles, and linens of high quality, plus the kinds of amenities you usually have to pay more for, like hair dryers, minifridges, alarm clocks, irons and ironing boards, in-room safes, and toiletries (VCRs were scheduled to be added at press time). Most rooms are street-facing and sunny; corner rooms tend to be brightest and noisiest. Ask for a darker, back-facing room if you crave total silence. There's a plain but pleasant sitting room off the lobby where you can relax and enjoy your morning coffee over a selection of newspapers and magazines. The staff is young and helpful, and the increasingly hip neighborhood makes a good base for exploring both midtown and downtown.

7 Times Square & Midtown West

VERY EXPENSIVE

Millennium Broadway & The Premier. 145 W. 44th St. (btw. Sixth Ave. and Broadway), New York, NY 10036. ☎ **800/622-5569** or 212/768-0847.

Fax 212/768-0847. www.millenniumbroadway.com. 752 units. A/C MINIBAR
TV TEL. $295–$345 double at Millennium, $395–$450 double at the Premier;
from $650 suite. Children under 13 stay free in parents' room. Inquire about
special deals and weekend packages (the Millennium's are regularly the best in
the Theater District), and check for Internet-only rates. AE, DC, CB, JCB,
MC, V. Valet parking $35. Subway: 1, 2, 3, 9, N, R to Times Square; B, D, F, Q
to 42nd St.

The Millennium Broadway is one of the top business hotels in the
city, but its prime Times Square location and well-priced packages
make it a good bet for leisure travelers, too. The spacious rooms have
a lovely art deco style, with black-and-white photos, rich red
mahogany, and black lacquer details. The textiles are of excellent
quality, the bathrooms have lots of marble counter space, and nice
extras include a writing desk, comfy streamline club chairs, and two-
line phones. Club rooms, on floors 46 to 52, feature additional extras like fax machines, coffeemakers, and free continental breakfast
and cocktails at the top-floor Club Lounge.

Adjoining the Millennium is the brand-new **Premier,** housing
125 high-tech luxury rooms done in a more contemporary style,
with blond ash, green glass, and natural fibers. The Omaha
mattresses—the same ones used in the far more expensive Four
Seasons—done up in Frette linens just may be the most glorious
beds in town. The rooms also feature larger-than-average workspace
with all the necessary gadgets, a love seat with its own cable-knit
throw for curling up, coffee maker, fax machine, CD player, and
oversized bathrooms with soaking tubs and separate showers. The
Premier also boasts its own lounge with continental breakfast, cocktails, and large flat-screen TV.

Dining: With very good New American cuisine and a friendly
staff, the highly regarded restaurant Charlotte is a classy choice for
pre- and post-theater dining as well as Sunday brunch.

Amenities: Fitness center with sauna, concierge, 24-hour room
service, valet service, twice-daily maid service, newspaper delivery,
express checkout, business center. Five-floor Manhattan Conference
Center, with 33 dedicated meeting rooms and 11,000 square feet of
exhibition space. Secretarial services, limo service, baby-sitting, and
in-room massage available.

✪ **The Royalton.** 44 W. 44th St. (btw. Fifth and Sixth aves.), New York, NY
10036. ☎ **800/635-9013** or 212/869-4400. Fax 212/869-8965. 205 units.
A/C MINIBAR TV TEL. $350–$550 double, from $500 suite. Ask about promo-
tional rates (sometimes as low as $260) and weekend deals. AE, DC, EURO,
MC, V. Valet parking $35. Subway: B, D, F, Q to 42nd St.

Thanks to the pioneering design of French superstar Phillippe Starck and the marketing savvy of hotelier Ian Schrager, the Royalton is still an ultra-modern show stopper: lighting fixtures that look like rhinoceros horns, attractive service people dressed in de rigueur black, furniture—even carpet—with attitude. Even more importantly, Starck and Schrager have reinvented the idea of hotel: This is hotel as public space, as gathering space, as *scene*. Never have you seen a lobby quite like this, buzzing with beautiful people and energy. This ain't exactly your average Hilton, baby.

Thankfully, comfort was never sacrificed for style. Beautifully designed with a loose cruise-ship theme in rich mahogany, cool slate, and white cotton duck, even the smallest guest room is spacious enough to have a cushioned banquette for reclining, a good-sized work desk, and a roomy bathroom with a five-foot round tub or an oversized shower stall (request one or the other when you book if it matters to you). All have a VCR, CD player, groovy Kiehl's toiletries, and two two-line speaker phones with direct-dial numbers and conference calling; some even have working fireplaces.

Dining/Diversions: 44 serves reliably good New American cuisine to publishing bigwigs and other power types; service can be lax if you're not one of the in-crowd. The perennially popular lobby features comfy seating nooks, an extensive martini list, a light menu of excellent finger foods, and the Round Bar, a 20-seat circular enclave done in high *Jetsons* style.

Amenities: Concierge, 24-hour room service, valet service, turndown service, *USA Today* delivery, video library, fitness room. Business/secretarial services, personal trainers, and massage available.

EXPENSIVE

✪ **The Algonquin.** 59 W. 44th St. (btw. Fifth and Sixth aves.), New York, NY 10036. ☎ **800/555-3000** or 212/840-6800. Fax 212/944-1419. www.camberleyhotels.com. 165 units. A/C TV TEL. $189–$329 double, $329–$529 suite. Extra person $25. Rates include continental breakfast. AE, CB, DC, DISC, EURO, JCB, MC, V. Parking $25 across the street. Subway: B, D, F, Q to 42nd St.

This 1902 hotel is one of the Theater District's best-known landmarks: This is where the *New Yorker* was born, where Lerner and Loewe wrote *My Fair Lady*, and—most famously—where some of the biggest names in 1920s literati, among them Dorothy Parker, met to trade boozy quips at the celebrated Algonquin Round Table. I'm happy to report that the past isn't just a memory here anymore—a complete 1998 restoration returned this venerable hotel to its full Arts-and-Crafts splendor. True to its tradition, the Algonquin is a very social hotel: The splendid oak-paneled lobby is the comfiest and most welcoming in the city, made for lingering over afternoon tea or a post-theater cocktail. While posher than ever, the small rooms are comfortable but cramped—fine for tourists out on the town all day, but not suitable for business travelers who may need to spread out and get some work done. Extras include stocked candy jars (a nice touch). The freshened baths boast short but deep soaking tubs, hair dryers, and bathrobes. Twins are the roomiest doubles. For the ultimate New York vibe, opt for one of the literary-themed suites.

Dining/Diversions: Cocktails, tea, coffee, and an all-day menu are served in the lobby and adjacent Rose Room. The Oak Room is one of the city's top cabaret rooms, featuring such big names as Andrea Marcovicci and the Monday-night Spoken Word program, with speakers as diverse as Stanley Tucci and Paul Theroux. Pub fare is available in the Blue Bar, home to a rotating collection of Hirschfeld drawings.

Amenities: Well-outfitted fitness and business centers, concierge, room service (daily 7am–11pm), twice-daily maid service, valet service; baby-sitting available.

Crowne Plaza Manhattan. 1605 Broadway (btw. 48th and 49th sts.), New York, NY 10019. ☎ **800/243-NYNY** or 212/977-4000. Fax 212/333-7393. www.crowneplaza.com. 770 units. A/C MINIBAR TV TEL. $229–$489 double, $479–$1,000 1-bedroom suite, $700–$1,350 2-bedroom suite. Ask about weekend rates, senior rates, and other discounts; check website for special deals. 2 children under 19 free in parents' room using existing bedding. AE, CB, DC, DISC, EURO, JCB, MC, V. Valet parking $35. Subway: 1, 9 to 50th St.; N, R to 49th St.

In the heart of Times Square and near most Broadway theaters, the 46-story glass tower is as good as a mass-market chain hotel gets—and you couldn't be better located for midtown's top attractions. The comfortable guest rooms boast contemporary furnishings and marble baths, plus extras like coffeemakers and all the features you've come to expect, like in-room safes. The top four floors are devoted to Crowne Plaza Club rooms, which also feature free continental breakfast, evening hors d'oeuvres, and other extras. Noted designer Adam Tihany is at work here through '99, so expect new zest in the public spaces. Rack rates are high, but discounted rates are often available, especially for weekend travelers.

Dining/Diversions: There are three satisfactory, if unmemorable, restaurants, including the well-situated Samplings Bar, which serves contemporary meals overlooking the lights of Broadway. The Lobby

Bar is a comfortable lounge that invites you to sink into a club chair, order up a martini, and stay awhile.

Amenities: Excellent fitness center with 50-foot pool and sauna, concierge, 24-hour room service, valet service, newspaper delivery, express checkout, business center, conference rooms, tour desk. Secretarial services available.

Doubletree Guest Suites. 1568 Broadway (47th St. at Seventh Ave.), New York, NY 10036. ☎ **800/222-TREE** or 212/719-1600. Fax 212/921-5212. www.doubletreehotels.com. 460 units. A/C MINIBAR TV TEL. $239–$350 2-room suite, from $400 family or conference suite. Extra person $20. Children under 12 free in parents' suite. Senior discounts and corporate rates available. Inquire about weekend package deals, which at press time included tickets to *The Lion King*. AE, DC, DISC, JCB, MC, V. Valet parking $30. Subway: N, R to 49th St.

For less than the cost of a normal room in many nearby Times Square hotels, you can get a suite at the Doubletree with a separate bedroom and living room with a pull-out sofa bed, a dining/work table, a refrigerator, a wet bar, a microwave, a coffeemaker, two TVs, and three phones with voice mail. For businesspeople, conference suites feature work stations with convenient dataports and outlets to plug in your laptop, and they're large enough for small meetings. What's more, this is a family-friendly hotel with a floor of childproof suites and special amenities for kids, such as the Kids Club for children 3 to 12, featuring a playroom, an arts-and-crafts center, and computer and video games. Cribs and strollers are available, as is a kids' room-service menu.

Dining/Diversions: There's a restaurant serving hotel-standard continental and American cuisine, plus a pleasant Broadway-themed piano bar.

Amenities: Fitness center, Kids Club with children's programs, concierge, 24-hour room service, valet service, newspaper delivery, express checkout, coin-op laundry room, guest services desk, business center with secretarial services available, newsstand and gift shop, meeting and banquet rooms.

The Gorham. 136 W. 55th St. (btw. Sixth and Seventh aves.), New York, NY 10019. ☎ **800/735-0710** or 212/245-1800. Fax 212/582-8332. www.gorhamhotel.com. 115 units. A/C TV TEL. $215–$400 single or double, $235–$475 suite. Children under 16 stay free in parents' room. Check website for seasonal deals and packages; at press time, theater packages included tickets to *The Lion King*. AE, CB, DC, EURO, JCB, MC, V. Parking $20. Subway: B, D, E to 53rd St.; B, N, R, Q to 57th St.

A major 1993 renovation reestablished the Gorham as an affordable choice in Midtown West, and a 1998 face-lift refreshed the bright new look. It's an especially good deal, considering that all of the large, pleasingly contemporary rooms have fully equipped kitchenettes with microwaves; 27-inch TVs with Nintendo; a spacious work desk; multiple multi-line phones with call waiting; two queen-size or one king bed; and marble baths with makeup mirrors and digital temperature controls. The suites feature a separate sitting room with a pull-out sofa bed and velour robes (two have Jacuzzi tubs). Rooms are equipped for the disabled with smoke detectors for the hearing impaired and Braille electronic key cards, and a number are wheelchair accessible.

Dining: Breakfast is served in a private breakfast room ($8.50 continental, $11.50 all-you-can-eat buffet).

Amenities: Fitness center, concierge, room service (daily 7am–10pm), valet service, express checkout, conference rooms. Secretarial services, baby-sitting, in-room massage, and access to nearby health club available.

New York Marriott Marquis. 1535 Broadway (btw. 45th and 46th sts.), New York, NY 10036. ☎ **800/843-4898** or 212/398-1900. Fax 212/704-8930. www.marriott.com. 1,919 units. A/C MINIBAR TV TEL. $210–$395 double, $250–$435 Concierge-level double, from $450 suite. Ask about AAA, AARP, and corporate discounts when booking. AE, CB, DC, DISC, JCB, MC, V. Parking $30. Pets allowed. Subway: 1, 2, 3, 9, N, R to Times Square; N, R to 49th St.

Though many New Yorkers love to hate this pedestrian-unfriendly, John Portman-designed 50-story hotel, it's a top choice of travelers. Its centerpieces are Portman's signature atrium, rising 37 floors to be the world's tallest, and the glass-enclosed elevators that zip up the atrium's center at knee-buckling speed. The surprisingly large guest rooms have two-line phones and coffee makers. Concierge Level amenities include free continental breakfast and evening hors d'oeuvres. In 1997, the hotel completed a $20-million redecoration, which, among many improvements, added work desks and ergonomic chairs to every room.

Dining/Diversions: If it's a clear night, head up to the three-story revolving rooftop restaurant, aptly named the View, for cocktails and skyline views, but dine elsewhere. There are several restaurants and lounges in the atrium.

Amenities: Health club with whirlpool and sauna, concierge, 24-hour room service, valet service, express checkout, business center, gift shop and newsstand, salon, American Express travel desk.

The Time. 224 W. 49th St. (btw. Broadway and Eighth Ave.), New York, NY 10019. ☎ **877/TIME-NYC** or 212/246-5252. Fax 212/320-2926. 192 units.

A/C MINIBAR TV TEL. $250–$400 double, from $375 suite. AE, DC, DISC, MC, V. Parking $20. Subway: 1, 9, C, E to 50th St.; N, R to 49th St.

This brand-new hotel will be fully up and running by the time you read this. The design buffs among you are likely to have heard the buzz on this first hotel designed by Adam Tihany, the man behind such incredible spaces as Le Cirque 2000, Jean-Georges, and Wolfgang Puck's Spago restaurants.

Despite the high-design pedigree and boutique-chic air that pervades the place, the guest rooms are surprisingly practical. They're done in a minimalist style in one of three primary color schemes: your choice of red, yellow, or blue, accented with black and gray. Everything is top quality but understated—think clean lines, low furnishings, and soft backlighting (including the cleverest bedside lighting I've seen). Nicely designed touches like a coffeemaker caddy and built-in valet make the rooms extra-efficient (some have double closets instead of drawer space, though, so ask if it matters to you). Amenities include a printer/copier/fax machine on the big worktable, Web TV, and Bose radios. Things get a bit silly with color-matched scents (yours to invoke only if you wish) and fruits, but the gimmicks don't intrude. Some of the baths are on the smaller side, but all have double-wide showers (suites have whirlpool tubs) and clever cubbyholes that provide additional storage space.

Dining/Diversions: The first New York restaurant from celebrity chef Jean-Louis Palladin, master of nouveau French cooking and mentor to such big-name chefs as Eric Ripert of Le Bernadin, Palladin is highly anticipated to be a major player on the restaurant scene. Time², the lobby-level lounge, is set to be another hotspot in the Royalton vein, with a tapas bar providing an individual twist.

Amenities: Concierge, 18-hour room service, valet service, turndown service, express checkout, gift shop, international newsstand, conference room, and fitness room. VCR and videos, mobile phones, and personal shopper service available.

MODERATE

✪ **Belvedere Hotel.** 319 W. 48th St. (btw. Eighth and Ninth aves.), New York, NY 10036. ☎ **888/HOTEL58** or 212/245-7000. Fax 212/265-7778. www.newyorkhotel.com/belvedere. 350 units. A/C TV TEL. $125–$240 double, depending on season (rates start at $150 in summer, $170 in fall and at holiday time). AAA discounts available; check website for special Internet deals. AE, DC, DISC, MC, V. Parking $17 on next block. Subway: C, E to 50th St.

Here's another excellent hotel from the Empire Hotel Group, the people behind the Upper West Side's Lucerne and Newton. Done with a sharp retro-modern deco flair, the public spaces are much more impressive than you'd expect to find in this price range. They lead to sizable, comfortable, attractive rooms with smallish but very nice baths with hair dryer as well as pantry kitchenettes with fridge, sink, and microwave (BYO utensils). Beds are nice and firm, textiles are of high quality, and you'll find voice mail and dataports on the telephones. The decor is pleasing in all rooms, but ask for a renovated one, where you'll get good-quality cherry-wood furnishings, plus an alarm clock and work desk (in all but a few). Also ask for a high floor (8 and above) for great views; usually they'll cost no more (ask when booking).

Extras that make the Belvedere one of the city's top values include dry cleaning and laundry service, a self-serve Laundromat, electronic luggage lockers, fax and Internet-access machines, a brand-new stylish breakfast room and light-bites cafe for guests, and the terrific Churrascaria Plataforma Brazilian restaurant. At press time, two change rooms for guests with late flights and a cocktail lounge were in the works. The neighborhood is loaded with great restaurants along Ninth Avenue and nearby Restaurant Row.

○ Broadway Inn. 264 W. 46th St. (at Eighth Ave.), New York, NY 10036. ☎ **800/826-6300** or 212/997-9200. Fax 212/768-2807. www. broadwayinn.com. 40 units. A/C TV TEL. $85–$95 single, $115–$170 double, $195 suite; $10 extra per person. Rates include continental breakfast. AE, DC, DISC, MC, V. Parking $16 at lot 3 blocks away. Subway: 1, 2, 3, 7, 9, S to 42nd St./Times Square; A, C, E to 42nd St.; N, R to 49th St.

More like a San Francisco B&B than a Theater District hotel, this lovely, welcoming inn is a real charmer. The second-floor lobby sets the homey, easygoing tone with stocked bookcases, cushy seating, and cafe tables where breakfast is served. The rooms are basic but comfy, outfitted in an appealing neo-deco style with firm beds and good-quality linens and textiles. The whole place is impeccably kept—neatniks won't have a quibble. Two rooms have king beds and Jacuzzi tubs, but the standard doubles are just fine for two if you're looking to save some dough. If there's more than two of you, or you're looking to stay awhile, the suites—with pullout sofa, microwave, minifridge, and lots of closet space—are a great deal. The location can be noisy, but double-paned windows keep the rooms surprisingly peaceful; still, ask for a back-facing one if you're extra-sensitive.

The inn's biggest asset is its terrific staff, who go above and beyond to make guests happy and at home in New York. And this corner of the Theater District is now porn-free and gentrifying nicely; it makes a great home base, especially for theatergoers. The inn has inspired a loyal following, so reserve early. However, there's no elevator in the four-story building, so overpackers and travelers with limited mobility should book elsewhere.

Comfort Inn Midtown. 129 W. 46th St. (btw. Sixth Ave. and Broadway), New York, NY 10036. ☎ **800/567-7720** or 212/221-2600. Fax 212/790-2760. www.applecorehotels.com. 80 units. A/C TV TEL. $109–$249 double, depending on season. Children under 14 stay free in parents' room. Rates include continental breakfast. Ask about senior, AAA, corporate, and promotional discounts; check www.comfortinn.com for online booking discounts. AE, DC, DISC, MC, V. Parking $20 nearby. Subway: 1, 2, 3, 9 to 42nd St./Times Square; N,R to 49th St.; B, D, F, Q to 47–50th sts./Rockefeller Center.

A major 1998 renovation brightened the former Hotel Remington's public spaces and small guest rooms, which now boast pretty floral patterns, neo-Shaker furnishings, and nice marble and tile baths (a few have showers only, so be sure to request a tub if it matters). Everything's fresh, comfortable, and new. In-room extras include hair dryers, coffee makers (oddly situated in the bathroom, but great for a morning cup o' joe nonetheless), blackout drapes, pay movies, and voice mail. Other plusses include a small fitness center and a business center; a coffee shop was in the works at press time. The location is excellent, steps from Times Square, Rockefeller Center, and the Theater District. We're not thrilled with Apple Core Hotels' (the management company that handles this Comfort Inn franchise) wide-ranging price schedule, but we found that it was relatively easy to get a well-priced room ($150 or less) even around holiday time, and rates drop as low as $79 in the off-season.

✪ **Hotel Metro.** 45 W. 35th St. (btw. Fifth and Sixth aves.), New York, NY 10001. ☎ **800/356-3870** or 212/947-2500. Fax 212/279-1310. 175 units. A/C TV TEL. $165–$250 double, $200–$325 suite. Extra person $25. Rates include continental breakfast. Off-season discounts may be available; check with airlines and other package operators for package deals. AE, DC, MC, V. Parking $20 nearby. Subway: B, D, F, Q, N, R to 34th St.

The Metro is the best choice in midtown for those who don't want to sacrifice either style or comfort for affordability. This lovely art deco-ish jewel has larger rooms than you'd expect for the price. They're outfitted with smart retro furnishings, playful textiles, and extras like voice mail and dataport on the phone as well as hair dryers and huge mirrors in the small but well-appointed bath. The neo-deco design gives the whole place an air of New York glamour that I've not otherwise seen in this price range. A great collection of black-and-white photos, from Man Ray classics in the halls to Garbo and Dietrich portraits in the lobby, adds to the vibe. Only about half the baths have tubs, but the others have shower stalls big enough for two. One of the really nice things about this hotel is its welcoming public spaces: The comfy lounge area off the lobby, where buffet breakfast is laid out and the coffeepot's on all day, is a popular hangout, and the well-furnished rooftop terrace boasts one of the most breathtaking views of the Empire State Building I've ever seen. Valet service, room service from the stylish Metro Grill, and a sizable fitness room add to the great value.

Quality Hotel & Suites Midtown. 59 W. 46th St. (btw. Fifth and Sixth aves.), New York, NY 10036. ☎ **800/567-7720** or 212/719-2300. Fax 212/921-8929. www.applecorehotels.com. 193 units. A/C TV TEL. $109–$249 double, $149–$299 suite, depending on the season. Children under 19 stay free in parents' room. Rates include continental breakfast. Ask about senior, AAA, corporate, and promotional discounts. AE, DC, DISC, MC, V. Parking $20 nearby. Subway: B, D, F, Q to 47th–50th sts./Rockefeller Center.

Here's a fine choice for those looking for your basic clean, well-outfitted hotel room for not too much money. Nice extras include coffee makers with free coffee; decent closets with iron and ironing board, and safe; smallish but fine bathrooms with hair dryers; and phones with voice mail, dataport, and free local calls (an excellent plus). The suites have king beds, pullout sleeper sofas in the living room, and two TVs, making them great for families. The 1902 landmark building, with a beaux arts facade and an attractive lobby, has been recently renovated to include a nice exercise room with cardio machines, two meeting rooms, and a business center with credit card-activated Internet access and fax and copy machines, as well as an ATM. The location, in the diamond district between Rockefeller Center and Times Square, is great for both business and pleasure. We're not thrilled with the management's wide-ranging price schedule, but we found that it was relatively easy to negotiate a good rate ($139 or less) even around holiday time, and rates drop as low as $79 in the off-season (you might even be able to get a suite for 99 bucks if your timing is right).

INEXPENSIVE

✪ **Hotel Edison.** 228 W. 47th St. (btw. Broadway and Eighth Ave.), New York, NY 10036. ☎ **800/637-7070** or 212/840-5000. Fax 212/596-6850. www.edisonhotelnyc.com. 869 units. A/C TV TEL. $125 single, $140 double, $155–$170 triple or quad, $160–$200 suite. Extra person $15. AE, CB, DC, DISC, MC, V. Valet parking $22. Subway: N, R to 49th St.; 1, 9 to 50th St.

There's no doubt about it—the Edison is one of the Theater District's best hotel bargains, if not *the* best. No other area hotel is so consistently value-priced. About 90% of the rooms were refurbished in 1998 (the rest should be done by the time you arrive), and they're *much* nicer than what you'd get for just about the same money at the nearby Ramada Inn Milford Plaza (which ain't exactly the "Lulla*buy* of Broadway!" these days). Don't expect much more than the basics, but you will find a firm bed (flat pillows, though), motel decor that's more attractive than most I've seen in this category, a phone with dataport, and a clean, perfectly adequate tile bath. Most double rooms feature two twins or a full bed, but there are some queens; request one at booking and show up early in the day for your best chance at one. Triple/quad rooms are larger, with two doubles.

Off the attractive deco-style lobby is Cafe Edison, a hoot of an old-style Polish deli that's a favorite among ladder-climbing theater types and downmarket ladies who lunch; Sofia's, an Italian restaurant; a tavern with live entertainment most nights; and a gift shop. Services are kept at a bare minimum to keep rates down, but there is a beauty salon and a guest services desk where you can arrange tours, theater tickets, and transportation. The hotel fills up with tour groups from the world over, but with nearly 1,000 rooms, you can carve out some space if you call early enough.

Hotel Wolcott. 4 W. 31st St. (at Fifth Ave.), New York, NY 10001. ☎ **212/ 268-2900.** Fax 212/563-0096. www.wolcott.com. 250 units. A/C TV TEL. $120 double, $140 triple, $170 suite. Discounted AAA, AARP, and promotional rates may be available. AE, JCB, MC, V. Parking $16 next door. Subway: B, D, F, Q, N, R to 34th St.

The Wolcott was one of the grande dames of Manhattan hotels at the start of the 20th century. Somewhat less than that now, it has been reinvented as a good-value option for bargain-hunting travelers. Only the lobby hints at the hotel's former grandeur; these days, the rooms are motel-standard, but they're well-kept and quite serviceable. Plusses include spacious bathrooms and voice mail, plus mini-fridges in most rooms. On the downside, some of the mattresses aren't as firm as I might like, and the closets tend to be on the small side. And some of the triples are poorly configured—the front door to one I saw hit up right against a bed—but they're plenty big enough for three, and come with two TVs to avoid before-bedtime conflicts (as do the suites). All in all, you get your money's worth here. One of the hotel's most recommendable features is its basement coin-op laundry, a rarity for Manhattan. There's also a tour desk and a snack shop where you can get your morning coffee; an Internet center was in the works at press time.

✪ **The Wyndham.** 42 W. 58th St. (btw. Fifth and Sixth aves.), New York, NY 10019. ☎ **800/257-1111** or 212/753-3500. Fax 212/754-5638. 140 units. AC TV TEL. $125–$140 single, $140–$155 double, $180–$225 1-bedroom suite, $320–$365 2-bedroom suite. AE, DC, MC, V. Parking $35 next door. Subway: N, R to Fifth Ave.; B, Q to 57th St.

This family-owned charmer is one of midtown's best hotel deals—and it's perfectly located to boot, on a great block steps away from Fifth Avenue shopping and Central Park. The Wyndham is stuck in the '70s on all fronts—don't expect so much as an alarm clock or hair dryer in your room, much less a dataport—but its guest rooms are enormous by city standards, comfortable, and loaded with character. The entire hotel features a wild collection of wallpaper, from candy stripes to crushed velvets, so some rooms definitely cross the ticky-tacky line. But others are downright lovely, with such details as rich oriental carpets and well-worn libraries, and the eclectic art collection that lines the walls boasts some real gems. Most important, you get a lot for your money: The rooms are universally large, and all feature huge walk-in closets (the biggest I've ever seen). The surprisingly affordable suites also have full-fledged living rooms, dressing areas, and cold kitchenettes (fridge only). If you're put in a room that's not to your taste, just ask politely to see another one; the staff is usually happy to accommodate. Valet service is available, as is limited room service (the restaurant should be in full swing by the time you arrive).

8 Midtown East & Murray Hill

VERY EXPENSIVE

Four Seasons Hotel New York. 57 E. 57th St. (btw. Park and Madison aves.), New York, NY 10022. ☎ **800/332-3442** in the U.S., 800/268-6282 in Canada, or 212/758-5700. Fax 212/758-5711. www.fourseasons.com. 370 units. A/C MINIBAR TV TEL. $565–$750 double, $1,050–$5,000 1-bedroom suite, $2,300–$2,800 2-bedroom suite; room with terrace $50 extra. One child under 19 stays free in parents' room. Check website for current package deals. AE, CB, DC, DISC, ER, JCB, MC, V. Valet parking $40. Subway: 4, 5, 6, N, R to 60th St.

Hollywood meets Manhattan in the grand but frosty lobby of this ultra-luxury, ultra-modern hotel. Aging rock stars spice the brew, as can anyone with a generous expense account or a wad of cash to drop. Designed by I. M. Pei in 1993, the limestone-clad tower rises 52 stories, providing hundreds of rooms with a view. You'll immediately know this place is special, even in super-luxe New York, where anything goes. The white-on-white guest rooms are among New York's largest (averaging 600 square feet) and have entrance foyers, sitting areas, desks with leather chairs, and sycamore-paneled dressing areas. The Florentine marble baths have separate tubs and showers. Other special touches include goose-down pillows, Frette linens, oversized bath towels, and cushy robes. You'd expect less? For this much money, you deserve *more.*

Dining/Diversions: Fifty-Seven, Fifty-Seven is a fine contemporary New American grill and popular power-breakfast and lunch spot. The snazzy Bar offers an extensive martini menu to wash down light meals. The Lobby Lounge features lunch, afternoon tea, cocktails, and hors d'oeuvres.

Amenities: Luxurious fitness center with Jacuzzi and sauna, concierge, 24-hour room service, valet service, twice-daily maid service, free newspaper delivery, express checkout, free coffee in lobby 5:30–7am, business center, conference rooms. Baby-sitting, secretarial services, and in-room massage available.

Morgans. 237 Madison Ave. (btw. 37th and 38th sts.), New York, NY 10016. ☎ **800/334-3408** or 212/686-0300. Fax 212/779-8352. 113 units. A/C MINIBAR TV TEL. $310–$375 double, from $425 suite. Rates include continental breakfast and afternoon tea. AE, DC, DISC, MC, V. Valet parking $33. Subway: 6 to 33rd St.; 4, 5, 6, 7, S to Grand Central.

Ian Schrager's first boutique hotel (also see the Royalton) opened in 1984 as a low-profile "anti-hotel" without a sign or a staff experienced in hotel management. There's still little to give away its Murray Hill location except for the limos occasionally dropping off some high-profile type, but today the staff is experienced and competent. The hotel's original designer, Andrée Putman, also renovated the stylish interior in 1995; it eschews the over-the-top elements of the Starck-designed Royalton for a more low-key, grown-up sensiblity. The rooms are done with gorgeous tactile fabrics in a soothing palette of taupe, ivory, and black. They're not huge, but furnishings designed low to the ground and beautiful custom maple-eye built-ins—including storage and cushioned window seats for both lounging and out-of-sight luggage storage—make them feel more spacious. Other pleasing extras include a VCR, CD player, spacious work desk, and a state-of-the-art phone system. The small baths are a Putman signature, with black-and-white checkered tile and stainless-steel sinks; most have double-wide stall showers, so request a tub when booking if you require one.

Dining/Diversions: Asia de Cuba serves surprisingly good fusion cuisine to a trendsetting crowd, becoming a white-hot velvet-rope bar scene later in the evening. In the cellar is Morgans Bar, a Rande

Gerber (of the Whiskey bars) late-night hotspot for musicians, art-ists, and models, this time done up as a postmodern salon. The lovely breakfast room is for guests only.

Amenities: Concierge, 24-hour room service, valet service, news-paper delivery on request, free access to nearby New York Sports Club. Fax machines, cell phones, and laptops available for use.

The Peninsula–New York. 700 Fifth Ave. (at 55th St.), New York, NY 10019. ☎ **800/262-9467** or 212/956-2888. Fax 212/903-3949. www.peninsula.com. 241 units. A/C MINIBAR TV TEL. $560–$680 double, from $850 suite. Extra person $20; 1 child under 12 stays free in parents' room. AE, CB, DC, DISC, EURO, JCB, MC, V. Valet parking $38. Small pets allowed. Subway: E, F to 53rd St./Fifth Ave.

After $45 million and ten months of downtime, the Peninsula re-opened in November 1998 as a state-of-the-art stunner. Work your way past the redecorated public floors and everything's brand new; the guest-room floors were totally gutted and laid out afresh, allow-ing for high-tech wiring, better room configurations, and what may be the most fabulous bathrooms in the city.

Rooted in an elegant gold-cream-black palette, the decor is a rich mix of art nouveau, vibrant Asian elements (including gorgeous silk bedcovers), and contemporary art. Every room boasts lots of stor-age and counter space, and fabulous linens (including the cushiest bathrobes I've seen). But the real news is the technology, which in-cludes a room-wide speaker system and mood lighting; an executive workstation with desk-level inputs, direct-line fax, and dual-line speakerphones; a bedside panel for everything, from climate controls to the DO NOT DISTURB sign; even a doorside weather display. But wait, there's more: In the huge marble baths, a tub-level panel allows you to control the speaker system, answer the phone, and, if you're in any room above the lowest (superior) level, control the bathroom TV. Simply fabulous—but why go this far and put VCRs and CD players in the suites only?

Dining/Diversions: Redone with a fresh contemporary feel, Adrienne now serves an admirable eclectic menu with Asian touches, plus lighter meals in the adjoining Bistro. With a wonderful library-like vibe, the Gotham Lounge offers an excellent afternoon tea, cocktails, and snacks. The Pen-Top Bar and Terrace offers rooftop cocktails and some of midtown's most dramatic views.

Amenities: Three-level rooftop health club and spa (one of New York's best), with heated pool, exercise classes, Jacuzzi, sauna, and sundeck. Concierge, 24-hour room service, valet service, newspaper delivery, twice-daily maid service, express checkout, business center, conference rooms, tour desk, salon. Secretarial services, baby-sitting, in-room massage available.

✪ **The Sherry-Netherland.** 751 Fifth Ave. (at 59th St.). ☎ **800/247-4377** or 212/355-2800. Fax 212/319-4306. www.sherrynetherland.com. 77 units. A/C TV TEL. $295–$450 double, $550–$825 1-bedroom suite, from $830 2-bedroom suite. Rates include continental breakfast at Cipriani's. AE, DC, DISC, ER, JCB, MC, V. Subway: N, R to Fifth Ave.

For a taste of genteel New York apartment living, come to the Sherry-Netherland. Housed in a wonderful 1927 neo-Romanesque building overlooking Fifth Avenue and Central Park, the Sherry is one of a kind: both a first-class hotel and a quietly elegant residential building where the guest rooms are privately owned co-ops. As a result, they vary greatly in style, but each is grandly proportioned with high ceilings, big bathrooms, and walk-in closets. These are the largest rooms I've seen in the city, and every one features high-quality furnishings and art, VCR, fax machine, Godiva chocolates upon arrival, and fridge with free soft drinks (voice mail was not yet in place at this writing, so check before you book if that matters). About half are suites with kitchenettes that have a cooktop or microwave, often both. The hotel is expensive, but at least you get a lot for your dollar here.

The most wonderful thing about the Sherry is its homeyness—even the standard doubles have a residential feel. You'll pay more for a lighter, park- or street-facing room; the views are stunning, but the lower floors can be noisy for light-sleepers. Interior-facing rooms are appreciably darker and quieter but no less fabulous, and a lot cheaper. One of my favorite suites is no. 814, an interior one-bedroom done in a playful art deco-contemporary style. If you'd prefer a more traditionally styled room, let the excellent staff know. The hotel is Old World formal—there are even attendants in gold-trimmed jackets manning the elevators around the clock—but not the least bit stuffy. A true New York classic.

Dining/Diversions: Packed with Armani-suited moguls, million-dollar models, and east side denizens, bustling Cipriani's is the ultimate power spot. The wildly expensive food is excellent, as is the tuxedoed service. Well worth the splurge.

Amenities: Concierge, room service (7am–midnight), valet service, newspaper delivery of any paper you choose, twice-daily maid service, fitness room, meeting room, barber shop, beauty salon, newsstand. Free access to library stocked with *The New York Times* best-sellers and a complete catalogue of Oscar-winning films.

EXPENSIVE

The Avalon. 16 E. 32nd St. (btw. Fifth and Madison aves.), New York, NY 10016. ☎ **888/HI-AVALON** or 212/299-7000. Fax 212/299-7001. www.theavalonny.com. 100 units. A/C MINIBAR TV TEL. $195–$350 double, $250–$390 junior suite, $300–$600 deluxe or executive suite. Rates include continental breakfast. Check website for special offers. AE, DC, MC, V. Valet parking $23. Subway: 6 to 33rd St.

New York's newest boutique hotel is a mostly suite-filled, amenity-laden ode to luxury—I challenge you to find another hotel in the city that offers 5-foot body pillows in every room (Craig Stoltz of the *Washington Post* claimed that one of these gave him his best night's sleep *ever*). The George Patero-designed interiors are attractively done in muted colors in a sophisticated but comfy Americana style. The basic doubles are on the small side, but even they come with desks with easy-access dataport and outlets, double-paned windows to block out noise, 27-inch TVs (VCRs on request), two-line speaker phones with conferencing (credit card and toll-free calls are free!), Egyptian cotton and Irish linens, lighted makeup mirrors in the marble bath, fluffy Frette bathrobes, coffee makers with free fixin's, and more—even umbrellas. All suites have pullout sofas and two TVs; expect even more in the most expensive ones, such as whirlpool tubs, cordless phones, and Bose radios. The stylish staff is professional, if a little aloof; still, you can expect to have all your desires met.

Dining/Diversions: The Coach House is the domain of star chef Larry Forgione (of An American Place), so come prepared to have your taste buds tantalized. An expanded continental breakfast is served in the library (7–11am), and tea is available in the afternoons.

Amenities: Clef d'Or concierge, room service (7am–midnight), valet service, newspaper delivery, high-tech conference room, secretarial services; airport "meet and greet" services available. A fitness center was in the plans at press time, but guests have complimentary access to a nearby Bally's Sports club.

The Waldorf-Astoria and Waldorf Towers. 301 Park Ave. (btw. 49th and 50th sts.), New York, NY 10022. ☎ **800/WALDORF,** 800/774-1500, or 212/355-3000. Fax 212/872-7272 (Astoria) or 212/872-4799 (Towers). www.hilton.com. 1,280 units (119 in the Towers). A/C MINIBAR TV TEL. Waldorf-Astoria: $229–$415 double, $300–$475 suite. Waldorf Towers: $309–$525 double, from $389–$1,445 suite. Ask about corporate, senior, seasonal, and weekend discounts; check online for special packages, with rates sometimes as low as $189 at the Astoria. AE, CB, DC, DISC, EURO, JCB, MC, V. Valet parking $37. Subway: 6 to 51st St.

There's hardly a more elegant address in town, and the legend lives on in much better shape thanks to the $200 million Hilton Hotels spent to renovate this legendary art deco masterpiece. Each room in the main hotel is uniquely decorated, but all feature marble baths and the luxury amenities befitting a hotel of this level. And Hilton deserves extra points for keeping rates comparatively affordable for a property of this stature.

The exquisite, and more exclusive, Waldorf Towers occupies floors 27 to 42 and has a separate entrance. These rooms and suites feature authentic and reproduction English and French antiques, and many have dining rooms, full kitchens, and maid's quarters. The Towers is renowned for its excellent butler service and respect for privacy. The Presidential Suite is aptly named, having cosseted many world leaders. It's quite a dramatic scene when the President is in residence, with paparazzi armed guards out front, stopped traffic in the street, and helicopters buzzing overhead.

Dining/Diversions: There are a number of restaurants to choose from, the most notable being Peacock Alley, the revitalized formal dining room; and Inagiku, serving excellent Japanese food. At the Cocktail Terrace, you can enjoy afternoon tea or evening drinks while a pianist tickles the ivories on Cole Porter's very own Steinway Grand.

Amenities: Fitness center, concierge, 24-hour room service, valet service, weekday newspaper delivery (executive rooms only), express checkout, business center. Tower services include butler service and two concierges.

MODERATE

Clarion Hotel Fifth Avenue. 3 E. 40th St. (at Fifth Ave.), New York, NY 10016. ☎ **800/252-7466** or 212/447-1500. Fax 212/213-0972. www.hotelchoice.com. 189 units. A/C TV TEL. $159–$375 double. Children under 18 stay free in parents' room; extra person $15. Ask about senior, AAA, corporate, and promotional deals; check website for online booking discounts. AE, CB, DC, DISC, EURO, JCB, MC, V. Parking $19 2 blocks away. Subway: B, D, F, Q to 42nd St.

The location, price, and quality of the accommodations make this former Quality Hotel the best value on midtown's east side. Across Fifth Avenue from the New York Public Library, near Grand Central and Rockefeller Center, the hotel is close to Times Square but a notch down on the hustle-and-bustle level. It isn't the most stylish place in town, but it's clean and comfortable, and a full renovation (in progress at press time) will only make things better. Rooms come with either one or two double beds or a queen, a work area, coffee maker, clock radio, iron and ironing board, and a phone with dataport and free local calls (a great value-added touch). For the best view, ask for a high-floor room ending with the number 5. Wonderful extras that you don't usually find in hotels in this price category include complimentary morning coffee and weekday newspaper, concierge service, limited room service, valet service, business services, and express checkout. You'll have access to a nearby health club for $15.

9   The Upper West Side

VERY EXPENSIVE

✪ **Trump International Hotel & Tower.** 1 Central Park West (at 60th St.), New York, NY 10023. ☎ **888/44-TRUMP** or 212/299-1000. Fax 212/299-1150. www.citysearch/nyc/trumphotel. 167 units. A/C MINIBAR TV TEL. $475–$525 double, $750–$950 1-bedroom suite, $1,500 2-bedroom suite. Children stay free in parents' room. AE, CB, DC, JCB, MC, V. Valet parking $42. Subway: 1, 9, A, B, C, D to Columbus Circle.

Forget all your preconceptions about The Donald—this is a surprisingly cultivated venture from the ultimate 1980s Bad Boy.

New in 1997, Trump International is housed on 14 lower floors of a freestanding 52-story mirrored monolith at the southwest corner of Central Park, with unobstructed views on all sides. The rooms are on the small side, but high ceilings and smart design make them feel uncluttered. They're beautifully done in an understated contemporary style, with clean-lined furniture, beautiful fabrics, and soothing earth tones. Floor-to-ceiling windows maximize the spectacular views, which are especially breathtaking on the park-facing side. Each room is equipped with a fax machine, VCR, CD stereo, Jacuzzzi tub in the marble bath, excellent bathrobes, umbrellas, and a telescope for taking in the views.

But what really sets this hotel apart is its signature services. Each guest is assigned a Trump Attaché who basically functions as your own personal concierge, providing comprehensive business and personal services and, following your stay, recording your preferences to have on hand for your next visit. For the ultimate in romance and convenience, you can arrange in advance to have a chef from Jean Georges cook and prepare a mulitcourse meal right in your suite's own kitchen.

Dining: Awarded the coveted four stars by the *New York Times,* Jean Georges serves excellent contemporary French cuisine by one of the city's most celebrated chefs. Word is that not enough reservations are put aside for guests, so be sure to book a table well ahead.

Uptown Accommodations & Dining

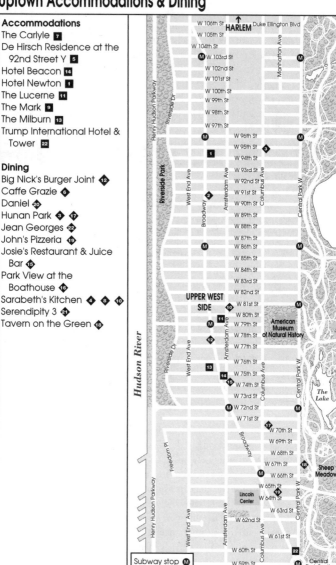

Accommodations
The Carlyle 7
De Hirsch Residence at the
  92nd Street Y 5
Hotel Beacon 14
Hotel Newton 1
The Lucerne 11
The Mark 9
The Milburn 13
Trump International Hotel &
  Tower 22

Dining
Big Nick's Burger Joint 12
Caffe Grazie 6
Daniel 20
Hunan Park 3 17
Jean Georges 22
John's Pizzeria 16
Josie's Restaurant & Juice
  Bar 15
Park View at the
  Boathouse 16
Sarabeth's Kitchen 4 8 10
Serendipity 3 21
Tavern on the Green 18

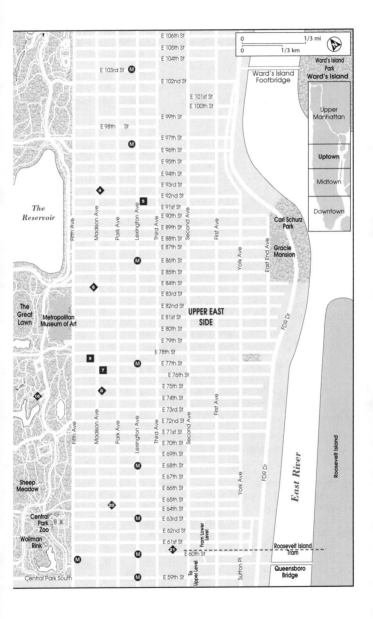

Amenities: Amazing 6,000-foot health and fitness spa with pool, steam rooms, saunas, personal trainers, and a full slate of spa treatments. Personal attaché service, 24-hour room service, valet service (with complimentary overnight pressing), free local phone calls, newspaper delivery, business center. Cell phones, computers, and printers upon request.

MODERATE

✪ **Hotel Beacon.** 2130 Broadway (at 75th St.), New York, NY 10023. ☎ **800/572-4969** or 212/787-1100. Fax 212/724-0839. www.beaconhotel.com. 210 units. A/C TV TEL. $145–$165 single, $170–$185 double, $205–$450 suite. Children under 17 stay free in parents' room; extra person $15. AE, DC, DISC, MC, V. Parking $25 nearby. Subway: 1, 2, 3, 9 to 72nd St.

Ideally located in one of the city's most desirable neighborhoods, the Beacon is one of the best deals in town, especially for families. Every generously sized room features a fully stocked kitchenette (with cooktop, coffee maker, minifridge, and microwave), roomy closet, alarm, voice mail, and new marble bathroom with hair dryer. Rooms won't win any personality awards, but they're freshly done in muted florals, and linens are plush. Virtually all standard rooms feature two double beds, and they're spacious enough to sleep a family on a budget. The big one- and two-bedroom suites are some of the best bargains in the city; each has two closets and a pull-out sofa in the well-furnished living room. The two-bedrooms have a second bathroom, making them well-outfitted enough to house a small army. Another fab family-friendly extra is the self-service laundromat. There's no room service, but with gourmet markets like Zabar's and Fairway nearby, cooking is an attractive alternative. Concierge and valet service are available, plus access to a terrific nearby health club for a daily fee. All in all, a great place to stay—and a great value to boot.

✪ **The Lucerne.** 201 W. 79th St. (at Amsterdam Ave.), New York, NY 10024. ☎ **800/492-8122** or 212/875-1000. Fax 212/579-2408. www.newyorkhotel.com/lucerne. 250 units. AC TV TEL. $150–$230 double, $190–$240 junior (queen) suite, $220–$450 1-bedroom suite. AE, DC, DISC, MC, V. AAA discounts offered; check website for special Internet deals. Parking $16 nearby. Subway: 1, 9 to 79th St.

Want top-notch comforts and service without paying top-dollar prices? Then book into this Mobil four-star, AAA three-diamond hotel, one of the best values in the city. As soon as the morning-suited doorman greets you at the entrance to the 1903 landmark building, you'll know you're getting more for your money than you expected. The bright marble lobby leads to comfortable guest rooms done in a tasteful Americana style. The standard rooms are big enough for a king, queen, or two doubles (great for those traveling with kids). All rooms have Nintendo, coffee makers, alarm, two-line phones with voice mail and dataport (although not always near the work desk), iron and ironing board, and attractive bathrooms with hair dryer, spacious travertine counters, and good toiletries. Everything is fresh and immaculate. The suites also boast kitchenttes with microwave and minifridge, terry robes, and a sitting room with a sofa and an extra TV and Nintendo set. The queen suites are a great deal for couples willing to spend a few extra dollars, while the larger suites with two queens or a king and pullout sofa give families the room they need (although Mom and Dad might get more space for their money at the Beacon).

The Lucerne prides itself on its excellent service record, so expect your needs to be promptly attended to. Amenities include a better-than-average fitness center with cardio machines and free weights, room service (7am–midnight), valet service, secretarial services (a business center was in the works at press time), and meeting space with a terrific rooftop sundeck. On site is Wilson's, an Upper West Side hotspot featuring good Continental fare and even better live jazz three or four nights a week.

INEXPENSIVE

✪ **Hotel Newton.** 2528 Broadway (btw. 94th and 95th sts.), New York, NY 10025. ☎ **888/HOTEL58** or 212/678-6500. Fax 212/678-6758. www.newyorkhotel.com/newton. 120 units (10 with shared bathroom). A/C TV TEL. $85 single or double with shared bathroom, $99–$135 single or double with private bathroom, $150 suite. Children under 17 stay free; extra person $15. AAA discounts available; check website for special Internet deals. AE, DC, DISC, MC, V. Subway: 1, 2, 3, 9 to 96th St.

Finally—an inexpensive hotel that's actually *nice*. Unlike many of its peers, the Newton doesn't scream "budget!" at every turn, or require you to have the carefree attitude of a college student to put up with it. As you enter the pretty lobby, you're greeted by a uniformed staff that's attentive and professional. The rooms are generally large, with good, firm beds, a work desk, and a sizable new bathroom, plus roomy closets in most (a few of the cheapest have wall racks only). Some are big enough to accommodate families with two doubles or two queen beds. The suites feature two queen beds in the bedroom, a sofa in the sitting room, plus niceties like a microwave, minifridge, iron and board, and hair dryer, making them well worth the few extra dollars. The bigger rooms and suites have been upgraded with cherry-wood furnishings, but even the older laminated furniture is much nicer than I usually see in this price range. The AAA-approved hotel is impeccably kept, and there was lots of sprucing up going on—new drapes here, fresh paint there—during my last visit. The nice neighborhood boasts lots of affordable restaurants, and a cute diner in the same block delivers room service from 6am to 1am. The 96th Street express subway stop is just a block away, providing convenient access to the rest of the city. A great bet all the way around.

The Milburn. 242 W. 76th St. (btw. Broadway and West End Ave.), New York, NY 10023. ☎ **800/833-9622** or 212/362-1006. Fax 212/721-5476. www.milburnhotel.com. 111 units. A/C TV TEL. $119–$145 studio double, $149–$175 1-bedroom suite, depending on season. Children under 12 stay free in parents' room; extra person $10. AE, CB, DC, MC, V. Parking $16–$20. Subway: 1, 2, 3, 9 to 72nd St.

On a quiet side street a block from the Beacon, the Milburn also offers rooms with kitchenettes in the same great neighborhood for less. The Milburn may not be quite as nice as the Beacon, but it offers equal value for your dollar, and arguably better in the less busy seasons, when a double studio goes for just $119. Every room is rife with amenities: dining area, safe, iron and ironing board, hairdryer, two-line phone with dataport, alarm, nice newish bath, and kitchenette with minifridge, microwave, coffee maker (with free coffee!), hot plate on request, and all the necessary equipment. The one-bedroom suites also boast a pullout queen sofa and a work desk. Don't expect much from the decor, but everything is attractive and in good shape. In fact, the whole place is spotless. But what makes the Milburn a real find is that it's more service-oriented than most hotels in this price range. The friendly staff will do everything from providing free copy, fax, and e-mail services to picking up your laundry at the dry cleaners next door. Additional facilities include a self-serve laundromat, VCR rentals, wheelchair-accessible rooms, discount dining programs at local restaurants, and use of the nearby Equinox health club for a special $15 fee (usually $35). At press time, a small workout room was in the works.

10 The Upper East Side

VERY EXPENSIVE

The Carlyle. 35 E. 76th St. (at Madison Ave.), New York, NY 10021. ☎ **800/227-5737** or 212/744-1600. Fax 212/717-4682. 180 units. A/C MINIBAR TV TEL. $375–$650 double, $600–$2,500 suite. AE, DC, MC, V. Valet parking $39. Pets are welcome. Subway: 6 to 77th St.

If you've ever wondered how the rich and famous live, check into the Carlyle. Countless movie stars and international heads of state (including JFK, who supposedly once was visited by Marilyn here) have laid their heads on the fluffy pillows. Why they choose the Carlyle is clear—its hallmark attention to detail. With a staff-to-guest ratio of about two-to-one, service is simply the best. The English manor-style decor is luxurious but not excessive, creating the comfortably elegant ambiance of an Upper East Side apartment. All rooms and suites have marble baths with whirlpool tubs and all the amenities you'd expect from a hotel of this caliber—even CD players and fax machines in every room.

Dining/Diversions: The Carlyle Restaurant features formal French dining in the evening as well as lavish breakfast and lunch buffets. Less stuffy but still dressy is Cafe Carlyle, the supper club where living legend Bobby Short and other big names entertain, which makes for an expensive but memorable night on the town. Both rooms serve up a legendary Sunday brunch, à la carte in the restaurant and buffet-style in the cafe. Charming Bemelmans Bar is a wonderful spot for cocktails, and the Gallery serves afternoon tea.

Amenities: High-tech fitness center with sauna and massage room, concierge, 24-hour room service, valet service, twice-daily maid service, banquet rooms. Business and secretarial services—as well as just about anything else you might need—are available.

The Mark. 25 E. 77th St. (btw. Fifth and Madison aves.), New York, NY 10021. ☎ **800/THE-MARK** in the U.S., 800/223-6800 in Canada, or 212/744-4300. Fax 212/744-2749. www.themarkhotel.com. 180 units. A/C MINIBAR TV TEL. $455–$530 double, from $650 suite. Children under 16 stay free in parents' room; extra person $30. Corporate rates available; ask about weekend packages, which can go as low as $299. AE, CB, DC, DISC, JCB, MC, V. Valet parking $35. Subway: 6 to 77th St.

After a $35-million renovation, the Mark positioned itself as the Carlyle's chief rival. Located in the heart of a tony neighborhood that makes an ideal base for museumgoers and boutique shoppers, it's superbly elegant and somewhat more contemporary in feeling than the Carlyle. Behind the 1929 building's art deco facade is a neoclassical decor and a wonderful air of tranquility. The lobby's custom-designed Biedermeier furniture and marble floors prepare you for the lovely guest rooms, which are larger than most and feature king-size beds with Frette triple sheeting, overstuffed chairs, upholstered sofas, and museum-quality art. Fresh flowers, two-line phones, fax machines, VCRs, terry robes, and even umbrellas are standard, and many rooms even have fully outfitted kitchenettes. The baths have oversized tubs, heated towel racks, and luxury toiletries. The GM has been named one of the top ten in the world, so it comes as no surprise that the service is beyond reproach.

Dining/Diversions: One of the best hotel restaurants in the city, Mark's serves consistently—and deservedly—high-rated New American-fusion cuisine in an elegant wood-paneled setting. The three-course pretheater dinner is an excellent value and the Sunday brunch is one of New York's best, while afternoon tea is a new institution among Upper East Side ladies. Mark's Bar serves hors d'oeuvres and cocktails.

Amenities: Award-winning concierge, 24-hour room service, fitness center with sauna, valet service, free newspaper delivery, twice-daily maid service, conference and banquet rooms, complimentary weekday car service to Wall Street, and Friday and Saturday evening car service to Theater District. Secretarial services, baby-sitting, and in-room massage available.

INEXPENSIVE

De Hirsch Residence at the 92nd Street Y. 1395 Lexington Ave. (at 92nd St.), New York, NY 10128. ☎ **888/699-6884,** or 212/415-5650. Fax 212/415-5578. www.92ndsty.org. 372 units (none with private bathroom). A/C. $69 single, $90 double; long-term stays (2 months or more) $795/month single, $1,100–$1,300/month double. Must be at least 18, and no older than 30 for long-term stays. AE, MC, V. Parking $20 nearby. Subway: 4, 5, 6 to 86th St.; 6 to 96th St.

Travelers on a tight budget should contact the 92nd Street Y well in advance. The de Hirsch Residence offers basic but comfortable rooms, each with either one or two single beds, a dresser, and bookshelves. Each floor has a large communal bathroom, a fully equipped kitchen/dining room with microwave, and laundry facilities. The building is rather institutional-looking but it's well-kept and secure, the staff is friendly, and the location is terrific. This high-rent Upper East Side neighborhood is just blocks from Central Park and Museum Mile, and there's plenty of cheap eats and places to pick up meal fixings within a few blocks. Daily maid service and use of the Y's state-of-the-art fitness facility (pool, weights, racquetball, aerobics) is included in the daily rates, making this a stellar deal. This is a great bet for lone travelers in particular, because the 92nd Street Y is a community center in a true sense of the word, offering a real sense of kinship and a mind-boggling slate of top-rated cultural happenings.

4

Dining

*A*ttention, foodies: Welcome to Mecca. Without a doubt, New York is the best restaurant town in the country, and one of the top in the world. Other cities might have particular specialties—Paris has better bistros, of course, Hong Kong better Chinese, Austin better barbecue—but no culinary capital spans the globe so successfully as the Big Apple.

RESERVATIONS   Reservations are always a good idea in New York, and a virtual necessity if your party is bigger than two. Do yourself a favor and call ahead as a rule of thumb so you won't be disappointed. If you're booking dinner on a weekend night, it's a good idea to call a few days in advance if you can.

For bookings at the city's most popular restaurants, call far ahead—a month is a good idea. If you're booking a holiday dinner, call earlier.

But if you didn't call well ahead and your heart's set on dinner at Le Cirque or Gramercy Tavern, don't despair. Often, early or late hours—between 6 and 7pm, or after 10pm—are available, especially on weeknights. And try calling the day before or first thing in the morning, when you may be able to take advantage of a last-minute cancellation. Or go for lunch, which is usually much easier to book without lots of advance notice. And if you're staying at a hotel with a concierge, don't be afraid to use them—they can often get you into hot spots that you couldn't get into on your own.

But What If They Don't *Take* Reservations?   Lots of city restaurants, especially at the affordable end of the price continuum, don't take reservations at all. One of the ways they're able to keep prices down is by packing people in as quickly as possible. This means that the best cheap and mid-priced restaurants often have a wait. Again, your best bet is to go early. Often, you can get in more quickly on a weeknight. Or just go knowing that you're going to have to wait if you head to a popular spot like Boca Chica, and hunker down with a margarita at the bar, taking in the festivities around you.

A Tipping Tip

Tipping is easy in New York. The way to do it: Double the 8¼% sales tax and voilà!, happy waitperson. In fancier venues, another 5% is appropriate for the captain. If the wine steward helps, hand him or her 10% of the bottle's price. Leave a dollar per item, no matter how small, for the checkroom attendant.

The Lowdown on Smoking   Following the national trend, New York City enacted strict no-smoking laws a few years back that made most of the city's dining rooms blessedly smoke-free. However, that doesn't mean that smokers are completely prohibited from lighting up. Here's the deal: Restaurants with more than 35 seats cannot allow smoking in their dining rooms. They can, however, allow smoking in their bar or lounge areas, and most do. Restaurants with fewer than 35 seats—and there are more of those in the city than you'd think—can allow or prohibit smoking as they see fit. This ruling has turned some of the city's restaurants into particularly smoker-friendly establishments, which might be a turn-off for non-smokers.

Whether you're a smoker or non-smoker, your best bet is to call ahead and ask about the smoking policy if it matters to you.

1   South Street Seaport & the Financial District

INEXPENSIVE

Mangia. 40 Wall St. (btw. Nassau and William sts.). ☎ **212/425-4040** or 212/363-9536. Main courses $5.95–$9.95. AE, DC, MC, V. Mon–Fri 7am–8pm. Subway: 4, 5 to Wall St.; J, M, Z to Broad St. GOURMET DELI.

This big, bustling gourmet cafeteria is an ideal place to take a break during your day of Financial District sightseeing. Between the giant salad and soup bars, the sandwich and hot entree counters, and an expansive cappuccino-and-pastry counter at the front of the cavernous room, even the most finicky eater will have a hard time deciding what to eat. Everything is freshly prepared and beautifully presented. Pay-by-the-pound salad bars don't get any better than this, hot meal choices (such as grilled mahi-mahi or cumin-marinated lamb kabob) are cooked to order, and sandwiches are freshly made as you watch. This place is packed with Wall Streeters between noon and 2pm, but things move quickly and there's enough seating that usually no one has to wait. Come in for a late breakfast or an afternoon snack, and you'll virtually have the place to yourself.

Lower Manhattan, TriBeCa & Chinatown

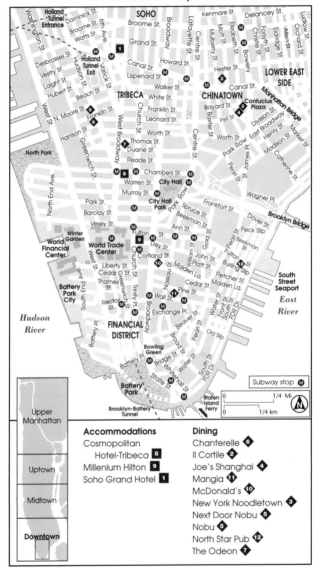

Accommodations
Cosmopolitan
  Hotel-Tribeca **8**
Millenium Hilton **9**
Soho Grand Hotel **1**

Dining
Chanterelle **6**
Il Cortile **2**
Joe's Shanghai **4**
Mangia **11**
McDonald's **10**
New York Noodletown **3**
Next Door Nobu **5**
Nobu **5**
North Star Pub **12**
The Odeon **7**

You Want Fries With That?

Wall Street's famous McDonald's, 160 Broadway, between Maiden
Lane and Liberty Street (☎ 212/385-2063), elevates the Happy Meal
to a whole new level. Ever been to another McDonald's where a doorman in tails greets you, a hostess finds you a table and sets
it with place mats, and a tux-clad pianist tickles the ivories at a
candelabra-topped baby grand? But lest you fear that Ronald has abandoned his winning formula, don't worry: Everything else, from the
quarter pounders to the ice-milk shakes, is comfortingly familiar.

In addition to the Wall Street location, Mangia also has two
cafeteria-style cafes in midtown that offer similar, if not such expansive, menus: at 50 W. 57th St., between Fifth and Sixth avenues
(☎ 212/582-5882); and at 16 E. 48th St., just east of Fifth Avenue
(☎ 212/754-7600).

North Star Pub. At South Street Seaport, 93 South St. (at Fulton St.). ☎ **212/
509-6757.** Main courses $7.50–$12.95. AE, CB, DC, MC, V. 11:30am–
10:30pm. Subway: 2, 3, 4, 5 to Fulton St. BRITISH.

This friendly place right at the entrance to the seaport is a refresh-
ing bit of authenticity in the mallified, almost theme park-like historic district. It's the spitting image of a British pub, down to the
chalkboard menus boasting daily specials like kidney pie and the
Guinness, Harp, and Fullers ESB on tap. We love the ale-battered
fish 'n' chips, good-quality fish deep-fried just right (not too greasy);
the excellent golden-browned shepherd's pie (just like grandma used
to make); the bangers 'n' mash, made with grilled Cumberland sausage; and the traditional Ploughman's, including very good pâté, a
sizable hunk of cheddar or stilton, fresh bread, and all the accompaniments (even Branston pickle!). All in all, a fun, relaxing place
to hang out and eat and drink heartily (and cheaply). There's also
an expansive menu of single-malt scotches and Irish whiskeys.

2 TriBeCa

VERY EXPENSIVE

✪ **Chanterelle.** 2 Harrison St. (btw. Hudson and Greenwich sts.). ☎ **212/
966-6960.** Reservations recommended well in advance. Prix-fixe lunch $35, à
la carte lunch $18.50–$24; prix-fixe dinner $75, tasting menu $89. AE, CB, DC,
DISC, MC, V. Mon 5:30–11pm, Tues–Sat noon–2:30pm and 5:30–11pm. Subway: 1, 9 to Franklin St. CONTEMPORARY FRENCH.

Here's a true special occasion restaurant. One of only five places to hold four stars from the *New York Times,* Chanterelle leaves you saying not only "The food was superb" or "The wine was sublime," but also "Thank you for a marvelous time." Overseen by husband-and-wife co-owners David and Karen Waltuch, the first-rate waitstaff—the best in the city—makes sure of it. There's no stuffiness here at all; everyone is encouraged to feel at home and relaxed. Your server will know the handwritten menu in depth and be glad to describe preparations in detail and suggests complementary combinations. The artful cuisine is based on traditional French technique, but Pacific and pan-European notes sneak into the culinary melodies, and lots of dishes are lighter than you'd expect. The seasonal menu changes every few weeks, but one signature dish appears on almost every menu: a marvelous grilled seafood sausage. Cheese lovers should opt for a cheese course—the presentation and selection can't be beat. The dining room is simple but beautiful, with a pressed-tin ceiling, widely spaced large tables, comfortable chairs, and gorgeous flowers. The wine list is superlative, but we wish there were more affordable options. Still, you don't come to Chanterelle on the cheap—you come to celebrate. Very expensive, but magnificent.

EXPENSIVE

✪ **Nobu/Next Door Nobu.** 105 Hudson St. (at Franklin St.). ☎ **212/ 219-0500** for Nobu; ☎ **212/334-4445** for Next Door Nobu. Reservations required far in advance at Nobu; reservations taken only for parties of 6 or more at Next Door Nobu. Most dishes $8–$32; sushi $3–$10 per piece. AE, DC, MC, V. Mon–Fri 11:45am–2:15pm, daily 5:45–10:15pm at Nobu; Mon–Thurs 5:45–midnight, Fri–Sat 5:45pm–1am. Subway: 1, 9 to Franklin St. NEW JAPANESE.

Chef Nobu Matsuhisa took New York by storm in 1994 with his innovative, pan-cultural preparations, and Nobu has been flying high ever since. Deeply rooted in Japanese tradition but heavily influenced by Latin American and Western techniques, his cooking is more than adventurous; it bursts with creative spirit. Unusual textures, impulsive combinations, and surprising flavors add up to a first-rate dining adventure that you won't soon forget. Virtually every creation hits its target, whether you opt for the new-style sashimi, seared whitefish in olive oil seasoned with garlic, ginger, and sesame; light-as-air rock shrimp tempura; or sublime broiled black cod in sweet miso, the best dish in the house. If Kobe beef is available, try this delicacy tataki style (with soy, scallions, and daikon). The knowledgeable staff will be happy to guide you on your culinary adventure. However, since most dinners are structured as a series of tasting plates, be aware that the bill can soar—wallet-watchers should keep a close eye on the tally. The excitement is heightened by the witty modern decor (check out the chopstick-legged chairs at the sushi bar). The only disappointment is the traditional sushi, which doesn't live up to the more creative dishes; head elsewhere for a full sushi meal.

But you can't get a reservation at Nobu? Take heart, for now there's **Next Door Nobu,** the slightly more casual version that has a firm no-reservations policy. This is great news in this exclusionary town: Just show up, wait your turn, and you get a table. Because waits can be as long as 90 minutes, the secret is to go early: We walked in at 6:30pm on a weeknight and the place was half-empty. This isn't cut-rate Nobu—you get the full treatment here, too. The modern room is highly stylized but comfortable, all the house specialties are available, and the service is equal to the main restaurant. Noodle dishes add a moderately priced dimension to the menu, but it takes a lot of willpower to keep the tab low. There's also a raw bar, the star of which is sea urchin served in the shell, a perfect juxtaposition of textures for bold palates.

MODERATE

The Odeon. 145 W. Broadway (at Thomas St.). ☎ **212/233-0507.** Reservations recommended for parties of 4 or more. Main courses $9–$25. AE, DC, MC, V. Mon–Wed noon–2am, Thurs–Fri noon–3am, Sat 11:30am–3am, Sun 11:30am–2am. Subway: 1, 2, 3, 9 to Chambers St. (walk 3 blks. north). AMERICAN/FRENCH.

The Odeon is always the first place that comes to mind when I crave a late-night meal, but this attractive hotspot is satisfying at any time of day. The striking deco-ish room is perennially trendy but universally welcoming—no velvet ropes here. Sure, you might see a famous face a couple of tables away, but it's the food that's the real draw. The restaurant crosses budget and culture lines: It's easy to eat cheap here if you stick to the burgers, vegetarian chili, and sandwiches, or you can spend a little more and go for excellent steak frites, roasted free-range chicken, braised lamb shank, and other top-notch brasserie-style dinners. The prices are lower than they have to be for food like this, and the wine list is equally reasonable. With rich wood paneling, Formica-topped tables, and leather banquettes, the Odeon even manages to be swanky and comfortable at the same time. As proof of its egalitarianism, there's even a kid's menu—and the chocolate pudding is scrumptious.

3   Chinatown & Little Italy

MODERATE

Il Cortile. 125 Mulberry St. (btw. Canal and Hester sts.). ☎ **212/226-6060.** Reservations recommended. Pastas $8.50–$22, meats and fish $16.50–$32. AE, DC, DISC, MC, V. Sun–Thurs noon–midnight, Fri–Sat noon–1am. Subway: 6, N, R to Canal St. NORTHERN ITALIAN.

The best restaurant in Little Italy stands out on Mulberry Street thanks to its warm, sophisticated demeanor amid the bright lights and bold decor of its lesser neighbors. There's a certain Old World elegance to the menu: Like a *billet doux* from the chef, it's folded and sealed with gold foil. The second sign that you're out of the Little Italy ordinary arrives with the warm basket of focaccia, crusty small loaves, golden-brown crostini, and crunchy breadsticks. The Northern Italian fare is well-prepared and pleasing: the greens fresh and crisp, the sauces appropriately seasoned, the pastas perfectly al dente. This is traditional cuisine, but not without a few welcome twists: The filet mignon carpaccio is rolled with onions and parsley, thick cut, and seared; shiitakes give an unexpected flair to the rigatoni. On my last visit, the best dish at our table was the polenta with mushrooms in a savory white wine sauce, a bargain at $10.50. The waitstaff, made up of career neighborhood waiters, is attentive and reserved in an appealing Old World style. The extensive wine cellar, hidden behind a beautiful wooden door that looks as if it may have been liberated from a grand European castle, contains a good number of well-priced selections.

INEXPENSIVE

Joe's Shanghai. 9 Pell St. (btw. Bowery and Mott sts.). ☎ **212/233-8888.** Reservations recommended for 10 or more. Main courses $4.25–$12.95. No credit cards. Sun–Thurs 11am–10pm, Fri–Sat 11am–10:30pm. Subway: N, R, 6 to Canal St; B, D, Q to Grand St. SHANGHAI CHINESE.

Tucked away on a little elbow of a side street just off the Bowery is this Chinatown institution, which serves up authentic cuisine to enthusiastic crowds nightly. The stars of the huge menu are the signature soup dumplings, quivering steamed pockets filled with hot broth and your choice of pork or crab, accompanied by a side of seasoned soy. Listed on the menu as "steamed buns" (item numbers 1 and 2), these culinary marvels never disappoint. Neither does the rest of the authentic Shanghai-inspired menu, which boasts such main courses as whole yellowfish bathed in spicy sauce; excellent "mock duck," a saucy bean-curd dish similar to Japanese yuba that's a hit with vegetarians and carnivores alike; and lots of well-prepared staples. The room is set mostly with round tables of ten or so, and you'll be asked if you're willing to share. I encourage you to do so; it's a great way to watch and learn from your neighbors (many of whom are Chinese), who are usually more than happy to tell you what they're eating. If you want a private table, expect a wait.

✪ **New York Noodletown.** 28½ Bowery (at Bayard St.). ☎ **212/349-0923.** Reservations accepted. Main courses $3.95–$10.95. No credit cards. Daily 9am–4am. Subway: N, R, 6 to Canal St. SEAFOOD/CHINESE.

This just may be the best Chinese food in New York City. Among its fans are Ruth Reichl, former restaurant critic for the *New York Times*, who constantly put it at the top of the heap. But don't expect fancy—this is two-star food served in no-star ambiance. So what if the room is reminiscent of a school cafeteria? The food is fabulous. The mushroom soup is a lunch in itself, thick with earthy chunks of shiitakes, vegetables, and thin noodles. Another appetizer that can serve as a meal is the hacked roast duck in noodle soup. The kitchen excels at seafood preparations, so be sure to try at least one: the salt-baked squid is sublime. The quick-woked Chinese broccoli or the crisp sautéed baby bok choy make great accompaniments. Other special dishes are sandy pot casseroles, hearty, flavorful affairs slow-simmered in clay vessels. Unlike most of its neighbors, New York Noodletown keeps very long hours, which makes it the best late-night bet in the neighborhood, too.

4 SoHo

EXPENSIVE

✪ **Quilty's.** 177 Prince St. (btw. Sullivan and Thompson sts.). ☎ **212/254-1260.** Reservations highly recommended. Main courses $10–$18.50 at lunch, $19.50–$29 at dinner; weekend brunch $8–$18.50. AE, DC, DISC, MC, V. Mon 6–11pm, Tues–Sat noon–3pm and 6–11pm, Sun 11am–3pm and 6–10pm. Subway: C, E to Spring St.; N, R to Prince St. CONTEMPORARY AMERICAN.

No matter how many restaurants I visit in this city, Quilty's remains one of my absolute favorites. Chef Katy Sparks and her crew just get it all right. The subtle, softly lit room is intimate and relaxing, with decently sized and spaced tables, comfortable seating, and an elegantly casual SoHo-goes-pastoral vibe that makes the restaurant feel special without being formal or stuffy. The greeting is warm, and the service professional yet personable. The feisty New American menu changes with the seasons, but you can expect bold, complex flavors that wow without overwhelming. There's always a lot going on in

The East Village & SoHo Area

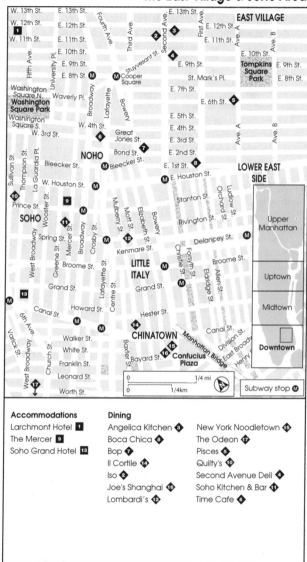

Accommodations

Larchmont Hotel **1**
The Mercer **9**
Soho Grand Hotel **13**

Dining

Angelica Kitchen **3**
Boca Chica **8**
Bop **7**
Il Cortile **14**
Iso **2**
Joe's Shanghai **16**
Lombardi's **12**

New York Noodletown **15**
The Odeon **17**
Pisces **5**
Quilty's **10**
Second Avenue Deli **4**
Soho Kitchen & Bar **11**
Time Cafe **6**

the dishes, but they're always harmonious. Last time I dined here (from the autumn menu), the fresh cepes baked in parchment and paired with harmony croutons and ricotta salata were a delicate symphony. And a reisling coriander jus was the ideal twist to the perfect comfort food: roasted organic chicken with buttermilk-battered onion rings. For dessert, the caramelized golden pineapple with vanilla bean–anise sauce was an ideal reinvention of the tropical fruit. The wine list is on the high side, but tends toward special vintages and rare labels; lively descriptions make it fun to choose, but the knowledgeable waitstaff is happy to suggest pairings if you prefer. Any way you look at it, Quilty's is a winner.

INEXPENSIVE

Lombardi's. 32 Spring St. (Mott and Mulberry sts.). ☎ **212/941-7994.** Reservations accepted for parties of 6 or more. Small pies (6 slices) $10.50–$16, large pies $12.50–$20. No credit cards. Mon–Thurs 11:30am–11pm, Fri–Sat 11:30am–midnight, Sun 11:30am–10pm. Subway: 6 to Spring St.; N, R to Prince St. PIZZA.

Lombardi's is a living gem in the annals of the city's culinary history. First opened in 1905, "America's first licensed pizzeria" still cooks some of New York's best pizza in its original coal brick oven. The wonderful, crispy-thin crust (a generations-old family recipe that Gennaro Lombardi hand-carried from Naples at the turn of the century) is topped with fresh mozzarella, basil, and tomatoes, Pecorino romano cheese, and virgin olive oil. From there, the choice is yours. Topping options are suitably Old World (pancetta, calamata olives, Italian sausage, and the like), but Lombardi's specialty is the fresh clam pie, with hand-shucked clams, oregano, garlic, romano, and pepper (no sauce). The main dining room is narrow but pleasant, with the usual checkered tablecloths and exposed brick walls. A big draw is the garden out back, where tables sport Cinzano umbrellas and a flowering tree shoots up through the concrete. Another plus: In a city where rudeness is a badge of honor, Lombardi's wait staff is extremely affable.

Soho Kitchen & Bar. 103 Greene St. (btw. Spring and Prince sts.). ☎ **212/925-1866.** Main courses $7.75–$18.50. AE, MC, V. Mon–Thurs 11:30am–midnight, Fri–Sat 11:30am–2am, Sun 12:30–11pm. Subway: N, R to Prince St.; C, E to Spring St. AMERICAN.

Even though the food is nothing special, the fun, easygoing atmosphere makes Soho Kitchen a regular stop on my agenda. This large, lofty space attracts an animated after-work and late-night crowd to its central bar, which dispenses more than 21 beers on tap, a whole slew of microbrews by the bottle, and more than 100 wines by the glass, either individually or in "flights" for comparative tastings. The menu offers predictable but affordable bar fare: buffalo wings, oversize salads, good burgers, and a variety of sandwiches and thin-crust pizzas. You won't spend more than 12 bucks or so on your main meal unless you graduate to entrees like the New York sirloin, which makes this a great bet for wallet-watchers.

5 The East Village

MODERATE

In addition to the choices below, also consider the NoHo branch of Time Cafe, 380 Lafayette St., at Great Jones Street (☎ 212/533-7000), which has a wonderful Moroccan-themed lounge called Fez (see chapter 6 for details).

✪ **Bop.** 325 Bowery (at 2nd St.). ☎ **212/254-7887.** Reservations accepted for parties of 4 or more. Main courses $12.95–$18.95. AE, MC, V. Mon–Sat 6pm–midnight, Sun 6–11pm; bar open daily from 5pm. Subway: 6 to Bleecker St.; F to 2nd Ave. KOREAN.

Bop may be on the fringes of Chinatown, but don't expect your average brightly-lit ethnic restaurant serving up the staples. This is a gorgeous space designed with the beautiful people in mind and dimly lit for ultimate effect. But that's where the pretensions end: The friendly, attentive staff serves wonderful modern Korean cuisine with pan-Asian twists. The signature dish is *bi bim bop,* rice served either sizzling in a hot stone bowl or warm in a wooden bowl with wild mountain vegetables, kimchee, and raw tuna or shredded beef. We prefer the sizzling variety, which actually cooks as you mix the ingredients with chili paste (you define the temperature by how much you add). For an even more interactive meal, dine at one of the tabletop barbecues, where you can have such specialties as short ribs brushed with sake and soy or squid marinated in chili sauce cooked right in front of you. Cocktail lovers shouldn't pass on the soju, a yummy, lightly sweet Korean vodka made from sweet potatoes that's beautifully served in a martini glass with cucumber slices.

Iso. 175 Second Ave. (at 11th St.). ☎ **212/777-0361.** Reservations not taken. À la carte sushi $2.50–$6; sushi rolls $4.50–$12.50; sushi combos and main courses $13.50–$21. AE, MC, V. Mon–Sat 5:30pm–midnight. Subway: 6 to Astor Place. SUSHI.

Iso is the top choice in town for fresh and beautifully presented sushi at affordable prices. The sushi and sashimi combos make a good-value starting point; supplement with your favorites or a few of the daily special fishes, which may include blue fin toro (tuna belly) or Japanese aji (horse mackerel). The menu also features light, greaseless tempura and entrees like chicken teriyaki and beef negamaki for the sushiphobes in your party. The attractive Keith Haring-themed room is tightly packed but still manages to be relatively comfortable, and service is better than at other sushi joints in this price range. Unless you arrive before 6pm, expect a line—but the high-quality fish and wallet-friendly pricing make Iso worth the wait.

✪ **Pisces.** 95 Ave. A (at 6th St.). ☎ **212/260-6660.** Reservations recommended. Main courses $8.95–$19.95; 2-course prix-fixe dinner (Mon–Thurs 5:30–7pm, Fri–Sun 5:30–6:30pm) $14.95. AE, CB, DC, MC, V. Mon–Thurs 5:30–11:30pm, Fri 5:30pm–1am, Sat 11:30am–3:30pm and 5:30pm–1am, Sun 11:30am–3:30pm and 5:30–11:30pm. Subway: 6 to Astor Place. SEAFOOD.

This excellent fish house serves up the best moderately priced seafood in the city. All fish is top-quality and fresh daily, and all smoked items are prepared in the restaurant's own smoker. But it's the creative kitchen, which shows surprising skill with vegetables as well as fish, that makes Pisces a real winner. The mesquite-smoked whole trout in sherry oyster sauce is sublime, better than trout I've had for twice the price; start with the phyllo-fried shrimp or the tuna ceviche with curried potato chips and roasted pepper coulis, and the world is yours. There are daily specials in addition to the menu; last time we dined here, I feasted on an excellent grilled mako shark with chard in a cockle stew. The wine list is appealing and very well priced, the decor suitably nautical without being kitschy, and the service friendly and attentive. For wallet-watchers, the early-bird prix-fixe makes an already terrific value even better. The Alphabet City locale gives Pisces a serious hip factor, but it's laid-back enough that even Grandma will be comfortable here. Tables spill out onto the sidewalk on warm evenings, giving you a ringside seat for the funky East Village show.

INEXPENSIVE

Angelica Kitchen. 300 E. 12th St. (just east of Second Ave.). ☎ **212/228-2909.** Reservations accepted for 6 or more Mon–Thurs. Main courses $5.95–$14.25; lunch deal (Mon–Fri 11:30am–5pm) $6.75. No credit cards. Daily 11:30am–10:30pm. Subway: L, N, R, 4, 5, 6, to 14th St./Union Sq. ORGANIC VEGETARIAN.

If you like to eat healthy, take note: This cheerful restaurant is serious about vegan cuisine. The kitchen prepares everything fresh daily; they guarantee that at least 95% of all ingredients are organically grown, with sustainable agriculture and responsible business practices additionally required before food can cross the kitchen's

The New York Deli News

There's simply nothing more Noo Yawk than hunkering down over a mammoth pastrami sandwich or a lox-and-bagel plate at an authentic Jewish deli, where anything you order comes with a bowl of lip-smacking sour dills and a side of attitude.

Opened in 1937, the **Stage Deli,** 834 Seventh Ave., between 53rd and 54th streets (**212/245-7850**), may be New York's oldest continuously run deli. The Stage is noisy and crowded and packed with tourists, but it's still as authentic as they come. Connoisseurs line up to sample the 36 famous specialty sandwiches named after many of the stars whose photos adorn the walls: The Tom Hanks is roast beef, chopped liver, onion, and chicken fat, while the Dolly Parton is—drumroll, please—twin rolls of corned beef and pastrami.

For the quintessential New York experience, head to the **Carnegie Deli,** 854 Seventh Ave., at 55th Street (☎ **212/757-2245**), where it's worth subjecting yourself to surly service, tourist-targeted pricing, and elbow-to-elbow seating to the best pastrami and corned beef in town. Even big eaters may be challenged by mammoth sandwiches with names like "fifty ways to love your liver" (chopped liver, hard-boiled egg, lettuce, tomato, and onion). Cheesecake can't get more divine, so save room!

The ✪ **Second Avenue Deli,** 156 Second Ave., at 10th Street (☎ 212/677-0606), is the best kosher choice in town (for all you goyem out there, that means no milk, butter, or cheese is served). There's no bowing to tourism here—this is the real deal. The service is brusque, the decor is nondescript, and the sandwiches don't have cute names, but the dishes served here are true New York classics: gefilte fish, matzoh ball soup, chicken livers, potato knishes, nova lox and eggs. And for $11 to $13—several bucks cheaper than midtown's Carnegie—you get a monster triple decker sandwich with a side of fries. The crunchy dills are to die for. Keep an ear tuned to the Catskills-quality banter among crusty wait staff.

threshold. But good-for-you (and good-for-the-environment) doesn't have to mean boring—this is flavorful, beautifully prepared cuisine served in a lovely country kitchen-style setting. Salads spill over with sprouts and all kinds of crisp veggies and are crowned with homemade dressings. The Dragon Bowls, a specialty, are heaping portions of rice, beans, tofu, and steamed vegetables. The daily seasonal specials feature the best of what's fresh and in season in such dishes as fiery three-bean chili, slow-simmered with sundried tomatoes and a blend of chile peppers; baked tempeh nestled in a sourdough baguette and dressed in mushroom gravy; and lemon-herb baked tofu layered with roasted vegetables and fresh pesto on mixed-grain bread. Breads and desserts are fresh baked and similarly wholesome (and made without eggs, of course).

Boca Chica. 13 First Ave. (at 1st St.). ☎ **212/473-0108.** Reservations accepted for parties of 6 or more Mon–Thurs only. Main dishes $7.50–$19.75 (most under $13). AE, MC, V. Sun–Thurs 6–11pm, Fri–Sat 6pm–midnight. Subway: F to Second Ave. SOUTH AMERICAN.

This lively, colorful joint is always packed with a gleefully mixed crowd working its way through a round of margaritas or a few pitchers of beer. The cuisine is a downmarket version of the pan-Latino favorites that have captivated palates farther uptown. The food at Boca Chica is a little closer to its hearty South American roots: well-prepared pork, beef, fish, and vegetarian dishes, most pleasingly heavy on the sauce and spice, accompanied by plantains, rice, and beans. There's also a bevy of interesting appetizers, including black bean soup well-seasoned with lime juice and terrific coconut-fried shrimp. While this approach to cooking now tends to be well out of reach of the under-$25 crowd, Boca Chica keeps things at an affordable level, much to the delight of those of us without bottomless wallets. *Be forewarned:* Getting in on weekends is about as hard as sneaking into Havana.

6 Greenwich Village

VERY EXPENSIVE

One If By Land, Two If By Sea. 17 Barrow St. (btw. W. 4th St. and Seventh Ave. South). ☎ **212/228-0822.** Reservations strongly recommended. Jacket recommended; tie optional. Main courses $29–$39; tasting menu $68. AE, DC, DISC, MC, V. Daily 5:30–11:30pm. Subway: 1, 9 to Christopher St. CONTINENTAL.

Ask just about any New Yorker to point you to the city's most romantic restaurant and you'll end up at this candlelit, rose-filled 18th-century carriage house once owned by Aaron Burr. This beautiful, intimate space has been a haven of lovers (and those who hope to be) for nearly 30 years. The fireplace crackles and a pianist fills the room with melody as you are escorted to your table for two by the tuxedoed maitre'd. Given the emphasis on romance, it's no wonder that food has always come second here. It has never been bad—just committedly retro in the way that makes food snobs turn

Greenwich Village

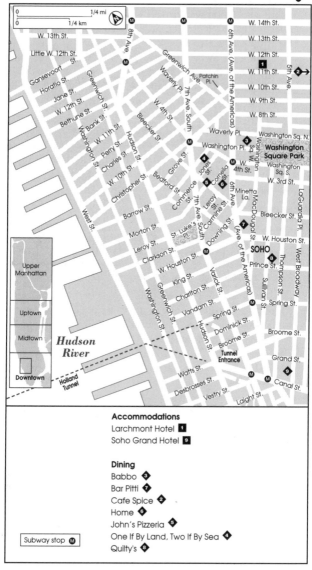

Accommodations

Larchmont Hotel **1**

Soho Grand Hotel **9**

Dining

Babbo **3**

Bar Pitti **7**

Cafe Spice **2**

Home **6**

John's Pizzeria **5**

One If By Land, Two If By Sea **4**

Quilty's **8**

Subway stop **Ⓜ**

85

up their noses ("Beef Wellington? Ugh!"). But now that chef David McInerney has taken over the kitchen, even gourmands are giving One If By Land a second look. It's still pleasingly Continental-classic, but a few modern touches have given the menu new life. Among the best appetizers are the foie gras terrine with wild field greens and warm brioche, and rosy seared tuna with fresh wasabi, baby fennel, and shiitakes. The pan-roasted duck breast is greaseless and perfectly accompanied by cherries and black lentils, and the rack of lamb is lightly smoked and roasted. And, of course, there's the beef Wellington with bordelaise sauce—still a classic, and outstanding. The formal service is attentive without being intrusive. The wine list boasts no bargains, but does have a number of celebratory champagnes.

EXPENSIVE

✪ **Babbo.** 110 Waverly Place (just east of Sixth Ave.). ☎ **212/777-0303.** Reservations highly recommended. Pastas $16–$19, meats and fish $19–$25; tasting menus $49–$59. AE, DC, DISC, MC, V. Tues–Sat 5:30–11:30pm, Sun 4–9:30pm. Subway: A, B, C, D, E, F, Q to W. 4th St. (use 8th St. exit). NORTHERN ITALIAN.

Chef Mario Batali may not be Emeril (yet), but his zesty, adventurous cooking has attracted a lot of attention since he began appearing on the Food Network. And justifiably so—Babbo is my pick for New York's top new restaurant.

As soon as we saw Babbo's inviting butter-yellow facade, we knew we were in for something special. The restaurant is warm and intimate, with well-spaced tables and a relaxed air that makes dining here feel special but comfortable, not formal. The greeting is welcoming and the service smart and friendly. That's a good thing, because you may need help choosing from the risk-taking menu. Batali has reinvented the notion of antipasti with such starters as fresh anchovies beautifully marinated in lobster oil, and legendary Faicco sopressata accented with roasted beets, shaved fennel, and Macintosh vinegar. The chef has no equal when it comes to creative pastas; ask anyone who's dined here and they'll wax poetic about the spicy lamb sausage in delicate clouds called mint love letters, quickly becoming Babbo's signature dish. Heavy with offals and game meats, the *secondi* menu features such wonders as tender fennel-dusted sweetbreads; smoky grilled quail in a gamey but heavenly fig and duck liver vinaigrette; and spicy two-minute calamari, a paragon of culinary simplicity. The knowledgeable sommelier can help you choose from the unusual but excellent wine list, all Italian and well priced.

MODERATE

✪ **Home.** 20 Cornelia St. (btw. Bleecker and W. 4th sts.) ☎ **212/243-9579.** Reservations highly recommended. Main courses $14–$18 at dinner. AE. Mon–Fri 9–11am, 11:30am–3pm, 6–11pm; Sat–Sun 11am–4pm and 6–11pm. Subway: A, B, C, D, E, F, Q to W. 4th St. (use W. 3rd St. exit). CONTEMPORARY AMERICAN HOME COOKING.

We just love Home. This cozy restaurant is the domain of a husband-and-wife team, chef David Page and co-owner Barbara Shinn, who have made homestyle cooking something to celebrate. Page and Shinn keep things fresh, popularly priced, and welcoming; as a result, their narrow, tin-roofed dining room is always packed. The menu changes regularly, but look for such signature dishes as the rich-and-creamy bleu cheese fondue; an excellent cumin-crusted pork chop on a bed of homemade barbecue sauce; a filleted-at-your-table brook trout; and perfectly moist roasted chicken with a side of spicy onion rings. Chocolate lovers should save room for the silky-smooth pudding. Weekend brunch is another great time to visit, with fluffy pancakes and excellent egg dishes. This is a quintessential Village restaurant, loaded with sophisticated charm, but it is tiny. Seating isn't uncomfortable and you won't feel intruded upon by your neighbors, but the tight room isn't built for large parties or those who want to spread out. The lovely garden is heated year-round, but is most charming in warm weather; book an outside table well ahead.

INEXPENSIVE

The original location of **John's Pizzeria** (p. 96), 278 Bleecker St. between Sixth and Seventh avenues (☎ **212/243-1680**), is a New York original and still one of the city's best. The pies are thin-crusted, properly sauced, and fresh, and served up piping hot in an authentic old-world setting. Sorry, no slices.

✪ **Bar Pitti.** 268 Sixth Ave. (btw. Bleecker and Houston sts.). ☎ **212/982-3300.** Reservations accepted only for 4 or more. Main courses $5.50–$12.50 (some specials may be higher). No credit cards. Daily noon–midnight. Subway: A, B, C, D, E, F, Q to W. 4th St. (use 3rd St. exit). TUSCAN ITALIAN.

This indoor/outdoor Tuscan-style trattoria is a perennially hip side-walk scene, and one of downtown's best dining bargains. Waiting for a table can be a chore, but all is forgiven once you take a seat, thanks to authentic, affordably priced cuisine and some of the friendliest waiters in town. Despite the tightly packed seating, Bar Pitti wins you over with its rustic Italian charm—it's the kind of place where the waiter brings over the list of daily specials to your table on a well-worn blackboard, and if you want more cheese, a block of Parmesan and a grater suddenly appears. Peruse the laminated menu, but don't get your heart set on anything until you see the board, which boasts the best of what the kitchen has to offer; the last time we dined here, they wowed us with a fabulous veal meatball special. Winners off the regular menu, which focuses heavily on pastas and panini, include excellent rare beef carpaccio, and spinach and ricotta ravioli in a creamy sage and Parmesan sauce. The all-Italian wine list is high-priced compared to the menu, but you'll find a few good value choices.

Cafe Spice. 72 University Place (at 11th St.). ☎ **212/253-6999.** Full dinners $13.50–$18. Mon–Wed 11:30am–3pm and 5pm–10:30pm, Thur–Sun 11:30am–3pm and 5pm–11:30pm, Sat and Sun 1pm–11:30pm. AE, MC, V. Subway: L, N, R, 4, 5, 6 to Union Square. INDIAN FUSION.

The owners of Dawat have opened an edgy, affordably priced restaurant that many (including yours truly) consider to be even better than their haute Indian uptowner. The restaurant has a groovy modern style; the room is all geometric shapes and vibrant colors. Each dish is artfully displayed and presented—a telltale sign of the not-quite-there-yet Indian fusion rage that has taken Manhattan this year. But, thankfully, the only thing that's really fusion about this menu is that it criss-crosses the sub-continent itself, from Punjab to Goa and back again, with a substantial side trip to southern India for spicy vegetarian along the way. The dishes are classic and confident. A great way to start is with the *palak papri chaat,* a well-spiced blend of spinach crisps, potatoes, and chickpeas in yogurt in tamarind; or with stuffed samosas, seasoned chicken or potatoes (skip the spiced tuna) in a light pastry shell. The tandooris (chicken, assorted veggies, or catch of the day) are all well prepared and pleasing, as are the other Indian basics: paneers, tikkas, and so on. All dinners come with basmati rice, fluffy naan, lentils, and a seasonal vegetable, making this an all-around great deal.

7 The Flatiron District & Union Square

To locate these restaurants, see the "Midtown Accommodations & Dining" map in chapter 3.

EXPENSIVE

✪ **Gramercy Tavern.** 42 E. 20th St. (btw. Broadway and Park Ave. South). ☎ **212/477-0777.** Reservations required well in advance. Main courses $18– $21 at lunch; 3-course prix-fixe lunch $33; 3-course prix-fixe dinner $62.

AE, DC, DISC, MC, V. Sun–Thurs noon–2pm and 5:30–10pm, Fri and Sat noon–2pm and 5:30–11pm. Subway: 6, R to 23rd St. CONTEMPORARY AMERICAN.

Thanks to warm service, a beautiful dining room that's the perfect blend of urban sophisitication and heartland rusticity, and faultless New American cuisine, Gramercy Tavern is one of the top dining rooms in the city. At the height of its game these days, it's a cut above almost any other contemporary restaurant in the city, including big sister Union Square Cafe. Owner Danny Meyer and chef Tom Colicchio assure that the restaurant exceeds expectations at every turn. You simply can't go wrong here.

The menu, which changes based on what's fresh and in season, is pleasing from start to finish. The foie gras appetizer exquisitely juxtaposes tender liver with a crunchy, acidic rhubarb relish. Saddle of rabbit will wow game lovers, and lowly chicken is elevated to new heights when it's poached and braised with salsify, pistachio, and truffles. The excellent cheese tray features top-notch farmstead selections from New York State, France, Spain, Italy, and England. Desserts are equally divine. Expensive, but well worth every penny.

MODERATE

Medusa. 239 Park Ave. South (btw. 19th and 20th sts.). ☎ **212/477-1500.** Reservations recommended. Pastas $10–$13, seafood and meat main courses $14–$19. Subway: L, N, R, 4, 5, 6 to 14th St./Union Square. MEDITERRANEAN.

If Medusa were just a little more expensive—a few dollars here, a few dollars there—there would be nothing special about it. It would be lost in the sea of overpriced Mediterranean boites that regularly come and go in the city. But what Medusa has going for it is *value*. In the increasingly high-rent, high-profile Flatiron District, Medusa has managed to keep its prices down to earth while still maintaining all the trappings of a downtown see-and-be-seen hotspot. And what's more, the food is good. The grilled octopus with baby greens, tomatoes, and steamed potatoes is a great way to start, and a bargain at $9. Or go with the attention-grabbing toasted herbed Medusa bread, topped with kefalotyri cheese flambéed in Sambuca—the restaurant's own successful twist on saganaki. All the pastas are fresh and well prepared, as are mostly seafood mains like oven-roasted Chilean sea bass. We've always been pleased with our meals at romantic, stylish Medusa; this is a place that manages to feel grown-up without the requisite high tab. There are a few concessions, such as on-the-cheap cafe chairs, but they're all but unnoticable in the romantically candlelit tomato-red space. Let's hope the people behind Medusa can keep up the good work.

✪ **The Tavern Room at Gramercy Tavern.** 42 E. 20th St. (btw. Broadway and Park Ave. South). ☎ **212/477-0777.** Reservations not taken. Starters $6–$9.50, main courses $12.50–$18. AE, DC, MC, V. Mon–Thurs and Sun noon–11pm, Fri–Sat noon–midnight. Subway: 6, N, R to 23rd St. CONTEMPORARY AMERICAN.

Unquestionably, Gramercy Tavern's main dining room is one of the finest in the city (see above). However, dining there requires reservations weeks in advance, and the prix-fixe prices almost demand a special occasion. Not so in the front Tavern Room, a friendly, informal bistro-style alternative where you can decide to eat at the last minute and still dine on some of the best food in town—without breaking the bank in the process. The compact but immensely appealing menu offers a lighter, more casual take on chef Tom Colicchio's excellent creative American fare. We love the perfectly roasted baby chicken with butternut squash succotash—nobody does chicken better. And where else are you going to get a filet mignon this good for less than $20? There's a good selection of salads, a terrific tomato garlic-bread soup, and a handful of fish dishes and sandwiches for lighter eaters, plus the restaurant's signature selection of cheeses and desserts. The room is very comfortable, with well-spaced tables and a pleasant energy that still allows for conversation; owner Danny Meyer's blanket no-smoking policy prevents any second-hand smoke from interfering with your meal. Service is top-notch, too. All in all, one of the best dining values in town.

INEXPENSIVE

✪ **Old Town Bar & Restaurant.** 45 E. 18th St. (btw. Broadway and Park Ave. South). ☎ **212/529-6732.** Reservations unnecessary. Main courses $6–$15. AE, MC, V. Mon–Sun 10am–12am. Subway: 4, 5, 6, L, N, R to 14th St./Union Sq. AMERICAN.

If you've watched TV at all over the last couple of decades, this place should look familiar: It was featured nightly in the old *Late Night with David Letterman* intro, starred as Riff's Bar in *Mad About You,* and appeared in too many commercials to count. But this is no stage set—it's a genuine tin-ceilinged 19th-century bar serving up good pub grub, lots of beers on tap, and a real sense of New York history. Sure, there are healthy salads on the menu, but everybody comes for the burgers. Whether you go low-fat turkey or bacon-chili-cheddar, they're perfect every time. Other good choices include spicy Buffalo wings with blue cheese, fiery bowls of chili sprinkled with cheddar cheese and dolopped with sour cream, and a Herculean Caesar salad slathered with mayo and topped with anchovies. Food comes up from the basement kitchen courtesy of ancient dumbwaiters behind the bar, where equally crusty bartenders would rather *not* make you a Cosmopolitan, thank you very much. If you want to escape the cigarettes and the predatory singles scene that pulls in on weekends, head upstairs to the blissfully smoke-free dining room.

8 Chelsea

To locate these restaurants, see the "Midtown Accommodations & Dining" map in chapter 3.

MODERATE

Cafeteria. 119 Seventh Ave. (at 17th St.). ☎ **212/414-1717.** Reservations recommended. Sandwiches $7.50–$12.95, main courses $10.95–$18.95. AE, DISC, MC, V. Open 24 hours. Subway: 1, 9 to 18th St. AMERICAN.

The greasy spoon goes glam at this round-the-clock Chelsea hotspot. More über-diner than nouvo automat, Cafeteria is all about high style, from the white-leather banquettes to the waifish waitstaff. Luckily, there's follow-through: Both the food and the service are better than they have to be in this veneer-happy town. The menu features modern takes on the blue-plate classics—meatloaf, chicken pot pie, fried chicken and waffles, and killer mac and cheese made with both cheddar and fontina (yum!)—as well as surprisingly successful neo-American fare, including a well-seared, thick cut tuna loin. On the downside, seating is tight—but that just puts you that much closer to the latest It-girls and boys, right? A great choice for those who want a dose of downtown's hippest crowd without paying the high tab that accompanies dinner at Moomba. Just put on your best basic black and you'll fit right in. Cafeteria is at its hippest after 10pm or so, but be sure to call ahead or you may be turned away at the door.

INEXPENSIVE

Empire Diner. 210 Tenth Ave. (at 22nd St.). ☎ **212/243-2736.** Reservations not accepted. Main courses $9.95–$16.95. AE, CB, DC, DISC, MC, V. Daily 24 hours. Subway: C, E to 23rd St. AMERICAN DINER.

Looking suspiciously like an Airstream camper plunked down on the corner, this throwback shrine to the slicked-up all-American diner boasts a timeless art deco vibe, honest coffee, and supreme mashed potatoes—Manhattan's best. The food is all basic and good: eggs, omelets, burgers, overstuffed sandwiches, and a very nice turkey platter. There's live music courtesy of a pianist every day at lunch and dinner, and at weekend brunch. If you want quiet, go early. If you want an eyeful, wait for the after-hours crowd; the hours between

1 and 3am offer the best people-watching, when Prada and Gucci meld with Phat Farm and Levi's. When the weather's warm, a sidewalk cafe appears, and the limited traffic this far over—mostly aiming for the Lincoln Tunnel—keeps the soot-and-fumes factor down.

9 Times Square & Midtown West

To locate these restaurants, see the "Midtown Accommodations & Dining" map in chapter 3.

VERY EXPENSIVE

✪ Le Bernardin. 155 W. 51st St. (btw. Sixth and Seventh aves.). ☎ **212/ 489-1515.** Reservations required 1 month in advance. Jacket required/tie optional. Prix-fixe lunch $32–$42, prix-fixe dinner $70; tasting menu $120. AE, DISC, MC, V. Mon noon–2:30pm and 6pm–10:30pm, Tues–Thurs noon–2:30pm and 5:30–10:30pm, Fri noon–2:30pm and 5:30–11pm, Sat 5:30–11pm. Subway: 1, 9 to 50th St.; N, R to 49th St. FRENCH/SEAFOOD.

If forced to choose, I'd peg Le Bernardin as one of my two favorite restaurants in the city (the other being Chanterelle). The seafood here is the best in New York, if not the world. Food doesn't get better than the flash-marinated black bass ceviche, awash in cilantro, mint, jalapeños, and diced tomatoes. Eric Ripert's tuna tartare always exhilarates, its Asian seasoning a welcome exotic touch. Among lightly cooked dishes that shine are herbed crabmeat in saffron ravioli and shellfish-tarragon reduction, and roast baby lobster tail on asparagus-and-cèpe risotto. The crusted cod, served on a bed of haricots verts with potatoes and diced tomatoes, is another favorite. The formal service is impeccable, as is the outrageously pricey wine list, and the room is uptown gorgeous. The prix-fixe lunches are a bargain, given the master in the kitchen. The desserts—especially the frozen rum-scented chestnut soufflé or the chocolate dome with crème brûlée on a macaroon—end the meal with a flourish.

"21" Club. 21 W. 52nd St. (btw. Fifth and Sixth aves.). ☎ **212/582-7200.** Reservations required. Jacket and tie required. Main courses $24–$41 (most $29 or more); prix-fixe lunch $29; pre-theater prix-fixe (5:30–6:30pm) $33; tasting menu $78. AE, DC, DISC, JCB, MC, V. Mon–Thurs noon–2:30pm and 5:30–10:15pm, Fri noon–2:30pm and 5:30–11pm, Sat 5:30–11pm. Closed Aug (or Sept). Subway: B, D, F, Q to 47th–50th sts./Rockefeller Center. AMERICAN.

A former speakeasy in the days of Prohibition, this landmark restaurant is ground zero for New York's old-school business and celebrity power set—and it has recently zoomed its way back onto the list of New York's most interesting dining rooms. After years of being more Ed McMahon than Johnny Carson, the place has a reinvigorated air. And that's due to new owners Orient-Express Hotels, who have made subtle changes in the decor and the menu, while keeping "21" classics like chicken hash, steak tartare prepared tableside, fried oysters, Maine lobster salad, and the famed burger— terribly expensive at $24, but worth it. The historic Bar Room is the best of the dining rooms, with its long mahogany bar, red-checkered tablecloths, and antique toys and other trinkets (many gifts of the celebs who consider "21" their second home) dangling playfully from the ceiling. A real New York classic.

EXPENSIVE

Cité. 120 W. 51st St. (btw. Sixth and Seventh aves.). ☎ **212/956-7100.** Reservations recommended. Main courses $19.75–$29.75; pre-theater 3-course prix-fixe $42.50 (5–7:30pm); Taste of the Grape 3-course dinner with wine $59.50 (8pm–midnight). AE, CB, DC, DISC, MC, V. Mon–Fri 11:30am–11:30pm, Sat–Sun 5–11:30pm. Subway: N, R to 49th St.; B, D, E to Seventh Ave. CONTINENTAL/STEAKS.

This pleasing art deco steakhouse has the air of a refined Parisian brasserie, making it a sophisticated—and value-wise—choice for a fine Theater District dinner. The standard pre-theater prix-fixe is a good value unto itself, offering a limited but pleasing number of choices, including the filet mignon steak frites, a mammoth cut that arrives perfectly grilled. But the real deal comes after 8pm, with Cité's fabulous "Taste of the Grape" offer: Choose any appetizer, main course, and dessert from the full dinner menu for $59.50, and enjoy unlimited quantities of the night's four featured wines on offer *at no extra charge.* They're not offering up the cheap stuff— Cité's wine guru Daniel Thames takes this program seriously, and has chosen well. Among the wines on recent offer were an '88 Burgess Cellars cabernet sauvignon, a '97 Acacia chardonnay, a Chalone Vinyard pinot noir reserve from '94, and a Nicolas Feuillate brut for celebrating. The full menu features an excellent selection of chops and steaks plus a fine spit-roasted garlic chicken and a stellar swordfish steak au poivre. Consider launching your meal with the creamy sweet corn chowder, and wrapping up with the classic Floating Island. The professional waitstaff is brisk and attentive, and the overall ambiance much friendlier than at clubbier, more masculine steak houses.

Molyvos. 871 Seventh Ave. (btw. 55th and 56th sts.). ☎ **212/582-7500.** Reservations recommended. Main courses $12.50–$20.50 at lunch, $18.50– $24.50 at dinner; prix-fixe lunch $20. AE, DC, DISC, MC, V. Mon–Fri noon–3pm and 5:30pm–11:30pm, Sat 5pm–midnight, Sun 5–11pm. Subway: N, R to 57th St.; B, D, E to Seventh Ave. GREEK.

Here's another terrific Greek restaurant, this one more like a cozy upscale taverna. Ruth Reichl, former restaurant critic of the *New York Times,* was so thrilled with its high quality and authenticity that she awarded Molyvos three stars (out of a possible four), and I concur wholeheartedly. The menu boasts beautifully prepared favorites—including superb taramosalata, tzatziki, and other traditional spreads—plus a few dishes with contemporary twists. The Greek country salad is generously portioned and as fresh as can be, while the baby octopus starter is grilled over fruit wood to tender, charred perfection. Among the main courses, the lemon and garlic-seasoned roasted free-range chicken is right on the mark: juicy, tender, and dressed with oven-dried tomatoes, olives, and russet potatoes. More traditional tastes can opt for excellent moussaka; rosemary-skewered souvlaki; or the day's catch, wood-grilled whole with lemon, oregano, and olive oil in traditional Greek style. Baklava fans shouldn't miss the restaurant's moist, nutty version, which is big enough to share. The room is spacious and comfortable, with a warm Mediterranean appeal that doesn't go overboard on the Hellenic themes, and service that's attentive without being intrusive. The sommelier will be happy to help you choose from the surprisingly good list of Greek wines, making Molyvos a winner on all counts.

MODERATE

Carmine's. 200 W. 44th St. (btw. Broadway and Eighth Ave.). ☎ **212/ 221-3800.** Reservations recommended before 6pm, after 6pm accepted only for 6 or more. Family-style main courses $15–$47. AE, DC, MC, V. Tues–Sat 11:30am–midnight, Sun–Mon 11:30am–11pm. Subway: N, R, S, 1, 2, 3, 7, 9 to 42nd St./Times Square. SOUTHERN ITALIAN FAMILY STYLE.

Everything is done B-I-G at this rollicking, family-style Times Square mainstay. The dining room is vast enough to deserve a map, massive platters of pasta hold Brady Bunch-size portions, and large groups wait to join in the rambunctious atmosphere at this sibling of the original Upper West Sider. This is a value-priced restaurant where the bang for your buck increases for every person you add to your party—but so does the wait, so come early or late to avoid the crowds. Caesar salad and a mound of fried calamari are a perfect beginning, followed by heaping portions of pasta topped with red or white clam sauce, mixed seafood, zesty marinara, and meatballs. The meat entrees include veal parmigiana, broiled porterhouse steak, chicken marsala, and shrimp scampi. The tiramisù is pie-size, thick and creamy, bathed in Kahlúa and marsala. Order half of what you think you'll need.

The original Carmine's at 2450 Broadway (☎ **212/362-2200**) is the same—but even B-I-G-G-E-R.

⊙ **Churrascaria Plataforma**. 316 W. 49th St. (btw. Eighth and Ninth aves.). ☎ **212/245-0505**. Reservations recommended. All-you-can-eat prix-fixe $27 at lunch, $31 at dinner. AE, DC, MC, V. Daily noon–midnight. Subway: C, E to 50th St. BRAZILIAN.

It's a carnival for carnivores at this upscale all-you-can-eat Brazilian rotisserie. A large selection of salad bar teasers like octopus stew, paella, and carpaccio may tempt you to fill up too quickly, but hold out for the never-ending parade of meat. Roving servers deliver beef (too many cuts to mention), ham, chicken (the chicken hearts are great, trust me), lamb, and sausage—more than 15 delectable varieties—and traditional sides like fried yucca, plantains, and rice right to your table until you cannot eat another bite. The food is excellent, and the service friendly and generous. A fun, festive family affair. The ideal accompaniment is a pitcher of Brazil's signature cocktail, called a *Caipirinha*: a margarita-like blend of limes, sugar, crushed ice, and raw sugarcane liquor; those in the know call Plataforma's the best in town.

Virgil's Real BBQ. 152 W. 44th St. (btw. Sixth and Seventh aves.). ☎ **212/ 921-9494**. Reservations recommended. Main courses $5.95–$24.95 (barbecue platters $12.95–$19.95). AE, DC, MC, V. Mon 11:30am–11pm, Tues–Sat 11:30am–12am, Sun 11:30am–11pm. Subway: 1, 2, 3, 7, 9, N, R to 42nd St./ Times Sq. SOUTHERN/BARBECUE.

Virgil's may look like a comfy theme-park version of a down-home barbecue joint, but this place takes its barbecue seriously. The meat is house-smoked with a blend of hickory, oak, and fruitwood chips, and most every regional school is represented, from Carolina pulled pork to Texas beef brisket to Memphis ribs. You may not consider this contest-winning chow if you're from barbecue country, but we less-savvy Yankees are thrilled to have Virgil's in the 'hood. I love to start with a plate of onion rings with bleu cheese for dipping. The ribs are lip-smackin' good, but the chicken is moist and tender—go for a combo if you just can't choose. Burgers, sandwiches, and other entrees (chicken-fried steak, anyone?) are also available if you can't face up to all that meat 'n' sauce. And cast that cornbread aside for a full order of buttermilk biscuits, which come with maple butter so good it's like dessert. So hunker down, pig out, and don't worry about making a mess; when you're through eating, you get a hot towel for washing up. The bar offers a huge selection of on-tap and bottled brews.

INEXPENSIVE

In addition to listings below, there's also a cafeteria-style branch of **Mangia** at 50 W. 57th St., between Fifth and Sixth avenues (☎ 212/582-5882). See the review in section 2, "South Street Seaport & the Financial District" for details.

✪ **Island Burgers & Shakes.** 766 Ninth Ave. (btw. 51st and 52nd sts.). ☎ **212/307-7934.** Reservations not accepted. Main courses $5.50–$8.75. No credit cards. Sat–Thurs 12pm–10:30pm, Fri 12pm–11:15pm. Subway: C, E to 50th St. GOURMET BURGERS/SANDWICHES.

This excellent aisle-sized diner glows with the wild colors of a California surf shop. A small selection of sandwiches and salads are on hand, but as the name implies, folks come here for the Goliath-sized burgers—either beef hamburgers or, the specialty of the house, churascos (flattened grilled chicken breasts). Innovation strikes with the more than 40 topping combinations: choose anything from the horseradish, sour cream, and black pepper burger to the Hobie's (with black pepper sauce, bleu cheese, onion, and bacon). Choose your own bread from a wide selection, ranging from soft sourdough to crusty ciabatta. Though Island Burgers serves fries now, you're meant to eat these fellows with their tasty dirty potato chips. Terrifically thick shakes and cookies are also available for those with a sweet tooth.

✪ **John's Pizzeria.** 260 W. 44th St. (btw. Broadway and Eighth Ave.). ☎ **212/391-7560.** Reservations accepted for 10 or more. Pizzas $9–$12.50 (plus toppings); pastas $6–8. AE, MC, V. Mon–Thurs 11:30am–11:30am, Fri–Sat 11:30am–1am, Sun noon–12:30am. Subway: A, C, E to 42nd St.–Port Authority; 1, 2, 3, 9, N, R, S, 7 to 42nd St.–Times Square. PIZZA.

Thin-crusted, properly sauced, and fresh, the pizza at John's has long been one of New York's best. Housed in the century-old Gospel Tabernacle Church, the split-level dining room is vast and pretty, featuring a gorgeous stained-glass ceiling and chefs working at classic brick ovens right in the room. More importantly, it's big enough to hold pre-theater crowds, so there's never too long of a wait despite the place's popularity. Unlike most pizzerias, at John's you order a whole made-to-order pie rather than by the slice, so come with friends or family. There's also a good selection of traditional pastas to choose from, such as baked ziti, and well-stuffed calzones.

Theme Restaurant Thrills!

Always the perennial favorite, New York's ✪ **Hard Rock Cafe,**
221 W. 57th St., between Broadway and Seventh Avenue (☎ **212/
459-9320**), is actually one of the originals of the chain, and a terrific realization of the concept. The memorabilia collection is terrific, with lots of great Lennon collectibles. The menu boasts all
the Hard Rock standards, including a surprisingly good burger and
fajitas, and the comfortable bar mixes up great cocktails.

Harley-Davidson Cafe, 1370 Sixth Ave., at 56th Street
(☎ **212/245-6000**), brings out the Hell's Angel in all of us. The
just-fine munchies do the trick, and memorabilia documents 90
years of Hog history.

The subterranean red planet-themed restaurant called **Mars
2112,** 1633 Broadway, at 51st Street (☎ **212/582-2112**), is a
hoot, from the simulated red-rock rooms to the Martian-costumed
waitstaff to the silly "Man Eats on Mars!" newspaper-style menu.
The eclectic food is better than you might expect, but skip the Star
Tours-style simulated spacecraft ride at the entrance if you don't
want to lose your appetite before you get to your table. The kids
won't mind, though—they'll love it, along with the extensive video
arcade.

Superstar athletes Andre Agassi, Wayne Gretzky, Ken Griffey
Jr., Joe Montana, Shaquille O'Neal, Monica Seles, and Tiger
Woods are the names behind the successful **Official All Star Cafe.**
1540 Broadway, at 45th Street (☎ **212/840-8326**). At center
court is a full-size scoreboard, on the sidelines are booths shaped
like baseball mitts, and video monitors guarantee that the great
plays in sports history live forever. The food is straight from the
ballpark—hot dogs and hamburgers, St. Louis ribs, Philly cheese
steak sandwiches, and the like.

Bruce Willis, Sly Stallone, and Ah-nuld are the moneymongers
behind **Planet Hollywood.** 140 W. 57th St., between Sixth and
Seventh avenues (☎ **212/333-7827**). Frankly, the movie memorabilia doesn't hold the same excitement as the genuine rock 'n'
roll goods over at the Hard Rock (didn't I see the R2D2 and C3PO
robots at three *other* PHs?), but it's still plenty of fun for Hollwyood
buffs nonetheless. Watch for a 2000 move to the new Planet
Hollywood hotel in Times Square.

This Theater District location is my favorite, but the original Bleecker Street location, at 278 Bleecker St., between Sixth and Seventh avenues (☎ **212/243-1680**), is loaded with old-world atmosphere. The locations near Lincoln Center, 48 W. 65th St. (☎ **212/721-7001**), and on the Upper East Side, 408 E. 64th St. (☎ **212/935-2895**), are also worth checking out.

La Bonne Soupe. 48 W. 55th St. (btw. Fifth and Sixth aves.). ☎ **212/586-7650.** Reservations recommended. Main courses $8.95–$18.25; "les bonnes soupes" prix-fixe $12.95; lunch and dinner prix-fixe $19.95. AE, DC, MC, V. Mon–Sat 11:30am–midnight, Sun 11:30am–11pm. Subway: E, F to Fifth Ave.; B, Q to 57th St. FRENCH BISTRO.

This little slice of Paris has been around forever; I remember discovering the magic of fondue here on a high school French Club field trip that took place more years ago than I care to think about. But for gourmet at good prices, it's still hard to best this authentic bistro, where you'll even see French natives seated elbow-to-elbow in the newly renovated dining room. "Les bonnes soupes" are satisfying noontime meals of salad, bread, a big bowl of soup (mushroom and barley with lamb is a favorite), dessert (chocolate mousse, crème caramel, or ice cream), and wine or coffee—a great bargain at just $12.95. The menu also features entree-sized salads (including a good niçoise), high-quality steak burgers, and traditional bistro fare like omelets, quiche Lorraine, croque monsieur, plus fancier fare like steak frites and filet mignon au poivre. Rounding out the menu are those very French fondues: emmethal cheese, beef, and yummy, creamy chocolate to finish off the meal in perfect style. Bon appetit!

Siam Inn Too. 854 Eighth Ave. (btw. 51st and 52nd sts.). ☎ **212/757-4006.** Reservations. Main courses $7.95–$15.95. AE, DC, MC, V. Mon–Fri 12pm–11:30pm, Sat 4pm–11:30pm, Sun 5pm–11pm. Subway: C, E to 50th St. THAI.

Situated on an unremarkable stretch of Eighth Avenue, the Siam Inn is an attractive outpost of very good Thai food. All of your Thai favorites are here, well prepared and served by a brightly attired waitstaff. Tom kah gai soup (with chicken, mushrooms, and coconut milk), chicken satay with yummy peanut sauce, and light, flaky curry puffs all make good starters. Among noteworthy entrees are the masaman and red curries (the former rich and peanuty, the latter quite spicy), spicy sautéed squid with fresh basil and chiles, and perfect pad thai. And unlike many of the drab restaurants in this neighborhood, there's a semblance of decor—black deco tables and chairs, cushy rugs underfoot, and soft lighting. Another branch, Siam Inn, is just 3 blocks up at Eighth at no. 854 (☎ **212/489-5237**).

10   Midtown East & Murray Hill

To locate these restaurants, see the "Midtown Accommodations & Dining" map in chapter 3.

VERY EXPENSIVE

✪ **Le Cirque 2000.** In the New York Palace hotel, 455 Madison Ave. (at 50th St.). ☎ **212/303-7788.** Reservations essential well in advance. Jacket and tie required. Main courses $28–$36; five-course prix-fixe dinner $90. AE, CB, DC, MC, V. Mon–Sat 11:45am–2:45pm and 5:45–11pm, Sun 5:30–10:30pm. Subway: 6 to 51st; E, F to Fifth Ave. FRENCH.

Iconic restaurateur Sirio Maccioni made a bold move when he relocated his legendary Le Cirque to the New York Palace a few years back, but it turned out to be a master stroke. Fine dining goes the way of the big top at Le Cirque 2000: Designer Adam Tihany festooned the gilded-age mansion's almost rococo interiors with jewel-toned circus colors, bright lights, touches of neon, and furniture with such outrageous lines that it looks like Tex Avery drew it for a Bugs Bunny cartoon. And guess what? It works. The fanciful setting is perfect for a magical night on the town. But that's where the reinvention ends—executive chef Sottha Khunn's haute French menu is classic Le Cirque. The food is excellently prepared if not innovative: lobster roasted with young artichokes and wild mushrooms; black Angus tenderloin in red wine sauce; rack of lamb roasted with savory potatoes. The starters are almost as pricey as the entrees, but we were won over by the flawlessly sautéed fois gras, and seared sea scallops with wild mushrooms and mesclun in a delicate Parmesan basket. The crème brûlée is a perfect realization of the classic dessert, but go with one of the chocolate choices for a suitably decadent finish. The wine list is remarkably well priced, relatively speaking; it seems that Maccioni has thus far avoided the current overcharging trend. There's spectacular courtyard dining in season.

EXPENSIVE

Michael Jordan's–The Steak House. In Grand Central Terminal, mezzanine level. ☎ **212/655-2300.** Reservations recommended. Main courses $16.95–$30.95; porterhouse for 2 $58.95. AE, DC, MC, V. Mon–Fri 11:30–2:30pm and 5pm–11pm, Sat noon–2:30pm and 5pm–11pm, Sun 1pm–2:30pm and 5pm–10pm. Subway: 4, 5, 6, 7, S to 42nd St./Grand Central. STEAKS.

The name may belong to one of sports' greatest heroes, but don't expect an overpriced burger factory with waiters in Bulls jerseys and basketball-shaped plates. Michael Jordan's new restaurant, an elegant steakhouse and richly appointed cigar lounge, is wholly a place for grown-ups. This gorgeous art deco space makes a great place to dine thanks to its magnificent location on the open mezzanine level overlooking the main concourse of newly restored Grand Central Terminal. With a perfect view of the legendary sky ceiling, this is more than just the city's best-looking steak house—it's an incredible only-in-New York dining experience.

And the food? Pure steakhouse fare: New York steaks, thick-cut filet mignons, tender rib eyes, and well-marbled sirloins, all prime aged cuts. The star of the show is the porterhouse for two, a whopping 44 ounces of top-quality cow, served suitably charred and salty on the outside. Other choices include buffalo sirloin for two, a pleasing lean cut as long as it's ordered on the rare side, and excellent braised short ribs. We didn't have a problem, but word is that on occasion a steak isn't cooked to order, an issue that should disappear as the kitchen establishes itself. In the meantime, don't be shy about sending yours back for another turn on the grill. Skip the more adventuresome starters and sides, such as the disappointing lobster salad, and stick with steak house classics like the perfectly creamed spinach, light-as-air fried onions, and the terrific crimini mushrooms in truffle oil. The wine list is overseen by a helpful sommelier, and service is similarly attentive.

✪ **Oyster Bar.** In Grand Central Terminal, lower level. ☎ **212/490-6650.** Reservations recommended. Main courses $9.45–$34.95. AE, CB, DC, DISC, JCB, MC, V. Mon–Fri 11:30am–9:30pm (last seating). Subway: 4, 5, 6, 7, S to 42nd St./Grand Central. SEAFOOD.

Here's one New York institution housed within another: the city's most famous seafood joint in the world's greatest train station, newly renovated Grand Central Terminal. Fully recovered from a 1997 fire, the restaurant is looking spiffy, too, with a main dining room sitting under an impressive curved and tiled ceiling, a more casual luncheonette-style section for walk-ins, and a wood-panelled saloon-style room for smokers. If you love seafood, don't miss this place. A new menu is prepared every day, since only the freshest fish is served. The oysters are irresistible: Kumomoto, Bluepoint, Malepeque, Belon—the list goes on and on. The list of daily catches, which can range from Arctic char to mako shark to ono (Hawaiian wahoo), is equally impressive. Most dinners go for between $19.95 and $24.95, and it's easy to jack up the tab by ordering live lobster (flown in directly from Maine) or one of the rarer daily specialties. But it's just as easy to keep the tab down by sticking with hearty fare like one of the excellent stews and panroasts (from $9.45 for oyster stew to $19.95 for a combo panroast rich with oysters, clams, shrimp, lobster, and scallops) or by pairing the New England clam chowder (at $4.50, an unbeatable lunch) with a smoked starter to make a great meal.

INEXPENSIVE

In addition to the listings below, there's also a cafeteria-style branch of **Mangia** at 16 E. 48th St., just east of Fifth Avenue (☎ 212/ 754-7600). See the review in section 2, "South Street Seaport & the Financial District" for details.

✪ **Ess-A-Bagel.** 831 Third Ave. (at 51st St.). ☎ **212/980-1010.** Sandwiches $1.35–$8.35. AE, DC, DISC, MC, V. Mon–Fri 6:30am–10pm, Sat–Sun 8am–5pm. Subway: 6 to 51st St.; E, F to Lexington Ave. BAGEL SANDWICHES.

Ess-A-Bagel turns out the city's best bagel, edging out rival H&H, who won't make you a sandwich. Baked daily on-site, the giant hand-rolled delicacies come in 12 flavors—plain, sesame, poppy, onion, garlic, salt, whole wheat, pumpernickel, pumpernickel raisin, cinnamon raisin, oat bran, and everything. They're so plump, chewy, and satisfying it's hard to believe they contain no fat, cholesterol, or preservatives. Head to the back counter for a baker's dozen or line up for a sandwich overstuffed with scrumptious salads and spreads. Fillings can range from a generous schmear of cream cheese to smoked Nova salmon or chopped herring salad (both have received national acclaim) to sundried tomato tofu spread. There are also lots of deli-style meats to choose from, plus a wide range of cheeses and salads (egg, chicken, light tuna, and so on). The cheerful dining room has plenty of bistro-style tables.

Prime Burger. 5 E. 51st St. (btw. Fifth and Madison aves.). ☎ **212/759-4729.** Reservations not accepted. Main courses $3.25–$7.95. No credit cards. Mon–Fri 5am–7pm, Sat 6am–5pm. Subway: 6 to 51st St.; E, F to Lexington/Third aves. and 53rd St. AMERICAN/HAMBURGERS.

Just across the street from St. Patrick's Cathedral, this coffee shop is a heavenly find. The burgers and sandwiches are tasty, the fries crispy and generous. The front seats, which might remind you (if you're old enough) of old wooden grammar-school desks, are great fun—especially when ever-so-serious suited-up New Yorkers quietly take their places at these oddities. A great quickie stop during a day of Fifth Avenue shopping.

11 The Upper West Side

To locate these restaurants, see the "Uptown Accommodations & Dining" map in chapter 3.

VERY EXPENSIVE

✪ **Jean Georges.** In the Trump International Hotel & Tower, 1 Central Park West (at 60th St./Columbus Circle). ☎ **212/299-3900.** Reservations required. Jacket required/tie optional. Main courses $22–$30 in Nougatine; lunch prix-fixe $28 in Nougatine, $45 in main restaurant; dinner prix-fixe $85; tasting menu $115. AE, CB, DC, MC, V. Mon–Fri noon–2:30pm and 5:30–11pm, Sat 5:30–11pm. Subway: A, B, C, D, 1, 9 to 59th St./Columbus Circle. FRENCH.

That smarmy Donald Trump can be a very smart guy. When he announced he had secured the services of star chef Jean-Georges Vongerichten to oversee the restaurant in his new hotel, everyone knew the rave reviews wouldn't be far behind. And they were right—Jean Georges was immediately awarded the coveted four stars by the *New York Times.*

Dining here is a sublime experience. In the elegantly restrained Adam Tihany–designed dining room, the menu is the best of Vongerichten's past successes taken one step further. French and Asian touches mingle with a new passion for offbeat harvests, like lamb's quarters, sorrel, yarrow, quince, and chicory. Spring garlic soup with thyme accompanied by a plate of sautéed frogs' legs with parsley makes a great beginning. The Muscovy duck steak with Asian spices and sweet-and-sour jus is carved tableside, while the lobster tartine with pumpkin seed, pea shoots, and a broth of fenugreek (one of Jean-Georges' signature aromatic plants) receives a final dash of spices seconds before you dig in. If the chestnut soup is on the menu, don't miss it. The food is equally excellent but more affordably priced in the more casual cafe Nougatine; don't expect equally comfy chairs or as much elbow room, however. If you're visiting in warm weather, try to get a table on the lovely outdoor terrace. The professional service is without fault in the main restaurant, and still attentive if not quite as well paced in the cafe. The wine list is also excellent, with a number of unusual choices in every price range.

EXPENSIVE

Tavern on the Green. In Central Park, Central Park West and W. 67th St. ☎ **212/873-3200.** www.tavernonthegreen.com. Reservations highly recommended, necessary on holidays (reservations available on-line). Main courses $20–$40; 3-course pre-theater prix-fixe (Mon–Fri until 6:15pm) $30–$40. AE, CB, DC, DISC, MC, V. Mon–Thurs 11:30am–3:30pm and 5:30–11:30pm, Fri 11:30am–3:30pm and 5–11:30pm, Sat 10am–3:30pm and 5–11:30pm, Sun 10am–3:30pm and 5:30pm–10:30pm. Subway: 1, 9 to 66th St./Lincoln Center. CONTEMPORARY AMERICAN/CONTINENTAL.

This legendary Central Park restaurant is a true one of a kind. Warner LeRoy's fantasy palace has one of the city's best settings.

Antiques and Tiffany glass fill the space, crystal chandeliers cast a romantic light, tiny twinkling lights glimmer on nearby trees, and the views over the park are wonderful. A festive spirit enlivens the Crystal Room, where you should ask to be seated. (A couple of the other dining rooms are so overdone as to cross the line into the realm of tacky.)

Since the passing of beloved executive chef Patrick Clark, the kitchen gets kudos for maintaining his legacy, though it's hard to be completely consistent in an operation this mammoth. The seasonal menus are surprisingly good, particularly if you stick with classic fare. The seared duck foie gras, served with a pear-and-pecan sticky bun and a balsamic-port syrup, is a wonderful beginning to any meal. The superb al dente pasta is handmade by pasta chef Renzo Barcatta. The grilled pork porterhouse is delicious and thick. Salmon is barbecued with Moroccan spices and served with a couscous cake. Despite its big reputation, the Tavern is known for its down-to-earth manner, and service is excellent. The crowd can be thick at holiday time, so book well ahead.

MODERATE

For fun, family-style Italian, there's also the original **Carmine's** at 2450 Broadway, between 90th and 91st streets (☎ **212/362-2200**), in addition to the choices below. For the review, see section 9, "Times Square & Midtown West."

✪ **Sarabeth's Kitchen.** 423 Amsterdam Ave. (btw. 80th and 81st sts.). ☎ **212/496-6280.** Reservations accepted for dinner only. Main courses $5–$11 at lunch and brunch, $10–$22 at dinner. AE, CB, DC, DISC, JCB, MC, V. Mon–Thurs 8am–10:30pm, Fri 8am–11pm, Sat 9am–11pm, Sun 9am–9:30pm. Subway: 1, 9 to 79th St. CONTEMPORARY AMERICAN.

Its 200-year-old family recipe for orange-apricot marmalade rooted Sarabeth's Kitchen into New York's consciousness, and now its fresh-baked goods, award-winning preserves, and creative American cooking keep a loyal following. This charming country restaurant with a distinct Hamptons feel is best known for its breakfast and weekend brunch, when the menu features such treats as porridge with wheatberries, fresh cream, butter, and brown sugar; pumpkin waffle topped with sour cream, raisins, pumpkin seeds, and honey (a sweet tooth's delight); and a whole host of farm-fresh omelets. But lunch and dinner are just as good and a lot less crowded. Lunch might be a generous Caesar salad with aged Parmesan, brioche croutons, and a tangy anchovy dressing accompanied by a hearty from-scratch soup, or some beautifully built country-style sandwiches.

Dinner is more sophisticated, with such specialties as hazelnut-crusted halibut in an aromatic seven-vegetable broth and oven-roasted lamb crusted in black mushrooms, with grilled leeks and Vidalia onion rings on the side. Leave room for the scrumptious desserts—Sarabeth Levine was just given the James Beard Award for Best Pastry Chef recently, an honor well deserved.

There are also two East Side locations: 1295 Madison Ave. (☎ 212/410-7335) and inside the Whitney Museum at 945 Madison Ave. (☎ 212/570-3670).

INEXPENSIVE

Near Lincoln Center, at 48 W. 65th St. between Columbus Avenue and Central Park West, there's a nice **John's Pizzeria** (☎ 212/721-7001), serving up one of the city's best pies (p. 98).

Big Nick's Burger Joint. 2175 Broadway (at 77th St.). ☎ **212/362-9238.** Reservations not necessary. Main courses $3.50–$11. No credit cards. Open 24 hours. Subway: 1, 9 to 79th St. AMERICAN.

A neighborhood legend since 1962, Big Nick's is one of the best spots in the city for a midnight snack. They offer a full menu 24 hours a day, which includes everything from killer French toast and pancakes to Nick's infamous gourmet beefburgers. The classic charbroiled burgers come in a whole host of varieties, from your all-American cheeseburger to the Mediterranean, stuffed with herbs, spices, and onions and topped with anchovies, feta, and tomato. Or how 'bout a Texasburger, with an egg on top for "egg-stra" energy (Nick's joke, not mine)? There's also a good selection of Big Nick-style pizzas, like the Gyromania, topped with well-seasoned gyro meat and onions. As the name suggests, Nick's is a real joint, specializing in homegrown Noo Yawk fare; however, the kitchen gets kudos for developing a dietwatchers menu, with such specialties as pizzas prepared with skim cheese and lean-ground veal and turkey burgers. The atmosphere is suitably lively, with waiters and buspeople scrambling about, cooks calling out orders, and crowded tables full of diners happily chowing down.

Hunan Park. 235 Columbus Ave. (btw. 70th and 71st St.). ☎ **212/724-4411.** http://members.aol.com/hunanpark/hunan.htm. Reservations accepted for groups of 5 or more. Main courses $5.25–$10.50 (Peking Duck $24). AE, MC, V. Sun–Thurs noon–11:30pm, Fri–Sat noon–12:30am. Subway: B, C, 1, 2, 3, 9 to 72nd St. HUNAN CHINESE.

This casual place has been earning broad-sweeping kudos for years from everybody from Zagat's to *New York* magazine to Alan Alda for its well-prepared, inexpensive Chinese standards. Everything about it—quality, service, decor—is a cut above the standard. Expect all the familiar favorites, plus satisfying specialties like ginger chicken, spicy four-flavor beef, and crispy sea bass in a rich Hunan sauce. Service is quick and efficient, and the convenient location makes this a cheap and easy post-Central Park or pre-Lincoln Center stop.

If you're farther uptown, there's a second location at 721 Columbus Ave., at 95th Street (☎ 212/222-6511).

Josie's Restaurant & Juice Bar. 300 Amsterdam Ave. (at 74th St.). ☎ 212/ 769-1212. Reservations recommended. Main courses $8–$16. AE, DC, MC, V. Mon 5:3–11pm, Tues–Fri 5:30pm–midnight, Sat 5pm–midnight, Sun 5–11pm. Subway: 1, 2, 3, 9 to 72nd St. HEALTH-CONSCIOUS.

You have to admire the sincerity of an organic restaurant that uses chemical-free milk paint on its walls. Chef/owner Louis Lanza doesn't stop there: His adventurous menu shuns dairy, preservatives, and concentrated fats. Free-range and farm-raised meats and poultry augment vegetarian choices like baked sweet potato with tamari brown rice, broccoli, roasted beets, and tahini sauce; eggless Caesar salad; and a great three-grain vegetable burger with homemade ketchup and caramelized onions. The yellowfin tuna wasabi burger with pickled ginger is another signature. Everything is made with organic grains, beans, and flour as well as organic produce when possible. You don't have to be a health nut to enjoy Josie's; Lanza's eclectic cuisine really satisfies. And nobody's gonna actually make you do without: If wheat grass isn't your thing, a full wine and beer list is served in this pleasing modern space, which boasts enough *Jetsons*-style touches to give the room a playful, relaxed feel.

12 The Upper East Side

To locate these restaurants, see the "Uptown Accommodations & Dining" map in chapter 3.

VERY EXPENSIVE

Daniel. 60 E. 65th St. (btw. Madison and Park aves.). ☎ 212/288-0033. Reservations required 1 month in advance. Jacket and tie required. Prix-fixe lunch $35–$42, 5-course tasting menu $69 at lunch; 3-course prix-fixe dinner $68, 6–8 course tasting menus $90–$120 at dinner. AE, DC, MC, V. Mon–Thurs noon–2:30pm and 5:45–11pm, Fri–Sat noon–2:30pm and 5:45–11:30pm. Subway: 6 to 68th St. FRENCH COUNTRY.

When chef/owner Daniel Boulud first opened Daniel in 1993, Patricia Wells named it one of the *world's* top 10 restaurants. In early '99, Boulud moved Daniel into this much larger space, previously occupied by Le Cirque. A fortune was spent on the renovation, and it shows. If Le Cirque 2000 sounds too over-the-top for your taste, this is the dining room for you: The room's gorgeous neo-Renaissance features—rich mahogany doors, sensuous arches, elegant Corinthian columns, and soaring terra-cotta-tiled ceilings—have been beautifully accented with a rich autumn color palette and custom furnishings with subtly playful curves. It's an ideal setting for Boulud's faultless country French cooking.

The menu is heavy with game dishes in elegant but unfussy preparations, plus Daniel signatures like black sea bass in a crisp potato shell, with tender leeks and a light Barolo sauce. Excellent starters include a frisee salad with crisp braised sweetbreads, pistachios, and black truffle, a dish that could convert the most committed offalphile. Don't neglect the specials menu; I was the envy of the table with my warm rabbit confit salad with foie gras. Sublime entrees may include braised Chatham cod with cockles and caviar, or chestnut-crusted venison with sweet potato puree. But you can't really go wrong with anything—the kitchen doesn't take a false turn. The service is a little stuffy for my taste and the sommelier not as interactive as I would like, but the wine list is excellent and features more affordable bottles than I usually see at a restaurant of this ilk. Divided between seasonal fruits and chocolates, the desserts are also uniformly excellent.

EXPENSIVE

Park View at the Boathouse. On the lake in Central Park, near 72nd St. and Park Dr. North (nearest park entrance is 72nd St. and Fifth Ave.). ☎ **212/517-2233.** Reservations highly recommended. Main courses $20–$32; weekend brunch $14–$23. AE, DISC, MC, V. Fall/Winter: Tues–Fri 6–10pm, Sat 11am–3pm and 6–10pm, Sun 11am–3pm. Spring/Summer: Mon–Fri 11:30am–10pm, Sat 11am–11pm, Sun 11am–9pm. Subway: 6 to 77th St. CONTEMPORARY AMERICAN.

Park View is a one-of-a-kind experience—there's no better alfresco dining in the city. What makes it so special? Beautifully set on the edge of the lake and surrounded by great green Central Park, it's quintessentially New York yet magically distant from the urban bustle. And now with acclaimed chef John Villa at the helm, the creative New American cuisine is almost as stellar as the surroundings. Villa particularly excels at dishes with an Asian flair: coriander spiced tuna loin on a crisp taro cake with mango salsa and cilantro vinaigrette was an ideal marriage of sweet and spice. Not everything works though—red snapper poached in milk?—so ask your waiter to help you steer past the menu's few pitfalls.

The restaurant opened year-round for the first time over the winter 1998–99 season, featuring a game menu served in a glass-walled, fireplace-lit dining room. Summer is the time to come, though; book ahead, since everybody wants to dine here, especially for weekend brunch. Twilight is enchanting, giving Park View the air of a tiny oasis lorded over by the distant twinkling skyline; try to arrive just before sunset if you can, even if it means coming early for a drink at the equally well-situated bar. You've no doubt heard about the dangers of wandering in Central Park after dark, but after 7pm a shuttle runs from Fifth Avenue and 72nd Street (inquire about the current schedule when you reserve).

MODERATE

If it's an excellent contemporary meal or a sweet treat you're after, head to **Sarabeth's Kitchen** (p. 103), which has two eastside locations: 1295 Madison Ave., at E. 92nd St. (☎ 212/410-7335), and at the Whitney Museum, 945 Madison Ave. (☎ 212/570-3670).

Caffe Grazie. 26 E. 84th St. (at Madison Ave.). ☎ **212/717-4407.** Reservations recommended. Main courses $12.50–$19.50; Sun brunch $12.95. AE, DC, MC, V. Mon–Sat 11:30am–11pm, Sun 11:30am–10pm. Subway: 4, 5, 6 to 86th St. ITALIAN.

This cheery, unpretentious Italian cafe is most notable for its convenient location near the Metropolitan Museum of Art, a neighborhood short of moderately priced, recommendable eats. It's perfect for sipping espresso between museum hops or lingering over an elegant dinner. Appetizers like the bruschetta assortment served with a small salad and the warm white-bean salad over prosciutto are generous enough to be a light meal in themselves. The pasta selection mixes staples (satisfying penne pomodoro and linguini pesto) with standouts (lasagna layered with grilled chicken, fresh tomatoes, cheese, and pesto). The entrees, like veal stuffed with prosciutto and spinach and jumbo shrimp with lemon-caper sauce, are fresh and flavorful. All in all, a hidden treasure in a needy neighborhood.

INEXPENSIVE

Serendipity 3. 225 E. 60th St. (btw. Second and Third aves.). ☎ **212/838-3531.** www.serendipity3.com. Reservations recommended for dinner. Main courses $5.50–$17.95; sweets and sundaes $4.50–$10. AE, DC, DISC, MC, V. Sun–Thurs 11:30am–midnight, Fri 11:30am–1am, Sat 11:30am–2am. Subway: 4, 5, 6 to 59th St.; N, R to Lexington Ave. AMERICAN.

You'd never guess that this whimsical place was once a top stop on Andy Warhol's agenda. Wonders never cease—and neither does the confection at this delightful restaurant and sweet shop. Tucked into a cozy brownstone a few steps from Bloomingdale's, Serendipity's small front-room curiosity shop overflows with odd objects, from jigsaw puzzles to silly jewelry. But the real action is behind the shop, where the quintessential American soda fountain still reigns supreme. Remember Farrell's? This is the better version (complete with candy to tempt the kids on the way out), and it's still going strong. Happy people gather at marble-topped ice-cream parlor tables for burgers and foot-long hot dogs, country meat loaf with mashed potatoes and gravy, and salads and sandwiches with cute names like "The Catcher in the Rye" (their own twist on the BLT, with chicken and Russian dressing—on rye, of course). The food isn't great, but the main courses aren't the point—just as they were at Farrell's, they're just an excuse to get to the desserts. The restaurant's signature is Frozen Hot Chocolate, a slushie version of everybody's cold weather favorite, but other crowd pleasers include dark double devil mousse, celestial carrot cake, lemon ice-box pie, and anything with hot fudge. So cast that willpower aside and come on in—Serendipity is an irony-free charmer to be appreciated by adults and kids alike.

5

Exploring New York City

*O*ne of the best ways to experience New York is to pick a neighborhood and just stroll it. Walk the prime thoroughfares, poke your head into shops, park yourself on a bench or at an outdoor cafe, and just watch the world go by. For tips on where to go, how to get there, and what highlights to be on the lookout for, see the "Manhattan's Neighborhoods in Brief" in chapter 2. If you'd prefer to explore with an expert at the helm, consider taking an organized tour; see "Organized Sightseeing Tours" later in this chapter.

1 In New York Harbor: Lady Liberty, Ellis Island & the Staten Island Ferry

✪ **Statue of Liberty.** On Liberty Island in New York Harbor. ✪ **212/ 363-3200** (general info) or 212/269-5755 (ticket/ferry info). www.nps.gov/stli. Ferry ticket/admission to Statue of Liberty and Ellis Island $7 adults, $6 seniors, $3 children under 17. Daily 9am–5pm; extended hours in summer. Subway: 4, 5 to Bowling Green; 1, 9 to South Ferry (the platform at this station is shorter than the train, so ride in the first 5 cars). From the station, walk south through Battery Park to Castle Clinton, the fort housing the ferry ticket booth.

For the millions who first came by ship to America in the last century—either as privileged tourists or needy, hopeful immigrants—Lady Liberty, standing in the Upper Bay, was their first glimpse of America. Few travel by boat anymore, so it probably won't be your first impression of New York, but you should make it one of the lasting ones. Designed by sculptor Freédéric-Auguste Bartholdi with the engineering help of Alexandre-Gustave Eiffel (responsible for the famed Paris tower) and unveiled on October 28, 1886, no monument so embodies the nation's, and the world's, notion of political freedom and economic potential. Even if you don't make it out to Liberty Island, you can get a spine-tingling glimpse from Battery Park, from the New Jersey side of the bay, or during a free ride on the Staten Island Ferry (see below).

Touring Tips: Ferries leave daily every half hour to 45 minutes from 9:30am to 3:15pm, with more frequent ferries in the morning and extended hours in summer. Try to go early on a weekday to avoid the crowds that swarm in the afternoon, on weekends, and on holidays. Be sure to arrive by noon if your heart's set on experiencing everything; go later, and you may not have time to make it to the crown. A stop at Ellis Island (see below) is included in the fare, but if you catch the last ferry, you can only visit the statue or Ellis Island, not both.

The ferry deposits you, in about 20 minutes, on Liberty Island, a short distance from the statue. Once on the island, you'll start to get an idea of the statue's immensity: She weighs 225 tons and measures 152 feet from foot to flame. Her nose alone is $4^1/2$ feet long, and her index finger is 8 feet long. You may have to wait as long as 3 hours to walk up into the crown (the torch is not open to visitors). If it's summer, or if you're just not in shape for it, you may want to skip it: It's a grueling 354 steps (the equivalent of 22 stories) to the crown, or you can cheat and take the elevator the first 10 stories up (an act I wholeheartedly endorse). But even if you take this shortcut, the interior is stifling once the temperature starts to climb. However, you don't have to go all the way up to the crown; there are a number of **observation decks** at different levels, including one at the top of the pedestal reachable by elevator. Even if you don't go inside, a stroll around the base is an extraordinary experience, and the views of the Manhattan skyline are stellar.

✪ **Ellis Island.** Located in New York Harbor. ☎ **212/363-3200** (general info) or 212/269-5755 (ticket/ferry info). www.ellisisland.org. For subway, hours, and ferry ticket details, see the Statue of Liberty directly above (ferry trip includes stops at both sights).

One of New York's most moving sights, the restored Ellis Island opened in 1990, slightly north of Liberty Island. Roughly 40% of Americans can trace their heritage back to an ancestor who came through here (myself included). For the 62 years when it was America's main entry point for immigrants (it closed in 1954), Ellis Island processed some 12 million people. The greeting was often brusque—especially in the early years of the century, when as many as 12,000 came through in a single day. The statistics and their meaning can be overwhelming, but the **Immigration Museum** skillfully relates the story of Ellis Island and immigration in America by putting the emphasis on personal experience.

Today you enter the Main Building's baggage room, just as the immigrants did, and then climb the stairs to the **Registry Room,** where millions waited anxiously for medical and legal processing. A step-by-step account of the immigrants' voyage is detailed in the **"Through America's Gate"** exhibit, with haunting photos and

Downtown Attractions

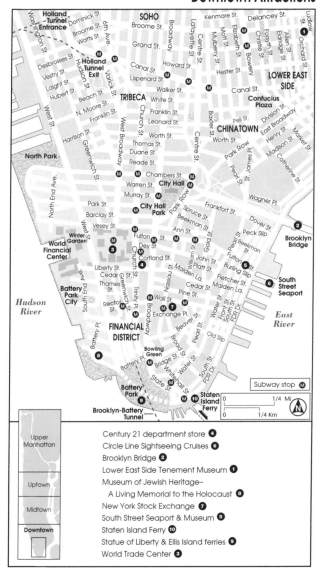

Century 21 department store ❹
Circle Line Sightseeing Cruises ❻
Brooklyn Bridge ❷
Lower East Side Tenement Museum ❶
Museum of Jewish Heritage–
   A Living Memorial to the Holocaust ❽
New York Stock Exchange ❼
South Street Seaport & Museum ❺
Staten Island Ferry ❿
Statue of Liberty & Ellis Island ferries ❾
World Trade Center ❸

touching oral histories. What might be the most poignant exhibit is **"Treasures from Home,"** 1,000 objects and photos donated by descendants of immigrants, including family heirlooms, religious articles, and rare clothing and jewelry. Outside, the **American Immigrant Wall of Honor** commemorates the names of hundreds of thousands of immigrants and their families who have been commemorated by their descendants, including George Washington's great-grandfather, John F. Kennedy's great-grandparents, Rudolph Valentino, Harry Houdini, and Marlene Dietrich (all catalogued on a computer registry as well). You can even research your own family's history at the **American Family Immigration History Center.** It's difficult to leave the museum unmoved.

Touring Tips: Ferries run daily to Ellis Island and Liberty Island from Battery Park and Liberty State Park at frequent intervals; see the Statue of Liberty (above) for details.

Staten Island Ferry. Departs from the Staten Island Ferry Terminal at the southern tip of Manhattan. ☎ **718/815-BOAT.** www.SI-Web.com/transportation/dot.htm. Free (fee charged for car transport). 24 hours; every 15–30 min weekdays, less frequently on off-peak and weekend hours. Subway: 1, 9, N, R to South Ferry.

Here's New York's best freebie—especially if you just want to glimpse the Statue of Liberty and not climb her steps. You get an enthralling hour-long excursion (round-trip) into the world's biggest harbor. This is not strictly a sightseeing ride, but commuter transportation to Staten Island (remember Melanie Griffith, in big hair and sneakers, heading to work in *Working Girl?*). As a result, during business hours, you'll share the boat with working stiffs reading papers and drinking coffee inside, blissfully unaware of the sights outside.

You, however, should go on deck and enjoy the busy harbor traffic. The old orange-and-green boats usually have open decks along the sides or at the bow and stern (try to catch one of these boats if you can; the newer white boats don't have decks). Go on a nice day if you can, as the outer decks are best. Grab a seat on the right side of the boat for the best view. On the way out of Manhattan, you'll pass the Statue of Liberty (the boat comes closest to Lady Liberty on the way to Staten Island), Ellis Island, and from the left side of the boat, Governor's Island; you'll see the Verranzano Narrows bridge stretching from Brooklyn to Staten Island in the distance.

When the boat arrives at St. George, Staten Island, everyone must disembark. Follow the boat loading sign on your right as you get off; you'll circle around to the next loading dock, where there's usually another boat waiting to depart for Manhattan. The skyline views are simply awesome on the return trip. Well worth the time spent.

2 Historic Lower Manhattan's Top Attractions

✪ **Brooklyn Bridge.** Subway: 4, 5, 6 to Brooklyn Bridge–City Hall; A, C to High St.

Its Gothic-inspired stone pylons and intricate steel-cable webs have moved poets like Walt Whitman and Hart Crane to sing the praises of this great span, the first to cross the East River and connect Manhattan to Brooklyn. Begun in 1867 and ultimately completed in 1883, the beautiful Brooklyn Bridge is now the city's best-known symbol of the age of growth that seized the city during the late 19th century. Walk across the bridge, and imagine the awe that New Yorkers of that age felt at seeing two boroughs joined by this monumental span. It's still astounding.

Walking the Bridge: Walking the Brooklyn Bridge is one of my all-time favorite New York activities. A wide wood-plank pedestrian walkway is elevated above the traffic, making it a relatively peaceful, and popular, walk. It provides a great vantage point from which to contemplate the New York skyline and the East River.

There's a sidewalk entrance on Park Row, just across from City Hall Park (take the 4, 5, or 6 train to Brooklyn Bridge–City Hall). But why do this walk *away* from Mahattan, toward the far less impressive Brooklyn skyline? For gorgeous Manhattan skyline views, take an A or C train to High Street, one stop into Brooklyn. From there, you'll be on the bridge in no time: Come above ground, then walk through the little park to Cadman Plaza East and head downslope (left) to the stairwell that will take you up to the footpath. (Following Prospect Place under the bridge, turning right onto Cadman Plaza East, will also take you directly to the stairwell.) It's a 20- to 40-minute stroll over the bridge to Manhattan, depending on your pace, the amount of foot traffic, and the number of stops you make to contemplate the spectacular views (there are benches along the way). The footpath will deposit you right at City Hall Park.

New York Stock Exchange. 20 Broad St. (between Wall St. and Exchange Place). ☎ **212/656-5165.** www.nyse.com. Free admission. Mon–Fri 9am–4:30pm (ticket booth opens at 8:45am). Subway: 2, 3, 4, 5 to Wall St.; J, M, Z to Broad St.

Wall Street—it's an iconic name, and ground zero for bulls and bears everywhere. This narrow 18th-century lane (you'll be surprised at how little it is) is appropriately monumental, lined with neoclassic towers that reach as far skyward as the dreams and greed of investors who built it into the world's most famous financial market. At the heart of the action is the New York Stock Exchange, the world's largest securities trader, where you can watch the billions change hands and get a fleeting idea of how the money merchants work.

While the NYSE is on Wall Street, the ticket kiosk is around the corner at 20 Broad St., where you'll be issued a ticket with a time on it; you must enter during the window of opportunity specified on your ticket. The staff starts handing out tickets at 8:45am, but get in line early if you want to be inside to see all hell break loose at the 9:30am opening bell. The 3,000 tickets issued per day are usually gone by noon; plan on having to return unless you're one of the first in line. Despite the number of visitors, things move pretty quickly.

Don't expect to come out with a full understanding of the market; if you didn't have one going in, you won't leave any more enlightened. Still, it's fun watching the action on the trading floor from the glass-lined, mezzanine-level **observation gallery** (look to the right, and you'll see the Bloomberg people sending their live reports back to the newsroom). You can stay as long as you like, but it doesn't really take more than 20 minutes or so to peruse the other jingoistic exhibits ("NYSE—our hero!"), which include a rather oblique explanation of the floor activities, interactive exhibits, and a short film presentation of the Exchange's history and present-day operations.

South Street Seaport and Museum. At Water and South sts.; museum is at 12–14 Fulton St. ☎ **212/748-8600.** www.southstseaport.org. Museum admission $6 adults, $5 seniors, $3 children. Museum, Apr–Sept Fri–Wed 10am–6pm, Thurs 10am–8pm; Oct–Mar Wed–Sun 10am–5pm. Subway: 2, 3, 4, 5 to Fulton St. (walk east, or downslope, on Fulton St. to Water St.)

This landmark district on the East River encompasses 11 square blocks of historic buildings, a maritime museum, several piers, shops and restaurants (including the authentically Old World North Star Pub; see chapter 4).

You can explore most of the seaport on your own. It's an odd place: The 18th- and 19th-century buildings lining the cobbled streets and alleyways are beautifully restored but nevertheless have a theme-park air about them, no doubt due to the J. Crews, Brookstones, and Body Shops housed within. The height of the seaport's cheesiness is **Pier 17,** a historic barge converted into a mall, complete with food court and cheap jewelry kiosks.

Despite its rampant commercialism, the seaport is worth a look. There's a good amount of history to be discovered here, most of it around the **South Street Seaport Museum,** a fitting tribute to the sea commerce that once thrived here.

Including the galleries—which house paintings and prints, ship models, scrimshaw, and nautical designs, as well as frequently-changing exhibitions—there are a number of historic ships berthed at the pier to explore. A few of the boats are living museums and restoration works in progress; others are available for private charters. But you can actually hit the high seas on the 1885 cargo schooner **Pioneer** (☎ **212/748-8786**), which offers two-hour public sails daily from early May through September. Tickets are $20 for adults, $15 for seniors and students, and $12 for children. Advance reservations are recommended; always call ahead to confirm sailing times.

At the gateway to the seaport, at Fulton and Water streets, is the **Titanic Memorial Lighthouse,** a monument to those who lost their lives when the ocean liner sank on April 15, 1912. It was erected overlooking the East River in 1913, and moved to this spot in 1968, just after the historic district was so designated.

✪ **World Trade Center.** Bounded by Church, Vesey, Liberty, and West sts. ☎ **212/323-2340** for observation deck, 212/435-4170 for general information. www.wtc-top.com. Admission to observation deck $12 adults, $9 seniors, $6 children under 12. Sept–May daily 9:30am–9:30pm; June–Aug 9:30am–11:30pm. Subway: C, E to World Trade Center; 1, 9, N, R to Cortlandt St.

Nowhere near as romantic as the Empire State Building, the World Trade Center is nevertheless just as heroic, having withstood a bombing in its basement garage in 1993 without so much as a flinch. Built in 1970, the center is actually an immense complex of seven buildings on 16 acres housing offices, restaurants, a hotel, an underground shopping mall, and an outdoor plaza with fountains, sculpture, and summer concerts and performances. But the parts you'll be interested in are the Twin Towers, which usurped the Empire State to become New York's tallest structures.

The box-like buildings are so nondescript that the local Channel 11 once used them to represent that number in their commercials. Each is 110 stories and 1,350 feet high. The **Top of the World** observation deck is high atop 2 World Trade Center, to the south. On the 107th floor, it's like a mini theme park, offering (besides the views, of course) a 6-minute simulated helicopter tour over Manhattan, high-tech kiosks, a food court, and a nighttime light show. But the reason to come is for those incredible views. The enclosed top floor offers incredible panoramas on all sides, with windows reaching right down to the floor. Go ahead, walk right up to one, and look down—*scaaary.*

Come on a clear day. If you're lucky, you'll be able to go out on the **rooftop promenade,** the world's highest open-air observation deck. (It's only open under perfect conditions; I've only been able to go out once in a lifetime of visits.) You thought inside was incredible? Wait 'til you see this. While you're up here, look straight down and wonder what Frenchman Philippe Petit could've been thinking when in August 1974 he shot a rope across to tower no. 1, grabbed his balancing pole, and walked gingerly across, stopping to lie down for a moment in the center.

You can have a similar view in more convivial conditions by going to the top of One World Trade Center, where you can linger over a drink and munchies—or put on some dancing shoes and Lindy to some hep-cat swing—at the **Greatest Bar on Earth** (see chapter 6).

3 The Top Museums

✪ **American Museum of Natural History.** On Central Park West, btw. 77th and 81st sts. ☎ **212/769-5100.** www.amnh.org. Suggested admission $8 adults ($13 with 1 IMAX movie, $16 with 2), $6 seniors and students ($7 with 1 IMAX movie, $12 with 2), $4.50 children 2–12 ($13 with 1 IMAX movie, $9 with 2). Sun–Thurs 10am–5:45pm, Fri–Sat 10am–8:45pm. Subway: B, C to 81st St.; 1, 9 to 79th St.

This four-block-square museum houses the world's greatest natural science collection in a group of buildings made of towers and turrets, pink granite and red brick—a mishmash of architectural styles, but overflowing with neo-Gothic charm. The diversity of the holdings is astounding: some 36 million specimens ranging from microscopic organisms to the world's largest cut gem, the Brazilian Princess Topaz (21,005 carats). It would take all day to see the entire museum, and then you still wouldn't get to everything. If you don't have a lot of time, you can see the best of the best on free **highlights tours** offered daily every hour at 15 minutes after the hour from 10:15am to 3:15pm. Free daily **spotlights tours,** thematic tours that change monthly, are also offered; stop by an information desk for the day's schedule. **Audio Expeditions,** high-tech audio tours that allow you to access narration in the order you choose, are also available to help you make sense of it all.

If you only see one exhibit, see the ✪ **dinosaurs,** which takes up the entire fourth floor. Recent restorations and redesign put new life in these old bones, making this the best of what the museum has to offer by far. Start in the **Orientation Room,** where a short video gives an overview of the 500 million years of evolutionary history that led to you. Continue to the **Vertebrate Origins Room,** where huge models of ancient fish and turtles hang overhead, with plenty of interactive exhibits and kid-level displays on hand to keep young minds fascinated. Next come the great **dinosaur halls,** with mammoth, spectacularly reconstructed skeletons and more interactive displays. **Mammals and Their Extinct Relatives** brings what you've learned in the previous halls home, showing how yesterday's prehistoric monsters have evolved into today's modern animals. Simply marvelous—you could spend hours in these halls alone.

Many other areas of the museum pale in comparison. The **animal habitat dioramas** and **halls of peoples** seem a bit dated but still have something to teach, especially the Native American halls. Other than peeking in to see the giant whale (viewable from the cafe below) skip the **ocean life** room altogether; let's hope this is next on the restoration agenda, because the current exhibit makes Disneyland's submarine ride look high-tech. The new **Hall of Biodiversity** is an impressive multimedia exhibit, but the doom-and-gloom story it tells about the future of rainforests and other natural habitats may be too much for the little ones. Kids five years and older should head to the **Discovery Room,** with lots of hands-on exhibits and experiments. (Be prepared, Mom and Dad—there seems to be a gift shop overflowing with fuzzy stuffed animals at every turn.)

The museum excels at **special exhibitions,** so I recommend checking to see what will be on while you're in town in case any advance planning is required. Highlights of the past year have included the magical Butterfly Conservatory, a walk-in enclosure housing nearly 500 free-flying tropical butterflies.

In addition, an **IMAX Theater** shows neat films like *Cosmic Voyage* and *Africa's Elephant Kingdom* on a four-story screen that puts you right in the heart of the action; you can buy tickets to

Museum-Going Tip

Many of the city's top museums—including the Natural History Museum, the Met, and MoMA—have late hours on Friday and/or Saturday nights. Take advantage of them. Most visitors run out of steam by dinnertime, so even on jam-packed weekends you'll largely have the place to yourself by 5 or 6pm—which, in most cases, leaves you hours left to explore, unfettered by crowds or screaming kids.

Midtown Attractions

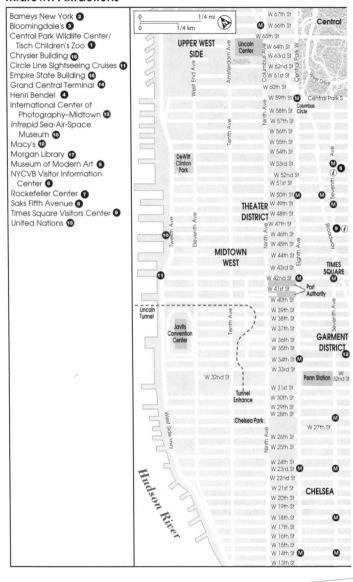

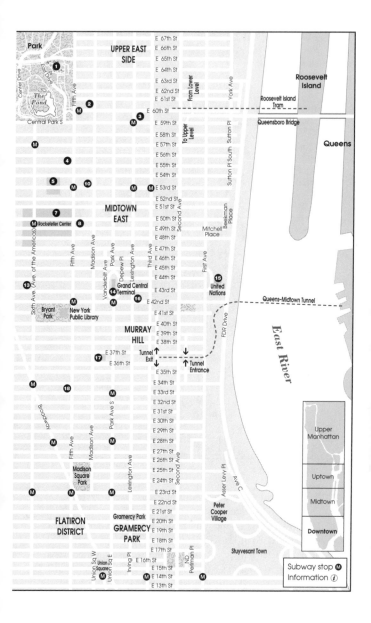

Park

The Pond

Central Park S

UPPER EAST SIDE

E 67th St
E 66th St
E 65th St
E 64th St
E 63rd St
E 62nd St
E 61st St
E 60th St
E 59th St
E 58th St
E 57th St
E 56th St
E 55th St
E 54th St
E 53rd St
E 52nd St
E 51st St
E 50th St
E 49th St
E 48th St
E 47th St
E 46th St
E 45th St
E 44th St
E 43rd St
E 42nd St
E 41st St
E 40th St
E 39th St
E 38th St
E 37th St
E 36th St
E 35th St
E 34th St
E 33rd St
E 32nd St
E 31st St
E 30th St
E 29th St
E 28th St
E 27th St
E 26th St
E 25th St
E 24th St
E 23rd St
E 22nd St
E 21st St
E 20th St
E 19th St
E 18th St
E 17th St
E 16th St
E 15th St
E 14th St
E 13th St

York Ave
From Lower Level
To Upper Level

Roosevelt Island

Roosevelt Island Tram

Queensboro Bridge

Queens

Sutton Pl South Sutton Pl

Beekman Place

Mitchell Place

MIDTOWN EAST

Fifth Ave
Madison Ave
Park Ave
Depew Pl
Vanderbilt Ave
Lexington Ave
Third Ave
Second Ave
First Ave

Rockefeller Center

Sixth Ave (Ave. of the Americas)

Bryant Park

New York Public Library

Grand Central Terminal

United Nations

Queens-Midtown Tunnel

FDR Drive

East River

MURRAY HILL

Tunnel Exit
Tunnel Entrance

Broadway
Fifth Ave
Madison Ave
Park Ave S
Lexington Ave

Madison Square Park

FLATIRON DISTRICT

Gramercy Park

GRAMERCY PARK

Union Sq W
Union Square
Union Sq E
Irving Pl
Peltman Pl

Aser Levy Pl
Ave C

Peter Cooper Village

Stuyvesant Town

Upper Manhattan

Uptown

Midtown

Downtown

Subway stop Ⓜ
Information ⓘ

Uptown Attractions

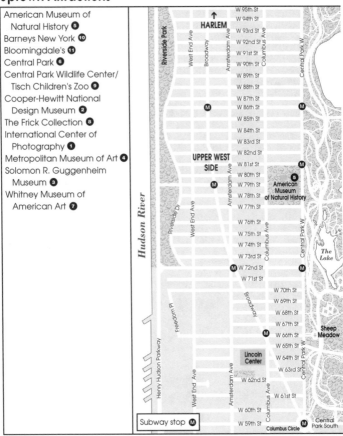

American Museum of
   Natural History ❺
Barneys New York ❿
Bloomingdale's ⓫
Central Park ❻
Central Park Wildlife Center/
   Tisch Children's Zoo ❾
Cooper-Hewitt National
   Design Museum ❷
The Frick Collection ❽
International Center of
   Photography ❶
Metropolitan Museum of Art ❹
Solomon R. Guggenheim
   Museum ❸
Whitney Museum of
   American Art ❼

screenings as part of your admission package (see above). IMAX tickets can also be ordered separately and in advance by calling ☎ 212/769-5200 or online at the museum's website. The **Hayden Planetarium** closed in 1997 for demolition and reconstruction that should be completed in early 2000, but Beavises and Buttheads (and I say that fondly) can still see **laser light shows**—including U2 and Laser Zeppelin in 3D—Friday and Saturday at 9 and 10pm. Tickets are $9; call ☎ **212/769-5200** to reserve.

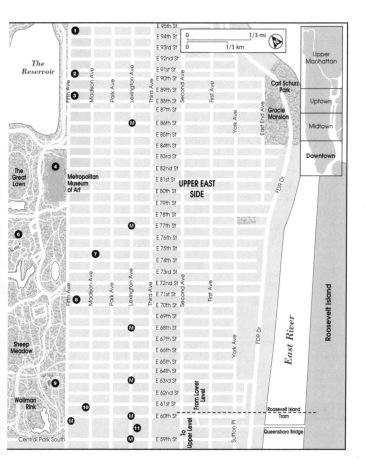

✪ **Metropolitan Museum of Art.** Fifth Ave. at 82nd St. ☎ **212/535-7710.** www.metmuseum.org. Suggested admission (includes same-day entrance to the Cloisters) $10 adults, $5 seniors and students, free for children under 12 when accompanied by an adult. Tues–Thurs and Sun 9:30am–5:15pm, Fri–Sat 9:30am–8:45pm. No strollers allowed Sun (back carriers available at 81st St. entrance coat-check area). Subway: 4, 5, 6 to 86th St.

Home of blockbuster after blockbuster exhibition, the Metropolitan Museum of Art attracts some 5 million people a year, more than any other spot in New York City. And it's no wonder this place is magnificent. At 1.6 million square feet, this is the largest museum in the Western Hemisphere. Nearly all the world's cultures are on display through the ages—from Egyptian mummies to ancient Greek statuary to Islamic carvings to Renaissance paintings to Native American masks to 20th-century decorative arts—and masterpieces are the rule. You could go once a week for a lifetime and still find something new on each visit.

So, unless you plan on spending your entire vacation in the museum (some people do), you cannot see the entire collection. My recommendation is to give it a good day—or better yet, two half days so you don't burn out. One good way to get an overview is to take advantage of the little-known **Highlights Tour.** Even some New Yorkers who've spent many hours in the museum could profit from this once-over. Call ☎ **212/570-3711** (Monday to Friday from 9am to 5pm) or visit the museum's website for a schedule of this and subject-specific tours (French Impressionists, Arts of Japan, and so on).

The least overwhelming way to see the Met on your own is to pick up a map at the round desk in the entry hall and choose to concentrate on what you like, whether it's 17th-century paintings, American furniture, or the art of the South Pacific. Highlights include the American Wing's **Garden Court,** the lower-level **Costume Hall,** and the **Frank Lloyd Wright room.** The newly reopened **Roman and Greek galleries** are overwhelming, but in a

---

Money- & Time-Saving Tip

CityPass just may be New York's best sightseeing deal. Pay one price ($27.50) for admission to six top attractions—the Top of the World observation deck at the World Trade Center, the Metropolitan Museum of Art, the Museum of Modern Art, the Empire State Building, the American Museum of Natural History, and the Intrepid Sea-Air-Space Museum—which would cost you fully twice as much if you paid for each one separately. More importantly, CityPass is not a coupon book; it contains actual admission tickets, so you can bypass lengthy ticket lines. CityPass is good for nine days from the first time you use it. It's sold at all participating attractions, and discounted rates are available for kids and seniors. If you want to avoid that first line, order your CityPass online at **www.citypass.net** or www.ticketweb.com. For phone orders, call Ticketweb at ☎ **212/ 269-4TIX.**

marvelous way, as is the collection of later **Chinese art.** The setting of the **Temple of Dendur** is dramatic, in a specially built glass-walled gallery with Central Park views. But it all depends on what your interests are. Don't forget the marvelous **special exhibitions,** which can range from "Jade in Ancient Costa Rica" to "Cubism and Fashion." If you'd like to plan your visit ahead of time, the museum's website is a useful tool; there's also a list of current exhibitions in the Friday and Sunday editions of the *New York Times.*

On **Friday and Saturday evenings,** the Met remains open late not only for art viewing but also for cocktails in the Great Hall Balcony Bar (4–8:30pm) and classical music from a string quintet or trio. A slate of after-hours programs (gallery talks, walking tours, family programs) changes by the week; call for this week's schedule.

✪ Museum of Modern Art. 11 W. 53rd St. (btw. Fifth and Sixth aves.). ☎ **212/708-9400.** www.moma.org. Admission $9.50 adults ($13.50 with audio tour), $6.50 seniors and students ($10.50 with audio tour), free for children under 16 accompanied by an adult; pay as you wish Fri 4:30–8:15pm. Sat–Tues and Thurs 10:30am–5:45pm, Fri 10:30am–8:15pm. Subway: E, F to Fifth Ave.; B, D, F, Q to 47–50th sts./Rockefeller Center.

The Museum of Modern Art (or MoMA, as it's usually called) boasts the world's greatest collection of painting and sculpture ranging from the late 19th century to the present, including everything from van Gogh's *Starry Night,* Picasso's early *Les Demoiselles d'Avignon,* Monet's *Water Lilies,* and Klimt's *The Kiss* to later masterworks by Frida Kahlo, Edward Hopper, Andy Warhol, Robert Rauschenberg, and many others. Top that off with an extensive collection of modern drawings, photography, architectural models and furniture (including the Mies van der Rohe collection), iconic design objects ranging from tableware to sports cars, and film and video (including the world's largest collection of D.W. Griffith films), and you have quite a museum. If you're into modernism, this is the place to be.

While not quite Met-sized, MoMa is probably still more than you can see in a day. In true modern style, the museum is efficient and well organized, so it's easy to focus on your primary interests; just grab a museum map after you pay your admission. For an overview, take the **self-guided tour** that stops at the collection's highlights, chosen by the different departments' curators. The sculpture garden—an island of trees and fountains in which to enjoy the works of Calder, Moore, and Rodin—is particularly of note. In addition, there's usually at least one beautifully mounted special exhibition in-house that's worth a special trip, whether it be the works of Finnish master architect Alvar Aalto, Julia Margaret Cameron's remarkable 19th-century photographs of women, or a celebration of sight gags in contemporary art.

MoMa boasts a good number of special programs. There's live jazz three evenings a week in **Sette MoMA** (☎ 212/708-9710), the museum's notable Italian restaurant overlooking the sculpture garden, or the Garden Cafe. A full slate of symposiums, gallery talks by contemporary artists, interactive family programs, and brown-bag lunches are always on offer; call ☎ **212/708-9781** or visit the museum's website to see what's on while you're in town. Additionally, there's always a multifaceted film and video program on the schedule; call the main number to see what's on. Films are included in the price of admission, but arrive early to make sure you get a seat.

Setting course for the 21st century, the Modern has embarked on a major expansion overseen by Japanese architect Yoshio Taniguchi. Don't look for this ambitious project to be completed anytime soon; but since it's expanding into adjacent space, it shouldn't appreciably affect your enjoyment of the museum as it currently exists.

Solomon R. Guggenheim Museum. 1071 Fifth Ave. (at 88th St.). ☎ **212/423-3500.** www.guggenheim.org. Admission $12 adults, $7 seniors, children under 12 free; Fri 6–8pm pay what you wish. Two-museum pass, which includes one admission to the SoHo branch valid for 1 week, $16 adults, $10 seniors. Sun–Wed 10am–6pm, Fri–Sat 10am–8pm. Subway: 4, 5, 6 to 86th St.

It has been called a bun, a snail, a concrete tornado, and even a giant wedding cake; bring your kids, and they'll probably see it as New York's coolest opportunity for skateboarding or in-line skating. Whatever description you choose to apply, Frank Lloyd Wright's only New York building, completed in 1959, is best summed up as a brilliant work of architecture—so consistently brilliant that it competes with the art for your attention. If you're looking for the city's best modern art, head to MoMA or the Whitney first; come to the Guggenheim to see the house.

It's easy to see the bulk of what's on display in two to four hours. Inside, a spiraling rotunda circles over a slowly inclined ramp that leads you past changing exhibits, which can range from modern masterworks from the *Centre Pompidou* to the *Art of the Motorcycle*. Usually the progression is counterintuitive: from the first floor up, rather than from the sixth floor down. If you're not sure, ask a guard before you begin. Permanent exhibits of 19th- and 20th-century art, including strong holdings of Kandinsky, Klee, Picasso, and French impressionists, occupy a stark annex called the **Tower Galleries,** an addition accessible at every level that some critics claimed made the original look like a toilet bowl backed by a water tank (judge for yourself—I think there may be something to that view).

The Guggenheim runs some interesting special programs, including free docent tours (there's a one-hour highlights tour daily at noon), film screenings, and the World Beat Jazz Series on Friday and Saturday evenings from 5 to 8pm.

✪ **Whitney Museum of American Art.** 945 Madison Ave. (at 75th St.). ☎ **212/570-3600** or 212/570-3676. www.echonyc.com/~whitney. Admission $9 adults, $7 seniors and students, free for children under 12; pay as you wish Thurs 6–8pm. Wed and Fri–Sun 11am–6pm, Thurs 11am–8pm. Subway: 6 to 77th St.

What is arguably the finest collection of 20th-century American art in the world belongs to the Whitney thanks to the efforts of Gertrude Vanderbilt Whitney. A sculptor herself, she organized exhibitions by American artists shunned by traditional academies, assembled a sizable personal collection, and founded the museum in 1930 in Greenwich Village.

Today's museum is an imposing presence on Madison Avenue— an inverted three-tiered pyramid of concrete and gray granite with seven seemingly random windows designed by Marcel Breuer, a leader of the Bauhaus movement. The rotating permanent collection consists of an intelligent selection of major works by Edward Hopper, George Bellows, Georgia O'Keeffe, Roy Lichtenstein, Jasper Johns, and other significant artists. A pleasing new fifth-floor exhibit space, the museum's first devoted exclusively to works from its permanent collection from 1900 to 1950, opened in 1998.

There are usually several simultaneous shows, commonly all well curated and more edgy than what you'd see at the MoMA or the Guggenheim. From April 1999 to February 2000, a substantial mulitmedia exhibition called "The American Century: Art and Culture 1900–2000" showcases the Whitney's innovative cultural-technological partnership with Intel as it explores the changing nature of American identity.

The Whitney is also notable for having the best museum restaurant in town: **Sarabeth's at the Whitney** (☎ **212/560-3670**), open for lunch Tuesday through Sunday and worth a visit in its own right (see chapter 6).

Free **gallery tours** are offered daily; call ☎ **212/570-3676** for the current schedule, or check at the Information desk when you arrive.

MORE MUSEUMS

Cooper-Hewitt National Design Museum. 2 E. 91st St. (at Fifth Ave.). ☎ **212/849-8300.** www.si.edu/ndm. Admission $5 adults, $3 seniors and students, free for children under 12; free to all Tues 5–9pm. Tues 10am–9pm, Wed–Sat 10am–5pm, Sun noon–5pm. Subway: 4, 5, 6 to 86th St.

Part of the Smithsonian Institution, the Cooper-Hewitt is housed in the Carnegie Mansion, built by steel magnate Andrew Carnegie in 1901. Some 11,000 square feet of gallery space is devoted to changing exhibits that are invariably well conceived, engaging, and educational. Exhibitions scheduled for late 1999–2000 include a retrospective on the work of Charles and Ray Eames and the National Design Triennial, featuring the work of both well-known and emerging talents as they address the pressing design issues of today.

✪ **The Frick Collection.** 1 E. 70th St. (at Fifth Ave.). ☎ **212/288-0700.** www.frick.org. Admission $7 adults, $5 seniors and students. Children under 10 not admitted; children under 16 must be accompanied by an adult. Tues–Sat 10am–6pm, Sun and minor holidays 1–6pm (closed all major holidays). Subway: 6 to 68th St./Hunter College.

To house his treasures and himself, steel magnate Henry Clay Frick hired architects Carrère & Hastings to build this 18th-century-French–style mansion (1914), one of the most beautiful remaining on Fifth Avenue. This is a living testament to New York's vanished Gilded Age: The interior still feels like a private home (albiet a really, really rich guy's home) graced with beautiful paintings, rather than a museum. Come here to see the classics, by some of the world's most famous painters: Titian, Bellini, Rembrandt, Turner, Vermeer, El Greco, and Goya, to name only a few. A highlight of the collection is the **Fragonard Room,** graced with the sensual rococo series *The Progress of Love.* The portrait of Montesquiou by Whistler is also stunning. Sculpture, furniture, Chinese vases, and French enamels complement the paintings and round out the collection. Included in the price of admission, the AcousticGuide audio tour is particularly useful, because it allows you to follow your own path rather than a prescribed route.

In addition to the permanent collection, the Frick regularly mounts small, well-focused temporary exhibitions, such as "Victorian Fairy Painting" and "Constable, A Master Draughtsman."

International Center of Photography and ICP—Midtown. Uptown branch: 1130 Fifth Ave. (at 94th St.) ☎ **212/860-1777.** Midtown branch: 1133 Sixth Ave. (at 43rd St.). ☎ **212/768-4682.** www.icp.org. Admission (includes both uptown and midtown locations) $6 adults, $4 seniors, $1 children under 13; Tues 5–8pm pay what you wish. Tues–Thurs 10am–5pm, Fri 10am–8pm, Sat and Sun 10am–6pm. Subway: 6 to 96th St. to ICP Uptown; B, D, F, Q to 42nd St. to ICP Midtown.

The ICP is one of the world's premier collectors and exhibitors of photographic art, mounting some of the most interesting changing art exhibits in the city. The original ICP is also worth a look, but the Midtown branch is the place to start since it's twice the size of the original and usually has two mounted exhibitions rather than just one. The emphasis is on contemporary photographic works, but historically important photographers aren't ignored. Topics can range from "Man Ray: Photography and its Double" to "Soul of the Game: Images and Voices of Street Basketball." A must on any photography buff's list.

Intrepid Sea-Air-Space Museum. Pier 86 (W. 46th St. at Twelfth Ave.). ☎ **212/245-0072.** www.intrepid-museum.com. Admission $10 adults; $7.50 veterans, seniors, and students; $5 children 6–11; first child under 6 free, each extra child $1. May–Sept, Mon–Sat 10am–5pm (last admission 4pm), Sun 10am–6pm (last admission 5pm); Oct–Apr, Wed–Sun 10am–5pm (last admission 4pm). Subway: A, C, E to 42nd St. Bus: M42 crosstown.

The most astonishing thing about the aircraft carrier USS *Intrepid* is how it can be simultaneously so big and so small. It's a few football fields long, holds 40 aircraft, and sometimes doubles as a ballroom for society functions. But stand there and think about landing an A-12 jet on the deck and suddenly, it's miniscule. Furthermore, in the narrow passageways below, you'll find it isn't quite the roomiest of vessels. Now a National Historic Landmark, the exhibit also includes the destroyer USS *Edison,* the submarine USS *Growler,* and the lightship *Nantucket,* as well as a collection of vintage and modern aircraft. Special exhibits are often mounted, such as 1998's tribute to 200 years of naval service by African-Americans. Kids just love this place. But think twice about going in winter— it's almost impossible to heat an aircraft carrier.

✪ **Lower East Side Tenement Museum.** Visitors' Center at 90 Orchard St. (at Broome St.). ☎ **212/431-0233.** www.wnet.org/tenement. $8 adults, $6 seniors and students for 1 tenement tour; $14 adults, $10 seniors and students for any 2 tours; $20 adults, $14 seniors and students for all 3 tours. Tenement tours depart Tues–Fri at 1pm and every half hour to 4pm; Thurs hourly 6pm–9pm; Sat–Sun every half-hour 11am–4:30pm. Subway: F to Delancey St.; B, D, Q to Grand St.

This decade-old museum is the first-ever National Trust for Historic Preservation site that was not the home of someone rich or famous. It's something quite different: a five-story tenement that 10,000 people from 25 countries called home between 1863 and 1935—people who had come to the United States looking for the American dream, and made 97 Orchard St. their first stop. This living history museum tells the story of the great immigration boom of the late 19th and early 20th centuries, when the Lower East Side was considered the "Gateway to America." A visit here makes a good follow-up to an Ellis Island trip—what happened to all the people who passed through that famous waystation?

The only way to see the museum is by guided tour. The primary tenement tour, offered on all open days, is a satisfying way to explore the museum. A knowledgeable guide leads you into the dingy urban time capsule, where several apartments have been faithfully restored to their exact lived-in condition, and recounts the real-life stories of the families who occupied them in fascinating detail. Tours are limited in number, so it pays to reserve ahead.

✪ **Morgan Library.** 29 E. 36th St. (at Madison Ave.). ☎ **212/685-0008.** www.shop.morganlibrary.org. Admission $7 adults, $5 seniors, children under 12 free. Tues–Thur 10:30am–5pm, Fri 10:30am–8pm, Sat 10:30am–6pm, Sun noon–6pm. Subway: 6 to 33rd St.

Here's an undiscovered New York treasure, boasting one of the world's most important collections of original manuscripts, rare books and bindings, master drawings, and personal writings. Among the remarkable artifacts on display under glass are stunning illuminated manuscripts (including Gutenberg bibles), a working draft of the U.S. Constitution bearing copious handwritten notes, and handwritten scores by the likes of Beethoven, Mozart, and Puccini. The collection of mostly 19th-century drawings—featuring works by Seurat, Degas, Rubens, and other great masters—has an excitement of immediacy about it that the artists' more well-known paintings often lack. This rich repository originated as the private collection of turn-of-the-century financier J. Pierpont Morgan and is housed in a landmark Renaissance-style palazzo building (1906) he commissioned from McKim, Mead & White to hold his masterpieces. Morgan's library and study are preserved virtually intact. The special exhibitions are particularly well chosen and curated; those scheduled for the coming year include "The Great Experiment: George Washington and the American Republic," tracing the first U.S. president's development from loyal British subject to leader of a radical revolution. A reading room is available by appointment.

Museum of Jewish Heritage—A Living Memorial to the Holocaust. 18 First Place (at Battery Place), Battery Park City. ☎ **212/968-1800.** www.mjhnyc.org. Admission $7 adults, $5 seniors and students, children under 5 free. Sun–Wed 9am–5pm, Thurs 9am–8pm, Fri and evenings of Jewish holidays 9am–2pm. Subway: 1, 9 to South Ferry; 4, 5 to Bowling Green.

Located in the south end of Battery Park City, this museum occupies a strikingly spare six-sided building designed by award-winning architect Kevin Roche, with a six-tier roof alluding to the Star of David and the 6 million Jews murdered in the Holocaust. The permanent exhibits—"Jewish Life a Century Ago," "The War Against the Jews," and "Jewish Renewal"—recount the daily pre-war lives, the unforgettable horror that destroyed them, and the tenacious renewal experienced by European and immigrant Jews in the years from the late 19th century to the present. Its power derives from the way it tells that story: through the objects, photographs, documents, and, most poignantly, through the videotaped testimonies of Holocaust victims, survivors, and their families, all chronicled by Steven Spielberg's Survivors of the Shoah Visual History Foundation.

Advance tickets are highly recommended to guarantee admission, and can be purchased by calling ☎ **212/786-0820, ext. 111** or TicketMaster (☎ **800/307-4007** or 212/307-4007; www. ticketmaster.com).

4 The Top Skyscrapers & Architectural Marvels

For details on the **World Trade Center,** see p. 115. For the **Brooklyn Bridge,** see p. 113.

Chrysler Building. 405 Lexington Ave. (at 42nd St.). Subway: 4, 5, 6, 7, S to 42nd St./Grand Central.

Built as Chrysler Corporation headquarters in 1930 (they moved out decades ago), this is perhaps the 20th century's most romantic architectural achievement, especially at night, when the lights in its triangular openings play off its steely crown. A recent cleaning added new sparkle. As you admire its facade, be sure to note the gargoyles reaching out from the upper floors, looking for all the world like streamline-Gothic hood ornaments.

The observation deck closed long ago, but you can visit the lavish ground-floor interior, which is art deco to the max. The ceiling mural depicting airplanes and other early marvels of the first decades of the 20th century evince the bright promise of technology. The elevators are works of art, masterfully covered in exotic woods (especially note the lotus-shaped marquetry on the doors).

✪ **Empire State Building.** 350 Fifth Ave. (at 34th St.). ☎ **212/736-3100.** www.esbnyc.com. Observatory admission $6 adults, $3 seniors and children under 12, free for children under 5. Daily 9:30am–midnight (tickets sold until 11:30pm). Subway: B, D, F, Q, N, R to 34th St.; 6 to 33rd St.

King Kong climbed it in 1933. A plane slammed into it in 1945. The World Trade Center superseded it in 1970 as the island's tallest building. And in 1997, a gunman ascended it to stage a deadly shooting. But through it all, the Empire State Building has remained one of the city's favorite landmarks, and its signature high-rise.

Completed in 1931, it rises 102 stories (1,454 feet) and now harbors the offices of fashion firms and, in its upper reaches, a jumble of high-tech broadcast equipment.

Always a conversation piece, the Empire State Building glows every night, bathed in colored floodlights to commemorate events of significance (red, white, and blue for Independence Day; green for St. Patrick's Day; red, black, and green for MLK Day; even lavender and white for Gay Pride Day). The familiar silver spire can be seen from all over the city. My favorite view of the building is from 23rd Street, where Fifth Avenue and Broadway converge: On a lovely day, stand at the base of the Flatiron Building and gaze up Fifth; the crisp, gleaming deco tower jumps out, soaring above the sooty office buildings that surround it.

But the views that keep nearly 3 million visitors coming every year are the ones from the 86th- and 102nd-floor **observatories.** The lower one is best—you can walk out on a windy deck (even inside at this height you feel the air whistling through the building) and look through coin-operated viewers (bring quarters!) over what, on a clear day, can be as much as an 80-mile visible radius. The citywide panorama is magnificent. The higher observation deck is glass-enclosed and cramped.

Light fog can create an admirably moody effect, but it goes without saying that a clear day is best. Dusk brings the most remarkable views, and the biggest crowds. Consider going in the morning, when the light is still low on the horizon, keeping glare to a minimum. Starry nights are pure magic.

Empire State Ticket-Buying Tip

Lines can be frightfully long at the concourse-level ticket booth, so be prepared to wait—or consider purchasing **advance tickets** online using a credit card at **www.esbnyc.org**. You'll pay a $2 service charge for the privilege, but it's well worth it, especially if you're visiting during a busy season, when the line can be shockingly long. You're not required to choose a time or date for your tickets in advance; they can be used on any regular open day. However, order them well before you leave home, because they're sent only by regular mail. Expect them to take 7 to 10 days to reach you (longer if you live out of the country). With tickets in hand, you're allowed to proceed directly to the second floor—past everyone who didn't plan as well as you did!

✪ **Grand Central Terminal.** 42nd St. at Park Ave. **www. grandcentralterminal.com**. Subway: 4, 5, 6, 7, S to 42nd St./Grand Central.

After more than two years and $175 million, Grand Central Terminal has come out from under the tarps and scaffolding. Rededicated with all the appropriate pomp and circumstance on October 1, 1998, the 1913 landmark has been reborn as one of the most magnificent public spaces in the country.

Come and visit, even if you're not catching one of the subway lines or Metro North commuter trains that rumble through the bowels of this great place. And even if you arrive and leave by subway, be sure to exit the station, walking a couple of blocks south, to about 40th Street, before you turn around to admire Jules-Alexis Coutan's neo-classical sculpture *Transportation* hovering over the south entrance, with a majestically buff Mercury, the Roman god of commerce and travel, as its central figure.

The greatest visual impact comes when you enter the vast **main concourse.** Cleaned of decades of grime and cheezy advertisements, it boasts renewed majesty. The high windows once again allow sunlight to penetrate the space, glinting off the half-acre Tennessee marble floor and the brass clock over the central kiosk. The masterful **sky ceiling,** again a brilliant greenish blue, depicts the constellations of the winter sky above New York. They're each lit with 59 stars, surrounded by dazzling 24-karat-gold and emitting light fed through fiber-optic cables, their intensities roughly replicating the magnitude of the actual stars as seen from Earth. Look carefully, and you'll see a patch near one corner left unrestored as a useful reminder of the neglect once visited on this splendid overhead masterpiece. On the east end of the main concourse is a grand **marble staircase** where there had never been one before, but as the original plans had always intended.

This dramatic beaux arts splendor serves as a hub of social activity as well. New retail shops and restaurants have taken over the mezzanine and lower levels. The highlight of the mezzanine is **Michael Jordan's—The Steak House,** a gorgeous art deco space that allows you to dine within view of the sky ceiling, and the famous lower-level **Oyster Bar,** also restored to its original old-world glory (see chapter 4).

✪ **Rockefeller Center.** Between 47th and 50th sts., from Fifth to Sixth aves. ☎ **212/632-3975.** Subway: B, D, F, Q to 47th–50th sts./Rockefeller Center.

A streamline modern masterpiece, Rockefeller Center is one of New York's central gathering spots for visitors and New Yorkers alike. A prime example of the city's skyscraper spirit and historic sense of optimism, it was erected mainly in the 1930s, when the city was deep in a depression as well as its most passionate art deco phase. Designated a National Historic Landmark in 1988, it's now the world's largest privately owned business-and-entertainment center, with 18 buildings on 21 acres.

For a dramatic approach to the entire complex, start at Fifth Avenue between 49th and 50th streets. The builders purposely created the gentle slope of the Promenade, known here as the **Channel Gardens** because it's flanked to the south by La Maison Française and to the north by the British Building (the Channel, get it?). You'll also find a number of attractive shops along here, including a big branch of the **Metropolitan Museum of Art Store,** a good stop for elegant gifts. The Promenade leads to the **Lower Plaza,** home to the famous ice-skating rink in winter (see next paragraph) and alfresco dining in summer in the shadow of Paul Manship's gilded bronze statue *Prometheus,* more notable for its setting than its magnificence as an artwork. All around the flags of the United Nations' member countries flap in the breeze. Just behind *Prometheus,* in December and early January, towers the city's official and majestic Christmas tree.

The **Rink at Rockefeller Plaza** (☎ 212/332-7654), is tiny but positively romantic, especially during the holidays, when the giant Christmas tree's multicolored lights twinkle from above. It's open from mid-October to mid-March, and you'll skate under the magnificent tree for the month of December.

The focal point of this "city within a city" is the **GE Building,** at 30 Rockefeller Plaza, a 70-story showpiece towering over the plaza. You can pick up a walking tour brochure highlighting the center's art and architecture at the main information desk in this building.

NBC television maintains studios throughout the complex. *Saturday Night Live,* the *Rosie O'Donnell Show,* and *Late Night with Conan O'Brien* originate in the GE Building; call ☎ 212/664-4000 for tips on getting tickets. If you're a fan of NBC's *Today Show,* the glass-enclosed studio from which the show is broadcast live weekdays from 7 to 9am is on the southwest corner of 49th Street and Rockefeller Plaza; come early if you want a visible spot, and bring your HI MOM! sign. Who knows? You may even get to chat with Katie, Matt, or Al in a segment. One-hour **NBC Studio Tours** (☎ 212/664-7174) are $10 per person (children under 6 are not admitted).

United Nations. At First Ave. and 46th St. ☎ **212/963-8687.** www.un.org. Guided tours $7.50 adults, $5.50 seniors, $4.50 students, $3.50 children (those under 5 not permitted). Daily tours every half hour 9:15am–4:45pm; closed weekends Jan–Feb. Subway: 4, 5, 6, 7, S to 42nd St./Grand Central.

In the midst of what some consider the world's most cynical city is this working monument to world peace. The U.N. headquarters occupies 18 acres of international territory—neither New York City nor the United States has jurisdiction here—along the East River from 42nd to 48th streets. Designed by an international team of architects (led by American Wallace K. Harrison and including Le Corbusier) and finished in 1952, the complex weds the 39-story glass slab Secretariat with the free-form General Assembly on beautifully landscaped grounds donated by John D. Rockefeller, Jr., along the East River. One hundred eighty nations use the facilities to arbitrate worldwide disputes.

Guided one-hour tours take you to the General Assembly Hall and the Security Council Chamber and introduce the history and activities of the United Nations and its related organizations. Along the tour you'll see donated objects and artwork, including charred artifacts that survived the atomic bombs at Hiroshima and Nagasaki, stained-glass windows by Chagall, a replica of the first *Sputnik*, and a colorful mosaic called *The Golden Rule,* based on a Norman Rockwell drawing, which was a gift from the United States in 1985.

The **Delegates' Dining Room** (☎ **212/963-7625**), which affords great views of the East River, is open to the public on weekdays for lunch 11:30am to 2:30pm (reserve in advance). The **post office** sells unique United Nations stamps that can be purchased and posted only here.

5 Organized Sightseeing Tours

DOUBLE-DECKER BUS TOURS

Taking a narrated sightseeing tour is one of the best ways to see and learn quickly about New York's major sights and neighborhoods. However, keep in mind that the commentary is only as good as the guide, who is seldom an expert. Enjoy the ride—and take the "facts" you hear along the way with a grain of salt.

Gray Line New York Tours. In the Port Authority Bus Terminal, Eighth Ave. and 42nd St. ☎ **212/397-2600.** www.graylinenewyork.com. Hop-on, hop-off bus tours from $22 adults, $13 children 5–11; basic full-city tour $33 adults, $21 children. Check website for online booking discounts (10% at press time). Operates daily. Subway: A, C, E to 42nd St.

Gray Line offers just about every sightseeing tour option and combination you could want. There are double-decker bus tours by day and by night that run uptown, downtown, and all around the town, as well as bus combos with Circle Line cruises, helicopter flights, museum entrances, and guided visits of sights. Two-day options are available, as are some out-of-town day trips (even a full day at Woodbury Commons, if you can't resist an opportunity for outlet shopping).

There's no real point to purchasing some combination tours—you don't need a guide to take you to the top of the World Trade Center or to the Statue of Liberty, and you don't save any money on admission by buying the combo ticket—but others, such as the Sunday Harlem Gospel tour, which features a tour of Harlem's top sights and a gospel service, is well worth the $33 price tag ($24 for kids 5–11). I've found Gray Line to put a higher premium on accuracy than the other big tour-bus operators, so this is your best bet among the biggies. There's also a sales office in the **Times Square Visitors Center,** 1560 Broadway, between 46th and 47th streets.

HARBOR CRUISES

If you'd like to sail the New York Harbor aboard the 1885 cargo schooner *Pioneer,* see the listing for South Street Seaport & Museum on p. 114.

✪ **Circle Line Sightseeing Cruises.** Departing from Pier 83, at W. 42nd St. and Twelfth Ave and Pier 16 at South Street Seaport. ☎ **212/563-3200.** Also departing from Pier 16 at South Street Seaport, 207 Front St. ☎ **212/630-8888.** www.circleline.com. Cruises from $12 adults, $6 children under 12; 3-hour full island cruise $22 adults, $12 children. Operates daily. Subway to Pier 83: A, C, E to 42nd St. Subway to Pier 16: J, M, Z, 2, 3, 4, 5 to Fulton Street.

Circle Line is the only tour company that circumnavigates the entire 35 miles around Manhattan, and I love this ride. It takes three hours and passes by the World Trade Center, the Statue of Liberty, Ellis Island, the Brooklyn Bridge, the United Nations, Yankee Stadium, the George Washington Bridge, and more, including Manhattan's wild northern tip. The panorama is riveting, and the commentary is surprisingly good. The big boats are basic but fine, with lots of deck room for everybody to enjoy the view. Snacks and drinks are available on-board for purchase.

If three hours is more than you or the kids can handle, go for either the 1¹/₂-hour **Semi-Circle** or **Sunset** cruise ($18 adults, $10 kids), both of which show you the highlights of the skyline. There's also a one-hour **Seaport Liberty** version ($12 adults, $6 kids) that sticks close to the south end of the island. But of all the tours, the kids might like **The Beast** best, a thrill-a-minute speedboat ride offered in summer only ($15 adults, $10 kids).

In addition, a number of adults-only **Music Cruises** are regularly on offer in summer. Call, check the website, or stop into the sales office in the **Times Square Visitors Center,** 1560 Broadway (between 46th and 47th streets), for details.

SPECIALTY TOURS

One of the most highly praised sightseeing organizations in New York is ✪ **Big Onion Walking Tours** (☎ **212/439-1090;** www. bigonion.com). Enthusiastic Big Onion guides (all hold an advanced degree in American history from Columbia or New York universities) peel back the layers of history to reveal the city's inner secrets. The two-hour walking tours are offered mostly on weekends, and subjects range from "Presidential New York" to a multi-ethnic eating tour of the Lower East Side, where you munch on everything from dim sum and dill pickles to fresh mozzarella. Tour prices range from $10 to $16 for adults, $8 to $14 for students and seniors. No reservations are necessary, but Big Onion strongly recommends that you call to verify schedules.

All tours offered by ✪ **Joyce Gold History Tours of New York** (☎ 212/242-5762; www.nyctours.com) are offered by Joyce Gold herself, an instructor of Manhattan history at New York University and the New School for Social Research. Her tours can really cut to the core of this town; Joyce is full of fascinating stories about Manhattan and its people. Tours are arranged around themes like "The Colonial Settlers of Wall Street" and "TriBeCa: The Creative Explosion." Tours are offered most weekends from March to December and last two to four hours. The price is $12 per person; no reservations are required.

For 18 years Larcelia Kebe, owner of **Harlem Your Way! Tours Unlimited** (☎ **212/690-1687;** www.harlemyourway.com), has been leading visitors around Harlem on bus and walking tours that take you beyond the snapshot stops at major sights (though they're all included). She shares Harlem's distinct culture—peppered with her own social commentary—on spirited tours of brownstones, churches, jazz clubs, and soul-food restaurants. Regularly scheduled tours include the Harlem "Sights and Sounds" tour, the Wednesday-night "Champagne Safari to the Apollo," the club-hopping "Champagne Jazz Safari," and the Sunday Gospel Tour. Walking tours are $25 to $48 per person, and bus tours are $35 to $55.

Free Neighborhood Tours

If you're looking to tour a specific neighborhood with an expert guide, call **Big Apple Greeter** (☎ **212/669-8159;** www.

bigapplegreeter.org). This non-profit organization is comprised of specially trained New Yorkers who volunteer to take visitors around town for a free 2- to 4-hour tour of a particular neighborhood. Reservations must be made in advance, preferably at least 1 week ahead of your arrival. Big Apple Greeter is also well-suited to accommodating disabled travelers; see "Tips for Travelers with Special Needs" in chapter 1 for details.

6 Central Park

Without this miracle of civic planning, Manhattan would be a virtual unbroken block of buildings. Instead, smack in the middle of Gotham, an 843-acre natural retreat provides a daily escape valve and tranquilizer for millions of New Yorkers.

While you're in the city, be sure to take advantage of the park's many charms—not the least of which is its sublime layout. Frederick Law Olmstead and Calvert Vaux won a competition with a plan that marries flowing paths with sinewy bridges, integrating them into the natural rolling landscape with its rocky outcroppings, man-made lakes and wooded pockets. The designers predicted the hustle and bustle to come, and tactfully hid traffic from the eyes and ears of parkgoers by building roads that are largely hidden from the bucolic view.

On just about any day, Central Park is crowded with New Yorkers and visitors alike. On nice days, especially weekends, it's the city's party central. Families come to play in the snow or the sun, depending on the season; in-line skaters come to fly through the crisp air and twirl in front of the bandshell; couples come to stroll or paddle the lake; and just about everybody comes to sunbathe at the first sign of summer. On beautiful days, the crowds are part of the appeal—everybody's come here to peel off their urban armor and relax, and the common goal puts a general feeling of camaraderie in the air. On these days, the people-watching is more compelling than anywhere else in the city. But one of Central Park's great appeals is that even on the most crowded days, there's always somewhere to get away from it all.

ORIENTATION & GETTING THERE Look at your map—that great green swath in the center of Manhattan is Central Park. It runs from 59th Street (also known as Central Park South) at the south end to 110th Street at the north end, and from Fifth Avenue on the east side to Central Park West (the equivalent of Eighth Avenue) on the west side. A 6-mile rolling road, **Central Park Drive,**

Central Park

Subway stop **M**

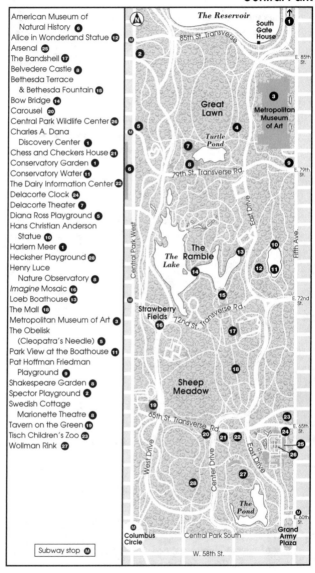

circles the park, and has a lane set aside for bikers, joggers, and in-line skaters. A number of **transverse** (crosstown) **roads** cross the park at major points—at 65th, 79th, 86th, and 97th streets—but they're built down a level, largely out of view, to minimize intrusion on the bucolic nature of the park.

A number of subway stops and lines serve the park, and which one you take depends on where you want to go. To reach the southernmost entrance on the west side, take an A, B, C, D, 1, or 9 to 59th Street/Columbus Circle. To reach the southeast corner entrance, take the N, R to Fifth Avenue; from this stop, it's an easy walk into the park to the Information Center in the **Dairy** (☎ 212/794-6564; open daily 11am to 5pm, to 4pm in winter), midpark at about 65th Street. Here you can ask questions, pick up park information, and purchase a good park map. If your time for exploring is limited, I suggest entering the park at 72nd or 79th streets for maximum exposure (subway: B, C to 72nd St. or 81st St./Museum of Natural History). From here, you can pick up park information at the visitor center at **Belvedere Castle** (☎ 212/772-0210; open Wednesday to Sunday 11am to 4pm), mid-park at 79th Street.

Food carts and vendors are set up at all of the park's main gathering points, selling hot dogs, pretzels, and ice cream, so finding a bite to eat is never a problem. You'll also find a fixed food counter at the **Conservatory,** on the east side of the park north of the 72nd Street entrance, and both casual snacks and more sophisticated dining at **Park View at the Boathouse** (for details on this and **Tavern on the Green,** see chapter 4).

GUIDED TOURS   Trolley tours of the park are offered weekdays from May through November; call ☎ 212/397-3809 for details. The **Charles A. Dana Discovery Center,** at the northeast corner of the park at Harlem Meer, hosts ranger-guided tours on occasion (☎ 212/860-1370).

FOR FURTHER INFORMATION   Call the main number at ☎ 212/360-3444 for recorded information, or 212/794-6564 to talk to a real person at the Dairy Information Center. The park also has a comprehensive website at **www.centralpark.org**.

SAFETY TIP   Even though the park has the lowest crime rate of any of the city's precincts, be wary, especially in the more remote northern end. It's a good idea to avoid the park entirely after dark, unless you're heading to one of the restaurants for dinner or to a Summerstage or Shakespeare at the Park event (see the "Calendar of Events" in chapter 1), when you should stick with the crowds.

EXPLORING THE PARK

The best way to see Central Park is to wander along its 58 miles of winding pedestrian paths, keeping in mind the following highlights.

Before starting your stroll, stop by the **Information Center** in the Dairy, midpark in a 19th-century-style building overlooking Wollman Rink at about 65th Street, to get a good park map and other information on sights and events, and to peruse the kid-friendly exhibit on the park's history and design.

The southern part of Central Park is more formally designed and heavily visited than the relatively rugged and remote northern end. Not far from the Dairy is the **carousel** with 58 hand-carved horses (open daily 10:30am to 6pm, to 5pm in winter; rides are 90¢); the **zoo** (see "Central Park Wildlife Center" below), and the **Wollman Rink** for roller- or ice-skating (see "Activities" below).

The Mall, a long formal walkway lined with elms shading benches and sculptures of sometimes forgotten writers, leads to the focal point of Central Park, **Bethesda Fountain** (along the 72nd Street transverse road). **Bethesda Terrace** and its grandly sculpted entryway border a large lake where dogs fetch sticks, rowboaters glide by, and dedicated early-morning anglers try their luck at catching carp, perch, catfish, and bass. You can rent a rowboat at or take a gondola ride from **Loeb Boathouse,** on the eastern end of the lake (see "Activities" below). Boats of another kind are at **Conservatory Water** (on the east side at 73rd Street), a stone-walled pond flanked by statues of both Hans Christian Andersen and Alice in Wonderland. On Saturdays at 10am, die-hard yachtsmen race remote-controlled sailboats in fierce competitions following Olympic regulations. (Sorry, model boats aren't for rent.)

If the action there is too intense, **Sheep Meadow** on the southwestern side of the park is a designated quiet zone, where Frisbee throwing and kite flying are as energetic as things get. Another respite is ✪ **Strawberry Fields,** at 72nd Street on the West Side. This memorial to John Lennon, who was murdered across the street at the Dakota apartment building (72nd Street and Central Park West, northwest corner), is a gorgeous garden centered around an

Where's Balto?

The people at Central Park say the question they're asked almost more than any other these days is "Where is the statue of Balto?" The heroic dog is just northwest of the zoo, mid-park at about 66th Street.

Italian mosaic bearing the title of the lead Beatle's most famous solo song, and his lifelong message: IMAGINE. In keeping with its goal of promoting world peace, the garden has 161 varieties of plants, donated by each of the 161 nations in existence when it was designed in 1985. This is a wonderful place for peaceful contemplation.

Bow Bridge, a graceful lacework of cast-iron designed by Calvert Vaux, crosses over the lake and leads to the most bucolic area of Central Park, **the Ramble.** This dense 38-acre woodland with spiraling paths, rocky outcroppings, and a stream is the best spot for bird-watching and feeling as if you've discovered an unimaginably leafy forest right in the middle of the city.

North of the Ramble, **Belvedere Castle** is home to **the Henry Luce Nature Observatory** (☎ **212/772-0210**), worth a visit if you're with children. From the castle, set on Vista Rock (the park's highest point at 135 feet), you can look down on the **Great Lawn,** which has emerged lush and green from renovations, and the **Delacorte Theater,** home to Shakespeare in the Park (see the "Calendar of Events" in chapter 1).

At the northeast end, **Conservatory Garden** (at 105th Street and Fifth Avenue), Central Park's only formal garden, is a magnificent display of flowers and trees reflected in calm pools of water. **Harlem Meer** and its boathouse were recently renovated, and look beautiful. The boathouse now berths the **Dana Discovery Center** (☎ **212/860-1370;** open daily 11am–5pm, to 4pm in winter), where children can learn about the environment and borrow fishing poles at no charge.

GOING TO THE ZOO

Central Park Wildlife Center/Tisch Children's Zoo. At Fifth Ave. and E. 64th St. ☎ **212/861-6030.** www.wcs.org/zoos. Admission $3.50 adults, $1.25 seniors, 50¢ children 3–12, under 3 free. Apr–Oct, Mon–Fri 10am–5pm, Sat–Sun 10:30am–5:30pm; Nov–Mar, daily 10am–4:30pm. Subway: N, R to Fifth Ave.

It has been nearly a decade since the zoo in Central Park was renovated, making it in the process both more human and more humane. Lithe sea lions frolic in the central pool area with beguiling style. The gigantic but graceful polar bears (one of whom, by the way, made himself a true New Yorker when he began regular visits with a shrink) glide back and forth across a watery pool that has glass walls through which you can observe very large paws doing very smooth strokes. The monkeys seem to regard those on the other side of the fence with knowing disdain.

Because of its small size, the zoo is at its best with its displays of smaller animals. The indoor, multi-level Tropic Zone is a real highlight, its steamy rainforest home to everything from black-and-white Colobus monkeys to Emerald tree boa constrictors to a leaf-cutter ant farm. So is the large penguin enclosure in the Polar Circle, which is better than the one at San Diego's Sea World. In the Temperate Territory, look for the Asian red pandas (cousins to the big black-and-white ones), which look like the world's most beautiful raccoons. Despite their pool and piles of ice, however, the polar bears still look sad.

The entire zoo is good for short attention spans; you can cover the whole thing in 1$^1/_2$ to 3 hours, depending on the size of the crowds and how long you like to linger. It's also very kid-friendly, with lots of well-written and -illustrated placards that older kids can understand. For the littlest ones, there's the $6-million **Tisch Children's Zoo.** With pigs, llamas, potbellied pigs, and more, this petting zoo and playground is a real blast for the five-and-under set.

ACTIVITIES

The 6-mile road circling the park, **Central Park Drive,** has a lane set aside for bikers, joggers, and in-line skaters. The best time to use it is when the park is closed to traffic: Monday to Friday 10am to 3pm (except Thanksgiving to New Year's) and 7 to 10pm. It's also closed from 7pm Friday to 6am Monday, but when the weather is nice, the crowds can be hellish. For a shorter jogging loop, try the midpark 1.58-mile track around the **Reservoir,** recently renamed for Jacqueline Kennedy Onassis, who often enjoyed a jog here (keep your eyes ready for spotting Madonna and other famous bodies). It's safest to jog only during daylight hours and where everybody else does.

BIKING   Off-road biking isn't permitted; stay on Central Park Drive or your bike may be confiscated by park police. You can rent 3- and 10-speed bikes as well as tandems in Central Park at the **Loeb Boathouse,** midpark near 74th Street and East Drive (☎ **212/ 861-4137** or 517-3623).

BOATING   From spring to fall, gondola rides and canoe rentals are available at the **Loeb Boathouse,** midpark near 74th Street and East Drive (☎ **212/517-3623**). Rentals are $10 for the first hour, $2.50 every 15 minutes thereafter, and a $30 deposit is required.

HORSE-DRAWN CARRIAGE RIDES   At the entrance to the park at 59th Street and Central Park South, you'll see a line of **horse-drawn carriages** waiting to take passengers on a ride through

Especially for Kids

Probably the best place of all to entertain the kids is in **Central Park**, which has kid-friendly diversions galore; see p. 136.

Kids of all ages can't help but turn dizzy with delight seeing incredible views from atop the **Empire State Building** (p. 129) and the **World Trade Center** (p. 115). The Empire State Building also offers the **New York Skyride** (☎ **888/SKYRIDE** or 212/279-9777; www.skyride.com), which offers a stomach-churning virtual tour of New York.

The **Children's Museum of Manhattan,** 212 W. 83rd St., between Broadway and Amsterdam Avenue on the Upper West Side (☎ **212/721-1234;** www.cmom.org), is a great place to take the kids when they're tired of being told not to touch. Interactive exhibits and activity centers encourage self-discovery, and a recent expansion means that there's now more than ever before to keep the kids busy and learning. The Time Warner Media Center takes children through the world of animation and helps them produce their own videos. Brand-new in 1999 is the Body Odyssey, a zany, scientific journey through the human body. Admission is $5 for kids and adults, $2.50 for seniors. Open Wednesday through Sunday from 10am to 5pm.

The **Sony Wonder Technology Lab,** at Sony Plaza, 550 Madison Ave., at 56th Street (☎ **212/833-8100**), is not as much of an infomercial as you'd expect. Both kids and adults love this high-tech science and tech center, which explores communications and information technology. You can experiment with robotics, explore the human body through medical imaging, mix a hit song, design a video game, and save the day at an environmental command center. Open Tuesday through Saturday from 10am to 6pm (until 8pm on Thursday), Sunday from noon to 6pm. Admission is free.

Also consider the following museums, discussed elsewhere in this chapter: The **American Museum of Natural History** (p. 116), whose dinosaur displays are guaranteed to wow both you and the kids; the **Intrepid Sea-Air-Space Museum** (p. 127), on a real battleship with an amazing collection of vintage and high-tech airplanes; the **Lower East Side Tenement Museum** (p. 127), whose living-history approach really intrigues school-age kids; and the **South Street Seaport & Museum** (p. 114), which little ones will love for its theme park–like atmosphere and old boats bobbing the harbor.

the park or along certain of the city's streets. You won't need me to tell you how forlorn most of these horses look; if you insist, a ride is about $50 for two for a half-hour, but I suggest skipping it.

IN-LINE SKATING   Central Park is the city's most popular place for blading. See the top of this section for details on **Central Park Drive,** main drag for skaters. On weekends, head to **West Drive** at 67th Street, behind Tavern on the Green, where you'll find trick skaters weaving through an NYRSA slalom course at full speed, or the **Mall** in front of the bandshell (above Bethesda Fountain) for twirling to tunes. In summer, **Wollman Rink** converts to a hotshot roller rink, with half-pipes and lessons available (see "Ice Skating" below).

You can rent skates for $15 a day weekdays and $25 a day weekends from **Blades East,** 160 E. 86th St. (☎ **212/996-1644**), and **Blades West,** 120 W. 72nd St. (☎ **212/787-3911**). April to October. Wollman also rents in-line skates for park use at similar rates.

ICE SKATING   Central Park's **Wollman Rink,** at 59th Street and Sixth Avenue (☎ **212/396-1010**), is the city's best outdoor skating spot. It's open for skating generally from mid-October to mid-April, depending on the weather. Rates are $7 for adults, $3.50 for seniors and kids under 12, and skate rental is $3.50; lockers are available.

PLAYGROUNDS   Nineteen Adventure Playgrounds are scattered throughout the park, perfect for jumping, sliding, tottering, swinging, and digging. At Central Park West and 81st Street is the **Diana Ross Playground,** voted the city's best by *New York* magazine. Also on the west side is the **Spector Playground,** at 85th Street and Central Park West, and, a little farther north, the **Wild West Playground** at 93rd Street. On the east side is the **Rustic Playground,** at 67th Street and Fifth Avenue, a delightfully landscaped space rife with islands, bridges, and big slides; and the **Pat Hoffman Friedman Playground,** right behind the Metropolitan Museum of Art at East 79th Street, is geared toward older toddlers.

7 Shopping Highlights

THE TOP SHOPPING STREETS & NEIGHBORHOODS
THE LOWER EAST SIDE

The bargains aren't quite what they used to be in the **Historic Orchard Street Shopping District**—which basically runs from Houston to Canal along Allen, Orchard, and Ludlow streets, spreading outward along both sides of Delancey Street—but prices on leather bags, shoes, luggage, fabrics on the bolt, and men's and women's clothes are still quite good. Be aware, though, that the hard sell on Orchard Street can be pretty hard to take. Still, the Orchard Street Bargain District is a nice place to discover a part of New York that's disappearing. Come during the week, since most stores are Jewish-owned, and therefore close Friday afternoon and all day Saturday. Sundays tend to be a madhouse.

Stop in first at the **Lower East Side's Visitor Center,** 261 Broome St., between Orchard and Allen streets (☎ **888/825-8374** or 212/226-9010; open Sun–Fri 10am–4pm; subway: F to Delancey St. or B, D, Q to Grand St.) for a shopping guide to the bargain district. There's also a free walking tour offered Sundays at 11am from April to December.

SoHo

People love to complain about super-fashionable SoHo—it's become too trendy, too tony, too Mall of America. True, **J. Crew,** 99 Prince St. (☎ **212/966-2739**), is only one of many big names that have supplanted the artists and galleries who used to inhabit its historic cast-iron buildings. But SoHo is still one of the best shopping 'hoods in the city—and few are more fun to browse. It's the epicenter of cutting-edge fashion, and still boasts plenty of unique boutiques. The streets are chock-full of tempting stores, so your best bet is to just come and browse.

SoHo's prime shopping grid is from Broadway east to Sullivan Street, and from Houston down to Broome, although Grand Street, on block south of Broome, has been sprouting shops of late. Broadway is the most commercial strip, with such recognizable names as **Pottery Barn** and **Banana Republic.** Most compelling along here are gourmet supermarket **Dean & Deluca,** at Prince St. (☎ **212/431-1691**), and **Canal Jean Co.,** between Spring and Broome streets (☎ **212/226-1130**), for well-priced jeans and other youth-oriented streetwear.

Among the designers in residence in SoHo are **Anna Sui,** 113 Greene St. (☎ **212/941-8406**), whose slinky fashions have a glammy edge; wild, colorful retro-inspired designs from golden boy **Todd Oldham,** 123 Wooster St. (☎ **212/226-4668**); trend-busting British designs from the legendary **Vivienne Westwood,** 71 Greene St. (☎ **212/334-5200**); pretty and playful Asian motifs from **Vivienne Tam,** 99 Greene St. (☎ **212/966-2398**); Prada off-shoot **Miu Miu,** 100 Prince St. (☎ **212/334-5156**); and sleek-chic from **Cynthia Rowley** 112 Wooster St. (☎ **212/334-1144**). Additionally, uptown names like **Louis Vuitton,** 116 Greene St. (☎ **212/274-9090**), have been migrating downtown of late.

If you're less interested in designer fashions and more interested in reasonable wearables, consider **Harriet Love,** 126 Prince St. (☎ **212/966-2280**), for women who like a lacy, Stevie Nicks-ish retro look; the incomparable **Eileen Fisher**'s new flagship at 395 West Broadway (☎ **212/431-4567**); and **Phat Farm,** 129 Prince St. (☎ **212/533-PHAT**), for upscale hip hop wear.

SoHo is also fabulous for accessories. The cobbled streets boast stores galore, from chic **Calvin Klein Shoes,** 133 Prince St. (☎ **212/505-3549**), and **Omari,** 132 Prince St. (☎ **212/219-0619**), to trendier styles at **Otto Tootsi Plohound,** 413 W. Broadway (☎ **212/925-8931**), and **John Fluevog,** 104 Prince St. (☎ **212/ 431-4484**). **Kate Spade,** 454 Broome St. (☎ **212/274-1991**), has revolutionized the handbag market with her practical yet chic rect-angular carry-alls.

Fashion is only half the story at **Anthropologie,** 375 W. Broad-way (☎ **212/343-7070**), whose funky-chic affordable wearables mix with fun gifts and home decorating items—much like Urban Outfitters for grown-ups.

High-end home stores are another huge part of the Soho scene. Hot potter **Jonathan Adler** has a cool new shop at 465 Broome St. (☎ **212/941-8950**)—anybody who has been reading shelter mags over the last year will recognize his bold vases instantly. **Global Table,** 107 Sullivan St. (☎ **212/431-5839**), is a great source for beautiful tableware from around the world (including lots of Japa-nese stuff), much of it affordable.

NoLiTa

Less than a handful of years ago, Elizabeth Street was a nondescript adjunct to Little Italy and the no-man's land east of SoHo. Today, it's the grooviest shopping strip in town, star of the neighborhood known as NoLiTa. Elizabeth and neighboring Mott and Mulberry streets are dotted with an increasing number of shops between Houston and Spring streets, with a few pushing one more block south to Kenmare. It's an easy walk from the Broadway–Lafayette stop on the B, D, F, Q line to the neighborhood, since it starts just east of Lafayette Street.

This may be a burgeoning neighborhood, but don't expect cheap—NoLiTa is clearly the stepchild of SoHo. Its boutiques are largely the province of sophisticated shopkeepers specializing in high-quality, fashion-forward products and design. Highlights include **Jamin Puech,** 252 Mott St. (☎ **212/334-9730**), for some of the most beautiful and unusual daytime and evening bags I've ever seen, all handmade in France by a husband-and-wife design team; **Sigerson Morrison,** 242 Mott St. (☎ **212/219-3893**), for eyepopping original shoe designs for women; **Daily 235,** 235 Elizabeth St. (☎ **212/334-9728**), a candy store for artsy grown-ups; and **Shì,** 233 Elizabeth St. (☎ **212/334-4330**), dedicated to new artists with an eye for innovation in home decor.

THE EAST VILLAGE

The East Village remains the international standard of bohemian hip. The easiest subway access is the 6 train to Astor Place, which lets you right out at **Kmart,** Astor Place at 770 Broadway (☎ **212/673-1540**); from here, it's just a couple blocks east to the prime hunting grounds. Note that some East Village shops don't open until 2pm, so your best bet is to come in the afternoon; most stay open until 8pm, some later.

East 9th Street between Second Avenue and Avenue A has become one of my favorite shopping strips in the entire city. Lined with an increasingly smart collection of boutiques, it proves that the East Village isn't just for kids anymore. Up-and-coming designers selling good-quality and affordably priced original fashions for women have set up shop along here, the best of which is the utterly fabulous ✪ **Jill Anderson,** at 311 E. 9th St. (☎ **212/253-1747**), one of New York's few designers creating clothes for real women to wear for real life—not just for 22-year-old size-2s to match with a pair of Pradas and wear out clubhopping. For stylish gifts and little luxuries, there's **H,** at no. 335 (☎ **212/477-2631**), with wonderful Japanese-inspired and other collectibles, from slinky vases to rice-paper coasters. There's also the factory store for super-hip **Manhattan Portage,** at no. 333 (☎ **212/995-1949**), if you're looking for something to stash your booty in.

If it's strange, illegal, or funky, it's probably available on **St. Marks Place,** which takes over for 8th Street, running east from Third Avenue to Avenue A. This skanky strip is a permanent street market, with countless T-shirt and boho jewelry stands. The height of the action is between Second and Third avenues, which is prime hunting grounds for used-record collectors.

GREENWICH VILLAGE

The West Village is great for browsing and gift shopping. Specialty book- and record stores, antiques and craft shops, and gourmet food markets dominate. Attention gourmands: Don't miss **Balducci's,** at Sixth Avenue and 9th Street (☎ **212/673-2600**), if you can help it. The best **Tower Records** in the country is at West 4th Street and Broadway (☎ **212/505-1500**). Except for NYU territory—8th

Street between Broadway and Sixth Avenue for trendy footwear and affordable fashions, and Broadway from 8th Street south to Houston, anchored by **Urban Outfitters** at 628 Broadway (☎ 212/475-0009) and dotted with skate and sneaker shops—the Village isn't much of a destination for fashion hunters. Clothes hounds looking for volume shopping are better off elsewhere.

The prime drag for strolling is bustling **Bleecker Street,** where you'll find lots of leather shops and record stores interspersed with a good number of interesting and artsy boutiques. Narrow **Christopher Street** is another fun street to browse, because it's loaded with genuine Village character.

THE FLATIRON DISTRICT & UNION SQUARE

When 23rd Street was the epitome of New York Uptown fashion more than a hundred years ago, the major department stores stretched along **Sixth Avenue** for about a mile from 14th Street up. These elegant stores stood in huge cast-iron buildings that were long ago abandoned and left to rust. In the last few years, however, the area has been rezoned and turned into the city's discount shopping center, with superstores and off-pricers filling up the renovated spaces: **Filene's Basement, TJMaxx,** and **Bed Bath & Beyond,** are all at 620 Sixth Ave., while witty **Old Navy,** the cheaper version of the Gap, is next door.

The city's best **Barnes & Noble** towers over Union Square at 22 E. 17th St. (☎ 212/253-0810). On the other side of the square is the city's second **Virgin Megastore,** 52 E. 14th St., at Broadway (☎ 212/598-4666). Just a few blocks north of Union Square is ♻ **ABC Carpet & Home,** 888 Broadway at 19th St. (☎ 212/473-3000), a magnet for aspiring Martha Stewarts.

Upscale retailers who have rediscovered the architectural majesty of **lower Fifth Avenue** include retro-inspired **Restoration Hardware,** at 22nd Street (☎ 212/260-9479), plus national mainstays like **Victoria's Secret.** You won't find too much that's new along here, but it's a pleasing stretch nonetheless.

HERALD SQUARE & THE GARMENT DISTRICT

Herald Square—where 34th Street, Sixth Avenue, and Broadway converge—is dominated by **Macy's,** the self-proclaimed world's biggest department store, and other famous-name shopping, like **Toys '✱' Us** at 34th and Broadway (☎ 212/594-8697). At Sixth Avenue and 33rd Street is the **Manhattan Mall** (☎ 212/465-0500), home to mall standards like **Foot Locker** and **Radio Shack.**

A long block over on Seventh Avenue, not much goes on in the grimy, heavily industrial Garment District. This is, however, where you'll find that quintessential New York experience, the sample sale; point your web browser for **www.samplesale.com** for the latest on sales in New York City.

TIMES SQUARE & THE THEATER DISTRICT

This neighborhood has become increasingly family-oriented: hence, **Disney** and **Warner Bros.** outposts at the crossroads of Times Square, Richard Branson's rollicking **Virgin Megastore,** Broadway at 45th St. (☎ **212/921-1020**), and **Skechers** for teenybopping tennies on Seventh Avenue just south of 42nd Street (☎ **212/ 354-8110**).

West 47th Street between Fifth and Sixth avenues is the city's famous **Diamond District.** Apparently, more than 90% of the diamonds sold in the United States come through this neighborhood first, so there are some great deals to be had if you're in the market for a nice rock or another piece of fine jewelry. Be ready to wheel and deal with the largely Hasidic dealers, who offer quite a juxtaposition to the crowds that people the rest of the area. For a complete introduction to the district, including smart buying tips, point your web browser to **www.47th-street.com**. For semiprecious stones, head one block over to the **New York Jewelry Mart,** 26 W. 46th St. (☎ **212/575-9701**). Virtually all of these dealers are open Monday through Friday only.

You'll also notice a wealth of electronics stores throughout the neighborhood, many trumpeting GOING OUT OF BUSINESS sales. These guys have been going out of business since the Stone Age. That's the bait and switch; pretty soon you've spent too much money for not enough stereo. If you want to check out what they have to offer, go in knowing what going prices are on that PDA or digital camera you're interested in. You can make a good deal if you know exactly what the market is, but these guys will be happy to suck you dry given half a chance.

FIFTH AVENUE & 57TH STREET

The heart of Manhattan retail is the corner of Fifth Avenue and 57th Street. Time was, only the very rich could make this sacred crossroads their ground-zero shopping site. Not anymore, now that the world's most famous jeweler, **Tiffany & Co.,** which has long reigned supreme at Fifth Avenue and 57th Street (☎ **212/ 755-8000**), sits across the street from a **Warner Bros. Studio Store**

(☎ 212/754-0300). Nearby are **Niketown,** 6 E. 57th St. (☎ **212/ 891-6453**), and the dazzling new **NBA Store,** Fifth Avenue and 52nd Street (☎ **212/515-NBA1**). In addition, a good number of mainstream retailers like **Liz Claiborne** have set up their flagships along Fifth (at 50th Street; ☎ **212/956-6505**), further democratizing the avenue.

Fifth Avenue has only a few big-name designer boutiques left in the 50s, although the opening of the **Gianni Versace** shop at 647 Fifth Ave. (☎ **212/317-0224**) just before his death has heralded a new era of respect for the avenue. Other deluxe designer tenants are **Gucci,** at no. 685 (☎ **212/826-2600**), and **Christian Dior,** no. 703 (☎ **212/223-4646**). You'll also find big-name jewelers like **Van Cleef & Arpels,** at no. 744 (☎ **212/644-9500**). Chi-chi department stores like **Bergdorf Goodman, Henri Bendel,** and **Saks Fifth Avenue** have also helped the Avenue maintain its classy cachet.

While 57th Street has similarly changed in the last few years, many big names are still hanging on. Italian knit queen **Laura Biagiotti** is at 4 W. 57th St. (☎ **212/399-2533**); **Chanel** is at 15 E. 57th St. (☎ **212/355-5050**); and **Prada** is at 45 E. 57th St. (☎ **212/308-2332**).

MADISON AVENUE

Madison Avenue from 57th to 79th streets has usurped Fifth Avenue as *the* tony shopping street in the city. In fact, in 1998, it vaunted ahead of Hong Kong's Causeway Bay to become the most expensive retail real estate in the world. Bring lots of plastic.

This strip of Madison is home to the most luxurious designer boutiques in the world, with **Barneys New York** as the anchor. **Calvin Klein** is all chrome and clean edges at 654 Madison Ave., between 60th and 61st streets (☎ **212/292-9000**), hawking magnificent threads for men and women with megabucks, plus home furnishings. **Giorgio Armani** holds minimalist court at 760 Madison Ave. (☎ **212/988-9191**), while Italian super-chic is at home at **Dolce & Gabanna,** no. 825 (☎ **212/249-4100**). **Ralph Lauren**'s stunner of a store at no. 867 (☎ **212/606-2100**) is the ultimate in all-American style. Look for **Donna Karan** to open a flagship on Madison between 68th and 69th; her more accessible **DKNY** store at Madison and 60th will be open by the time you arrive.

For those of us without unlimited fashion budgets, the good news is that stores like **Crate & Barrel,** at 59th Street (☎ **212/ 308-0011**), and the fabulous **Ann Taylor** flagship, at 60th Street (☎ **212/832-2010**), make the untouchable Madison Avenue seem approachable and affordable. Shoe freaks from budget to deluxe should be on the lookout for **Cole-Haan** at no. 667 (☎ **212/421-8400**), where style triumphs over trendiness; **Timberland,** no. 709 (☎ **212/754-0434**), for the best in rugged footwear; and **Sergio Rossi,** no. 835 (☎ **212/396-4814**), for glamorous mules, sexy slingbacks, and classic pointy-toe pumps.

THE TOP DEPARTMENT STORES

Barney's New York. 660 Madison Ave. (at 61st St.). ☎ **212/826-8900.** Subway: N, R to Fifth Ave.

New York's self-made temple of chic has been plagued with financial woes (and the accompanying publicity storm) over the last few years, so severe that they forced the closure of the original Chelsea location. You wouldn't know it by walking into the Madison Avenue store, though—its eight floors of menswear and eight floors of womenswear and accessories exude impeccable high style. While the store focuses on hot-off-the-runway womenswear, its menswear runs the gamut from classic to cutting-edge. Chelsea Passage, the gift/tabletop department, is one of the world's best such spaces. Bring your platinum card, because nothing comes cheap here.

✪ **Bloomingdale's.** 1000 Third Ave. (Lexington Ave. at 59th St.). ☎ **212/705-2000.** Subway: 4, 5, 6 to 59th St.

This is my favorite of New York's big department stores. It's more accessible than Barneys or Bergdorf's and more affordable than Saks, but still has the New York pizzazz that Macy's and Lord and Taylor now largely lack. Taking up the space of a city block, Bloomie's has just about anything you could want, from clothing (both designer and everyday basics) and fragrances to housewares and furniture. The main entrance is on Third Avenue, but pop up to street level from the 59th Street station and you'll be right at the Lexington Avenue entrance.

✪ **Century 21.** 22 Cortlandt St. (btw. Broadway and Church St.). ☎ **212/227-9092.** Subway: 1, 9, N, R to Cortlandt St.; 4, 5 to Fulton St.; C, E to World Trade Center.

Just across from the World Trade Center, Century 21 long ago achieved legend status as *the* designer discount store. If you don't mind wrestling with the aggressive, ever-present throngs, this is where you'll find those $20 Todd Oldham pants or the $50 Bally loafers you've been dreaming of—not to mention underwear, hosiery, and ties so cheap that they're almost free. Don't think that

$250 Armani blazer is a bargain? Look again at the tag—the retail price on it is upwards of $800.

Henri Bendel. 712 Fifth Ave. (at 56th St.). ☎ **212/247-1100.** Subway: N, R to Fifth Ave.

This beautiful Fifth Avenue store is a lot of fun to browse. It feels like you're shopping in the townhouse of a confident, monied old lady who doesn't think twice about throwing on a little something by Anna Sui and a outrageously wide-brimmed hat to go out shopping for the day—and she's got the panache to pull it off. It's a super-stylish, high-ticket collection, but the sales are good, and there's always some one-of-a-kind accessories that make affordable souvenirs (and earn you one of their black-and-white striped shopping bags, the best in town). The interior is so divine that you should remember to take a break from perusing the racks to look up, down, and around every once in awhile.

Macy's. At Herald Square, W. 34th St. and Broadway. ☎ **212/695-4400.** Subway: 1, 2, 3, 9, B, D, F, Q, N, R to 34th St.

A four-story sign on the side of the building trumpets, "MACY'S, THE WORLD'S LARGEST STORE"—a hard fact to dispute, since the ten-story behemoth covers an entire city block, even dwarfing Bloomie's on the other side of town. Macy's is a hard place to shop: The size is unmanageable, the service is dreadful, and the incessant din from the crowds on the ground floor alone will kick your migraine into action. But they do sell *everything*. Massive renovation over the past few years has redesigned many departments into more manageable "mini-stores"—there's a Metropolitan Museum Gift Shop, a Swatch boutique, and cafes and make-up counters on several floors—but the store's one-of-a-kind flair that I remember so well from my childhood is just a memory now. Still, sales run constantly, holiday or no (one-day sales are popular on Wednesdays and Saturdays), so bargains are guaranteed.

Saks Fifth Avenue. 611 Fifth Ave. (btw. 49th and 50th sts.). ☎ **212/753-4000.** Subway: B, D, F, Q to 47–50th sts.–Rockefeller Center; E, F to Fifth Ave.

There are branches of Saks all over the country now, but this is it: Saks *Fifth Avenue*. This legendary flagship store is well worth an hour or two, and the smaller-than-most size makes it manageable in that amount of time. Saks carries a wide range of clothing; departments err on the pricey designer side but run the gamut to affordable house brands. As department stores go, there's something for everyone here. Some call this men's department the finest in the city. The cosmetics and fragrance departments on the main floor are justifiably noteworthy, since they carry many hard-to-find and brand-new brands. Don't miss the holiday windows.

6

New York City After Dark

For the latest, most comprehensive arts and entertainment listings, pick up a copy of *Time Out New York,* or the free weekly *Village Voice,* the city's legendary alterna-paper. Another great weekly is *New York* magazine. The *New York Times* features terrific nightlife coverage, particularly in the two-part Friday "Weekend" section.

Some of your best, most comprehensive and up-to-date information sources for what's going on about town are in cyberspace, of course. Excellent sources worth scanning are **www.newyork.sidewalk.com**, **www.newyork.citysearch.com**, and **www.nytoday.com**, plus **www.papermag.com** for opinionated coverage of the downtown club and bar scenes.

1 The Theater Scene

Nobody does theater better than New York. No other city—not even London—has a theater scene with so much breadth and depth, with so many wide-open alternatives. Broadway, of course, gets the most ink and the most airplay, and deservedly so: Broadway is where you'll find the big stage productions and the moneymakers, from crowd-pleasing warhorses like *Cats* to phenomenal newer successes like *The Lion King.* But today's scene is thriving beyond the bounds of just Broadway: With bankable stars on stage, crowds lining up for hot tickets, and hits popular enough to generate major-label cast albums, off-Broadway isn't just for culture vultures anymore.

Despite this vitality, plays and musicals close all the time, often with little warning, so I can't tell you precisely what will be on while you're in town. Your best bet is to check the publications and websites listed at the start of this chapter to get an idea of what you might like to see. A particularly useful source is the **Broadway Line** (☎ **888/BROADWAY** or 212/302-4111; www.broadway.org), where you can obtain details and descriptions on current Broadway shows, hear about special offers and discounts, and choose to be transferred to Tele-charge to buy tickets. **NYC/Onstage** (☎ **212/768-1818**; www.tdf.org) offers similar service for both Broadway and off-Broadway productions.

ADVANCE TICKET-BUYING TIPS

Phone ahead or go online for tickets to the most popular shows as far in advance as you can—in the case of shows like *The Lion King* and, thus far, *Cabaret,* it's never too early.

Buying tickets can be simple, if the show you want to see isn't sold out. You need only call such general numbers as **Tele-Charge** (☎ 212/239-6200; www.telecharge.com), which handles most Broadway and off-Broadway shows and some concerts; or **TicketMaster** (☎ 212/307-4100; www.ticketmaster.com), which also handles Broadway and off-Broadway shows and most concerts. If you use the **Broadway Line** or **NYC/Onstage** services discussed above to select your show, you can be automatically transferred to the appropriate ticket agency.

If you're an American Express gold card holder, see if tickets are being sold through **American Express Gold Card Events** (☎ 800/ 448-TIKS; www.americanexpress.com/gce). You'll pay full price, but AmEx has access to blocks of preferred seating specifically set aside for gold-card holders, so you may be able to get tickets to a show that's otherwise sold out, or better seats than you would be able to buy through other outlets.

Theatre Direct International (TDI) is a ticket broker that sells tickets to select Broadway and off-Broadway shows direct to individuals and travel agents. Check to see if they have seats to the shows you're interested in by calling ☎ 800/334-8457 or pointing your web browser to **www.theatredirect.com**. (Disregard the discounted prices, unless you're buying for a group of 20 or more; tickets are full price for smaller quantities). With a service charge of $12.50 per ticket, you'll do better by trying TicketMaster or Tele-charge first; but because they act as a consolidator, TDI may have tickets left for a specific show even if the major outlets don't. Other reputable ticket brokers include **Keith Prowse & Co.** (☎ 800/669-8687; www.keithprowse.com) and **Edwards & Edwards Global Tickets** (☎ 800/223-6108).

If you don't want to pay a service charge, try calling the **box office** directly. Broadway theaters don't sell tickets over the telephone, but a good number of off-Broadway theaters do.

GETTING TICKETS WHILE YOU'RE HERE

Once you arrive in the city, getting your hands on tickets can take some street smarts—and failing those, good hard cash. Even if it seems unlikely that seats are available, always **call or visit the box office** before attempting any other route. Single seats are often easiest to obtain, so people willing to sit apart may find themselves in luck.

You should also try the **Broadway Ticket Center** at the Times Square Visitors Center, 1560 Broadway, between 46th and 47th streets (open daily 8am to 8pm). They often have tickets available for otherwise sold-out shows, and only charge $4 extra per ticket.

Even if saving money isn't an issue for you, check the boards at the ✪ **TKTS Booth** at Duffy Square, 47th Street and Broadway (open 3 to 8pm for evening performances, 10am to 2pm for Wednesday and Saturday matinees, from 11am on Sunday for all performances), which sells same-day tickets for both Broadway and off-Broadway shows. Tickets for that day's performances are usually offered at half price, with a few reduced only 25%, plus a $2.50 per ticket service charge. Boards outside the ticket windows list available shows; you're unlikely to find certain perennial or outsize smashes, but most other shows turn up. Cash and traveler's checks only are accepted. There's often a huge line, so show up early for the best availability and be prepared to wait—but frankly, the crowd is all part of the fun. If you don't care much what you see and you'd just like to go to a show, you can walk right up to the window later in the day and something's always available.

Run by the same group and offering the same discounts is the **TKTS Lower Manhattan Theatre Centre,** on the mezzanine of Two World Trade Center (open Monday to Friday 11am to 5:30pm, Saturday 11am to 3:30pm). All the same policies apply. The advantages to coming down here is that the lines are generally shorter; your wait is sheltered indoors; and matinee tickets are available the day before, so you can plan ahead.

In addition, your **hotel concierge** may be able to arrange tickets for you. These are usually purchased through a broker and a premium will be attached, but they're usually good seats and you can count on them being legitimate. If you want to deal with a licensed broker direct, **Global Tickets Edwards & Edwards** has a local office that accommodates drop-ins at 1270 Sixth Ave., on the 24th floor (☎ **212/332-2435;** open Monday to Saturday 9am to 9pm, Sunday noon to 7pm).

If you buy from one of the **scalpers** selling tickets in front of the theater doors, you're taking a risk. They may be perfectly legitimate—a couple from the 'burbs whose companions couldn't make it for the evening, say—but they could be swindlers passing off fakes for big money. It's a risk not worth taking.

2 The Performing Arts: Major Concert Halls & Companies

Brooklyn Academy of Music. 30 Lafayette Ave., Brooklyn. ☎ **718/636-4100.** www.bam.org. Subway: 2, 3, 4, 5, D, Q to Atlantic Ave.; B, M, N, R to Pacific Ave.

BAM, as it's known, is the city's most renowned contemporary arts institution. Offerings have included historically informed presentations of baroque opera by William Christie and Les Arts Florissants; Marianne Faithfull singing the music of Kurt Weill; dance by Mark Morris, Merce Cunningham, and Mikhail Baryshnikov; the Royal Dramatic Theater of Sweden directed by Ingmar Bergman; and many more experimental works by both renowned and lesser-known international artists as well as visiting companies from all over the world. Of particular note is the **Next Wave Festival,** from September through December, this country's foremost showcase for new experimental works.

Carnegie Hall. 881 Seventh Ave. (at 57th St.). ☎ **212/247-7800.** www.carnegiehall.org. Subway: N, R or B, Q to 57th St.

Perhaps the world's most famous performance space, the 2,804-seat main hall welcomes visiting orchestras from across the country and the world. Many of the world's premier soloists and ensembles give recitals. The legendary hall is both visually and acoustically brilliant; don't miss an opportunity to experience it if there's something on that interests you. There's also the intimate 284-seat **Weill Recital Hall,** usually used to showcase chamber music and vocal and instrumental recitals.

City Center. 131 W. 55th St. (btw. Sixth and Seventh aves.). ☎ **212/581-7907.** Subway: N, R or B, Q to 57th St.; B, D, E to Seventh Ave.

Modern dance usually takes center stage in this Moorish dome-topped performing arts palace. Regular performances by the companies of Merce Cunningham, Paul Taylor, Trisha Brown, Alvin Ailey, Twyla Tharp, and the American Ballet Theatre are often on the calendar. Don't expect cutting edge—but do expect excellence. Sightlines are terrific from all corners.

Joyce Theater. 175 Eighth Ave. (at 19th St.). ☎ **212/242-0800.** www.joyce.org. Subway: C, E to 23rd St.; 1, 9 to 18th St.

Housed in an old art deco movie house, the Joyce has grown into one of the world's greatest modern dance institutions. You can see everything from Native American ceremonial dance to Maria Benites Teatro Flamenco to the innovative works of Pilobolus to the Martha

Graham Dance Company. In residence annually is Ballet Tech, which WQXR radio's Francis Mason called "better than a whole month of namby-pamby classical ballets."

✪ **Lincoln Center for the Performing Arts.** 70 Lincoln Center Plaza (at Broadway and 64th St.). ☎ **212/546-2656.** www.lincolncenter.org. Subway: 1, 9 to 66th St.

New York is the world's premier performing arts city, and Lincoln Center is its premier institution. Lincoln Center's many buildings serve as permanent homes to their own companies as well as major stops for world-class performance troupes from around the globe.

Resident companies include the **Metropolitan Opera** (☎ 212/362-6000; www.metopera.org), whose full productions of the classics, regularly starring world-class grand sopranos and tenors, make the Met the world's premier opera house. The opera house also hosts the **American Ballet Theatre** (www.abt.org) each spring, as well as such visiting companies as the Kirov, Royal, and Paris Opéra ballets.

The New York State Theater (☎ **212/870-5570** or ☎ 212/307-4100) is home to the **New York City Opera** (www.nycopera.com), a superb company that attempts to reach a wider audience than the Metropolitan with its more "human" scale and signifcantly lower prices. It's also committed to adventurous premieres, newly composed operas, and American operettas, plus the occasional avant-garde work. Also based here is the world-renowned **New York City Ballet** (www.nycballet.com), founded by George Balanchine and highly regarded for its unsurpassed technique. The cornerstone of the annual season is the Christmastime production of *The Nutcracker.*

Symphonywise, you'd be hard-pressed to do better than the phenomenal **New York Philharmonic** (☎ **212/875-5030** or 212/721-6500 for tickets; www.newyorkphilharmonic.org), performing at Avery Fisher Hall. The country's oldest philharmonic orchestra is under the strict but ebullient guidance of music director Kurt Masur. He's retiring in 2002, so don't miss this chance to see the master conductor leading his orchestra. **Jazz at Lincoln Center** (☎ **212/875-5299;** www.jazzatlincolncenter.org), is led by the incomparable Wynton Marsalis, with the orchestra usually performing at Alice Tully Hall. The **Chamber Music Society of Lincoln Center** (☎ **212/875-5788;** www.chamberlinc.org) performs at Alice Tully Hall or the Rose Rehearsal Studio, often in the company of such high-caliber guests as Anne Sofie Von Otter and Midori.

The **Film Society of Lincoln Center** (☎ **212/875-5600;** www.filmlinc.com), screens a daily schedule of movies at the Walter

Reade Theater, and hosts a number of important annual film and video festivals.

Most of the companies' **major seasons** run from about October to May or June. **Special series** like Great Performers help round out the calendar. Indoor and outdoor events are held in warmer months; check the "Calendar of Events" in chapter 1 or Lincoln Center's website to see what events will be on while you're in town.

Tickets for all performances at Avery Fisher and Alice Tully halls can be purchased through **CenterCharge** (☎ **212/721-6500**) or online at www.lincolncenter.org. Tickets for all Lincoln Center Theater performances can be purchased through **Tele-Charge** (☎ **212/239-6200;** www.telecharge.com). Tickets for New York State Theater productions are available through **TicketMaster** (☎ **212/307-4100;** www.ticketmaster.com), while film tickets can be bought via **Movie Phone** (☎ **212/777-FILM;** www. 777film.com; the theater code is 954).

92nd Street Y. 1395 Lexington Ave. (at 92nd St.). ☎ **212/996-1100.** www.92ndsty.org. Subway: 4, 5, 6 to 86th St.; 6 to 96th St.

This community center offers a phenomenal slate of top-rated cultural happenings. Just because you see "Y," don't think this place is small potatoes: The greatest classical performers—Isaac Stern, Janos Starker, Nadja Salerno-Sonnenberg—give recitals here. In addition, the full concert calendar often includes musical programs from luminaries such as Max Roach and John Williams; Jazz at the Y from Dick Hyman and guests; plus regular chamber music and cabaret programs. The lectures and literary readings calendar is unparalleled, with featured speakers ranging from Lorne Michaels to Ann Richards to Charles Frazier. Best of all, readings and lectures are usually priced between $10 and $15 for non-members (although select lectures can be priced as high as $30), and concert tickets generally go for $25 to $35—half or a third of what you'd pay at comparable venues.

Radio City Music Hall. 1260 Sixth Ave. (at 50th St.). ☎ **212/247-4777,** or 212/307-1000 for tickets. www.radiocity.com. Subway: B, D, F, Q to 49th St./ Rockefeller Center.

This stunning 6,200-seat art deco theater opened in 1932 and continues to be a choice venue, where the theater alone adds a dash of panache to any performance. Star of the Christmas season is the **Radio City Music Hall Christmas Spectacular,** starring the legendary Rockettes. Visiting chart-toppers, from Stevie Nicks to Radiohead, also perform here. Thanks to perfect acoustics and uninterrupted sightlines, there's hardly a bad seat in the house. The theater also hosts a number of annual awards shows—such as the ESPYs and anything MTV is holding in town—so this is a good place to celeb-spot on show nights. The theater is currently under renovation, mainly to bring it up to ADA accessibility code, and is scheduled to reopen by October 1999. In the meantime, the box office remains open.

3 Live Rock, Jazz, Blues & More

Below you'll find only a handful of special venues; there are far more than these around town, and there's always something going on. Check the listings in the *Village Voice* or *Time Out New York* to see what's on around town while you're here.

If you're looking for a rock or pop show by a national act, see what's happening at **The Bottom Line,** 15 W. 4th St. (☎ **212/ 228-7880** or 212/228-6300), one of the city's most comfortable and well-respected venues, especially for acoustic acts; the ✪ **Bowery Ballroom,** 6 Delancey St., at Bowery (☎ **212/533-2111**), a marvelous space accommodating a crowd of 500 or so; **Irving Plaza,** 17 Irving Place, at 15th Street (☎ **212/777-6800**), another pleasing midsized hall; **Roseland,** 239 W. 52nd St. (☎ **212/247-0200**), an old warhorse of a general-admission venue that has hosted everybody from Big Bad Voodoo Daddy to Busta Rhymes to Jeff Beck; and the **Hammerstein Ballroom,** at the Manhattan Center, 311 W. 34th St. (☎ **212/564-4882**), a general admission hall with very good sound and sightlines.

Arlene Grocery. 95 Stanton St. (btw. Ludlow and Orchard sts.). ☎ **212/ 358-1633.** www.arlene-grocery.com. Subway: F to Second Ave.

Live music is always free at this Lower East Side club, which boasts a friendly bar and a good sound system. Arlene Grocery primarily serves as a showcase for unknown bands looking for a deal or promoting their self-pressed record. Still, there's little risk involved thanks to the no-cover policy, and bookers who know what they're doing. The crowd is an easygoing mix of club hoppers, rock fans looking for a new fix, and industry scouts looking for new blood.

✪ **Blue Note.** 131 W. 3rd St. (at Sixth Ave.). ☎ **212/475-8592.** www. bluenote.net. Subway: A, B, C, D, E, F, Q to W. 4th St.

The Blue Note attracts the biggest names in jazz to its intimate setting, from B.B. King to Manhattan Transfer to the superb Oscar Peterson. The sound system is excellent, and every seat in the house has a sightline to the stage. A night here can get expensive, but how often do you get to enjoy jazz of this caliber? Dinner is served (main courses are $19 to $29); also consider a Sunday brunch show.

Cafe Wha? 115 MacDougal St. (btw. Bleecker and W. 3rd sts.). ☎ **212/254-3706.** Subway: A, B, C, D, E, F, Q to W. 4th St.

You'll find a carefree crowd dancing in the aisles of this casual basement club just about any night of the week. From Wednesday through Sunday, the stage features the house's own Wha Band, which does an excellent job cranking out crowd-pleasing covers of familiar rock-and-roll hits from the '70s, '80s, and '90s. Monday night is the hugely popular Brazilian Dance Party, while Tuesday night is Funk Night. Expect to be surrounded by lots of Jersey kids and out-of-towners on the weekends, but so what? You'll be having as much fun as they are.

CBGB's. 315 Bowery (at Bleecker St.). ☎ **212/982-4052,** or 212/677-0455 for CB's 313 Gallery. www.cbgb.com. Subway: 6 to Bleecker St.; F to Second Ave.

The original downtown rock club has seen much better days, but no other spot is so rich with rock-and-roll history—this was the launching pad for New York punk and New Wave. The occasional names still show up (at press time, Tom Tom Club was doing a special 25th Anniversary show) but most acts performing here these days you've never heard of. Never mind—CBGB's still rocks. Expect loud and cynical, and you're unlikely to come away disappointed. Come early if you have hopes of actually seeing the stage, and avoid the bathrooms at all costs.

More today than yesterday is ✪ **CB's 313 Gallery,** a welcome spin-off that showcases alternative art on the walls and mostly acoustic singer/songwriters on stage. Within striking distance of the history, but much more pleasant all the way around.

Chicago B.L.U.E.S. 73 Eighth Ave. (btw. 13th and 14th sts.). ☎ **212/924-9755.** Subway: A, C, E, L to 14th St.

Here's the best blues joint in the city, with a genuine Windy City flair. The contrived decor makes the place feel more theme-park than roadhouse, but the music is the real thing. Kick back on the comfortable couches for some of the best unadulterated blues around, which can include big names like Buddy Miles and Lonnie Brooks.

Iridium. 44 W. 63rd St. (at Columbus Ave., below the Merlot Bar & Grill). ☎ **212/582-2121.** www.iridiumjazz.com. Subway: 1, 9 to 66th St.; 1, 9, A, B, C, D to Columbus Circle.

This well-respected and snazzily designed basement boîte across from Lincoln Center books accomplished acts that play crowd-pleasing standards and transfixing new compositions. The Les Paul Trio still plays every Monday night, and other top-notch performers who often appear include the Frank Foster Quintet, McCoy Tyner, and the excellent Jazz Messengers.

The Knitting Factory. 74 Leonard St. (btw. Broadway and Church St.). ☎ **212/219-3006.** www.knittingfactory.com. Subway: 1, 9 to Franklin St.

New York's premier avant-garde music venue has four separate spaces, each showcasing performances ranging from experimental jazz and acoustic folk to spoken-word and poetry readings to out-there multimedia works. Regulars who use the Knitting Factory as their lab of choice include former Lounge Lizard John Lurie; around-the-bend experimentalist John Zorn; and guitar gods Vernon Reid, Eliot Sharp, and David Torn. (If these names mean nothing to you, chances are good that the Knitting Factory is not for you.) The schedule is peppered with edgy star turns from the likes of Taj Mahal, Faith No More's Mike Patton, and folky charmer Jill Sobule ("I Kissed a Girl"). There are often two shows a night in the remarkably pleasing main peformance space.

✪ **Mercury Lounge.** 217 E. Houston St. (at Essex St./Ave. A). ☎ **212/260-4700.** Subway: F to Second Ave.

The Merc is everything a top-notch live music venue should be: unpretentious, extremely civilized, and outfitted with a killer sound system. The rooms themselves are nothing special: a front bar and an intimate back-room performance space with a low stage and a few tables along the wall. The calendar is filled with a mix of accomplished local rockers and up-and-coming national acts. The crowd is grown-up and easygoing. The only downside is that it's consistently packed thanks to the high quality of the entertainment and all-around pleasing nature of the experience.

✪ **S.O.B's.** 204 Varick St. (at W. Houston St.). ☎ **212/243-4940.** Subway: 1, 9 to Houston St.

This is the city's top world-music venue, specializing in Brazilian, Caribbean, and Latin sounds. The packed house dances and sings along nightly to calypso, samba, mambo, African drums, reggae, or other global grooves, united in the high-energy, feel-good vibe. Bookings include top-flight performers from around the globe; luminaries who have graced the stage include Marc Anthony, Astrud Gilberto, King Sunny Ade, and the unsurpassed Celia Cruz. The room's Tropicana Club style has island pizzazz that carries through to the Caribbean-influenced cooking and tropical drinks menu. This place is so popular that it's an excellent idea to book in advance, especially if you'd like table seating.

The Village Vanguard. 178 Seventh Ave. South (just below 11th St.). ☎ **212/255-4037.** Subway: 1, 2, 3, 9 to 14th St.

What CBGB's is to rock, the Village Vanguard is to jazz. One look at the photos on the walls will show you who's been through: Coltrane, Monk, Miles, and many, many more. Thankfully, this legendary club is just as vital as ever. Expect a mix of established names and high-quality local talent, including the Vanguard's own jazz orchestra. The sound is great but sightlines are terrible, so come early for a front table.

4   Cabaret & Stand-Up Comedy

CABARET

✪ **Cafe Carlyle.** In the Carlyle hotel, 781 Madison Ave. (at 76th St.). ☎ **212/744-1600.** Subway: 6 to 77th St. Closed July–Aug.

Cabaret doesn't get any better than this. Nothing evokes the essence of Manhattan more than an evening with Bobby Short, the quintessential interpreter of Porter and the Gershwins. When he's not in residence, you'll find such rarefied talents as Eartha Kitt, Betty Buckley, and Michael Feinstein. The room is intimate and as swanky as they come. Expect a high tab—admission is $50 with no minimum, but add dinner and two people could easily spend $300—but if you're looking for the best of the best, look no further. On most Mondays, Woody Allen joins the Eddy Davis New Orleans Jazz Band on clarinet to swing Dixie style.

Joe's Pub. At the Joseph Papp Public Theater, 425 Lafayette St. (btw. Astor Place and 4th St.). ☎ **212/539-8777** or Telecharge at 212/239-6200 (for advance tickets). www.publictheater.org. Subway: 6 to Astor Place.

The newest entry on the cabaret circuit is a beautiful new cabaret and supper club eloquently named for the legendary Joseph Papp. The sophisticated crowd comes for top-notch music and spoken word that ranges from legendary Broadway duo Betty Comden and Adolph Green to fiery flamenco dancing to pop golden boy Duncan Sheik. Don't be surprised if Broadway actors show up on off-nights to exercise their substantial chops.

The Oak Room. At the Algonquin hotel, 59 W. 44th St. (btw. Fifth and Sixth aves.). ☎ **212/840-6800.** Subway: B, D, F, Q to 42nd St.

The Oak Room is one of the city's most intimate, elegant, and so-phisticated spots for cabaret. Headliners include such first rate talents as Andrea Marcovicci, Julie Wilson, and cool-cat jazz guitarist John Pizzarelli, plus occasional lesser names destined for greatness. Monday night is Spoken Word night, with speakers as diverse as Spalding Gray and Paul Theroux.

COMEDY

Cover charges are generally in the $8 to $15 range (with all-star Caroline's going as high as $25 on occasion), plus a two-drink minimum.

Caroline's. 1626 Broadway (btw. 49th and 50th sts.). ☎ **212/757-4100.** Subway: 1, 9 to 50th St.; N, R to 49th St.

Caroline Hirsch presents today's hottest headliners in her upscale Theater District showroom. You're bound to recognize at least one or two of the established names and hot up-and-comers on the bill in any given week; Robert Klein even takes the stage on occasion.

✪ **Comedy Cellar.** 117 MacDougal St. (btw. Bleecker and W. 3rd sts.). ☎ **212/254-3480.** Subway: A, B, C, D, E, F, Q to W. 4th St. (use 3rd St. exit).

This intimate subterranean club is the club of choice for stand-up fans in the know, thanks to the best, most consistently impressive lineups in the business. I'll always love the Comedy Cellar for introducing an uproariously funny unknown comic named Ray Romano to me a few years back.

Gotham Comedy Club. 34 W. 22nd St. (btw. Fifth and Sixth aves.). ☎ **212/367-9000.** www.citysearch.com/nyc/gothamcomedy. Subway: N, R or F to 23rd St.

Here's the city's trendiest and most sophisticated comedy club. The young talent—Tom Rhodes, Jeff Ross, Paul Mercurio—is red-hot. Look for theme nights like the lovelorn laugh riot "Breakup Girl Live!" and "A Very Jewish Thursday."

5 Bars & Cocktail Lounges

DOWNTOWN

Chumley's. 86 Bedford St. (btw. Grove and Barrow sts.). ☎ **212/675-4449.** Subway: 1, 9 to Christopher St.–Sheridan Square.

A classic. Many bars in New York date their beginnings to Prohibition, but Chumley's still has the vibe. The circa college-age crowd doesn't date back nearly as far, however. Come to warm yourself by the fire and indulge in a once-forbidden pleasure: beer. The door is unmarked, with a metal grille on the small window; another entrance is at 58 Barrow St., which takes you in through a back courtyard.

✪ **dba.** 41 First Ave. (btw. 2nd and 3rd sts.). ☎ **212/475-5097.** Subway: F to Second Ave.

Along with Temple Bar (below), this is my other favorite bar in the city. It has completely bucked the loungey trend that has taken over the city, instead remaining firmly and resolutely an unpretentious neighborhood bar, where everyone is welcome and at home. Most importantly, dba is a beer- and scotch-lover's paradise. Owner Ray Deter specializes in British-style cask-conditioned ales (the kind that you pump by hand) and stocks a phenomenal collection of 90 single-malt scotches. The relaxed crowd is a pleasing mix of connoisseurs and casual drinkers who like the unlimited choices and egalitarian vibe. Excellent jukebox, too.

✪ **The Greatest Bar on Earth.** 1 World Trade Center, 107th floor (on West St., btw. Liberty and Vesey sts.) ☎ **212/524-7000.** www. windowsontheworld.com. Subway: 1, 9, C, E to Church St.; N, R to Cortlandt St.

High atop the World Trade Center sits The Greatest Bar on Earth, whose name is only a slight exaggeration. This is a magical spot for cocktails and dancing (mostly swing); the music is loud, and the joint really jumps as the night goes on. No matter how many times I come up here, I'm wowed by the incredible views. The place is huge, but intimate nooks and a separate back room bring the scale down to comfortable proportions. The crowd is a lively mix of in-the-know locals and stylish out-of-towners. Quintessentially—and spectacularly—New York.

Idlewild. 145 E. Houston St. (btw. First and Second aves., on the south side of Houston). ☎ **212/477-5005.** Subway: F to Second Ave.

It may look unapproachable from the street, with nothing but an unmarked stainless-steel facade, but inside you'll find a fun, easygoing bar that's perfect for lovers of retro-kitsch. The interior is a larger-scale repro of a jet airplane, complete with reclining seats, tray tables, an Austin Powers-style bar to gather around at center stage, and too-small bathrooms that will transport you back to your favorite mid-air moments in no time. The DJ spins a listener-friendly mix of light techno, groovy disco in the Funkadelic vein, and '80s tunes from the likes of the Smiths and the Cure.

Lucky Cheng's. 24 First Ave. (btw. 1st and 2nd sts.). ☎ **212/473-0516.** Subway: F to Second Ave.

> You gotta have a gimmick if you want to get ahead, according to *Gypsy*—so why not go the RuPaul route? The Asian fusion food is beside the point at this silly place, so come simply to be entertained by the fabulous drag queens in the brand-new six-screen, state-of-the-art karaoke lounge with a goldfish pond under the plexiglass stage. It's pure camp—like stepping into a production of *The King and I* cast in a New Orleans bordello. You'll find a mixed crowd, suits and jeans, yuppies and gays, with bemused out-of-towners spicing the brew.

The Sporting Club. 99 Hudson St. (btw. Franklin and Leonard sts.). ☎ **212/ 219-0900.** www.thesportingclub.net. Subway: 1, 9 to Franklin St.

> The city's best sports bar is a guy's joint if there ever was one. The space is as big as a linebacker, with giant TV screens at every turn tuned to just about every game on the planet. (Wall Streeters bring their international cohorts here to catch everything from English football to Japanese sumo.) There's no better place for sports fans to get crazy at Super Bowl time and during March Madness. When the big games are over, this turns into a surprisingly popular singles place.

✪ **Temple Bar.** 332 Lafayette St. (just north of Houston St., on the west side of the street). ☎ **212/925-4242.** Subway: B, D, F, Q to Broadway/Lafayette St.; 6 to Bleecker St.

> This gorgeous art deco hangout is, hands down, my favorite lounge in the city. Members of the It crowd will tell you it's passe, which only serves to increase its appeal as far as I'm concerned—it's easy to get in now and, on weeknights at least, you can usually manage to find a comfy seat. Cocktails simply don't get any better than the classic martini or the smooth-as-penoir silk Rob Roy (Johnnie Walker Black, sweet vermouth, bitters). Bring a date—and feel free to invite me along anytime. Temple Bar is a little inconspicuous, so look for the petroglyph-like lizards on the facade.

Wall St. Kitchen & Bar. 70 Broad St. (btw. Beaver and S. William sts., about 1¹/₂ blocks south of New York Stock Exchange). ☎ **212/797-7070.** www.citysearch.com/nyc/wallstkitchen. Subway: 4, 5 to Bowling Green; J, M, Z to Broad St.

> Want to rub elbows with some genuine bulls and bears after a hard day of downtown sightseeing? Head to this surprisingly appealing and affordable bar, housed (appropriately enough) in a spectacular former bank in the heart of the financial district. Wall St. Kitchen

specializes in on-tap beers and "flight" menus of wines and microbrews for tasting. The familiar bar food is well prepared and reasonably priced.

MIDTOWN

Divine Bar. 244 E. 51st St. (btw. Second and Third aves.). ☎ **212/ 319-9463.** www.citysearch.com/nyc/divinebar. Subway: 6 to 51st St.; E, F to Lexington Ave.

This glowing hacienda-style wine bar is a big hit with a cute and sophisticated under-40 crowd (think up-and-coming media types and you'll get the picture), with a few older patrons in the mix who come for the excellent selection of wines and microbrews rather than the pick-up scene. The DJ plays a familiar, radio-friendly mix, and there's live acoustic music on Sundays. Good tapas and an extensive humidor round out the appeal.

Flute. 205 W. 54th St. (btw. Seventh Ave. and Broadway). ☎ **212/265-5169.** Subway: 1, 9 to 50th St.; B, D, E to Seventh Ave.

This sexy subterranean champagne lounge is a terrific place to linger over a glass of the bubbly and fancy finger foods. A DJ spins a funky dance mix later in the evening that makes conversation difficult, but that gives you a perfect excuse to cuddle even closer. If only the service weren't so lackadaisical. Still, a much-needed addition to the Theater District. Look carefully for the stairs leading to the entrance; they're on the north side of the street, about mid-block.

Joe Allen. 326 W. 46th St. (btw. Eighth and Ninth aves.). ☎ **212/581-6464.** Subway: A, C, E to 42nd St.

An upscale pub peopled with Broadway types gives this atmospheric place the edge on Restaurant Row. More than 30 bottled beers are on the shelves. The bar is always hopping, but the American food is reliable and well-priced if you'd rather sit down at a table for a bite. You'll thoroughly enjoy perusing the walls, which are covered with posters and other memorabilia from legendary Broadway flops.

✪ **King Cole Room.** At the St. Regis hotel, 2 E. 55th St. (at Fifth Ave.). ☎ **212/339-6721.** Subway: E, F to 53rd St.

The birthplace of the Bloody Mary, this theatrical spot may just be New York's best hotel bar. The Maxfield Parrish mural alone is worth the price of a classic cocktail. The sophisticated setting demands proper attire, so be sure to dress for the occasion. The *New*

York Times calls the bar nuts "the best in town," but there's an elegant bar food menu if you'd like something more substantial.

Oak Bar. At the Plaza Hotel, 768 Fifth Ave. (at 59th St.). ☎ **212/546-5330.** Subway: N, R to 60th St.

And they do mean oak! The warm wood sets an elegant tone throughout this clubby beer hall. Sumptuous red chairs and old-time waiters set the right mood for the after-work power crowd. The bar gets very crowded after 5pm, but the atmosphere always remains sophisticated and Old World.

Pete's Tavern. 129 E. 18th St. (at Irving Place). ☎ **212/473-7676.** Subway: 4, 5, 6, N, R, L to 14th St./Union Square.

This old-timer features sidewalk space for summer imbibing, Guinness on tap, and a St. Patrick's Day party that makes the neighbors crazy. But the best thing in Pete's (opened in 1864—while Lincoln was still president!) is the happy hour, where drinks are cheap and the crowd is a mix of locals from ritzy Gramercy Park and more down-to-earth types.

Pen-Top Bar & Terrace. On the 23rd floor of the Peninsula hotel, 700 Fifth Ave. (at 55th St.). ☎ **212/956-2888.** Subway: E, F to Fifth Ave.

This petite penthouse bar offers some of midtown's most dramatic views. Best of all is the huge rooftop patio—much bigger than the bar itself—which is midtown's best open-air spot on warm evenings. Expect an extremely well-heeled crowd that doesn't mind the big tab that follows cocktails here. This place is extremely popular, so don't be surprised if you can't get in, especially on nights when the weather isn't accommodating to alfresco revelers.

UPTOWN

✪ **Bemelmans Bar.** At the Carlyle hotel, 35 E. 76th St. (at Madison Ave.). ☎ **212/744-1600.** Subway: 6 to 77th St.

Named after children's book illustrator Ludwig Bemelmans, who created the Madeline books after he painted the whimsical mural here, this pub is a supremely luxurious spot for cocktails. Tuck into a dark, romantic corner and nurse a classic martini (both house bartenders have been on the job for 40 years) as you eye the best-heeled crowd in town. A pianist tickles the ivories throughout the evening.

O'Neal's. 49 W. 64th St. (btw. Broadway and Central Park West). ☎ **212/787-4663.** Subway: 1, 9 to 66th St.

O'Neal's easygoing, old-time atmosphere makes it a favorite among a grown-up neighborhood crowd as well as students from nearby Juilliard. Lincoln Center is a stone's throw away, making this a great place for a pre-theater cocktail or a reasonably priced, if unremarkable, bite to eat.

Shark Bar. 307 Amsterdam Ave. (btw. 74th and 75th sts.). ☎ **212/874-8500.** Subway: 1, 2, 3, 9 to 72nd St.

This perennially popular upscale spot is well known for its good soul food and even better singles' scene. It's also a favorite hangout for sports celebs, so don't be surprised if you spot a New York Knick or two.

6 Dance Clubs & Party Scenes

First things first: Finding and going to the latest hotspot are not worth agonizing over. Clubbers spend their lives obsessing over the scene. My rule of thumb is that if I know about a place, it must not be hip anymore. Even if I could tell you where the hippest club kids hang out today, they'll have moved on by the time you arrive in town.

You can find listings for the most current hotspots and moveable parties in the publications and online sources listed at the start of this chapter. Another good bet is to cruise hip boutiques in SoHo, the East Village, and the Lower East Side, where party planners usually leave flyers advertising the latest goings-on. No matter what, **always call ahead,** because schedules change constantly, and can do so at the last minute.

New York nightlife starts late: With the exception of places that have scheduled performances, it's almost useless to show up anywhere before about 11pm. Bring cash, and plan on dropping a wad at most places. Cover charges start out high—anywhere from $10 to $25—and often get more expensive as the night wears on.

China Club. 268 W. 47th St. (btw. Broadway and Eighth Ave.). ☎ **212/398-3800.** Subway: N, R to 49th St.

The China Club has been a top choice for club hoppers for years now, and it's still a great place to shake your booty. This huge club draws in the crowds with a top-flight sound system, fiber-optic lighting, and a good, accessible dance music mix. Trendy types gravitate to the bar and VIP lounge, where Broadway hopefuls mix with famous faces on occasion.

Life. 158 Bleecker St. (Sullivan & Thompson sts.). ☎ **212/420-1999.** Subway: A, B, C, D, E, F, Q to W. 4th St.

This velvet-drenched, faux-deco nightclub was *the* clubbers' hotspot a few years back, and it just keeps on going. The formula changes every night: Lifestyle Fridays draws a fabulous fashion crowd; Wednesdays offer the star-studded house party Legends as well as retro-campy Lust for Life, which books '80s throwbacks like the Human League alongside local glam acts; and Boy's Life Sundays draws beautiful Chelsea boys looking for the same.

✪ **Mother.** 432 W. 14th St. (at Washington St.). ☎ **212/366-5680.** Subway: A, C, E to 14th St.

Fabulous hipsters, both gay and straight, crowd this joint for a variety of hugely popular events. On Tuesday it's Jackie 60 (☎ **212/929-6060;** www.echonyc.com/~interjackie), which *Paper* magazine calls "the mother of all freak fests." Almost as popular is Saturday's Click + Drag, a futuristic techno-fetish party from the same team. Performance art, poetry readings, and other multimedia fun round out the goings-on. Call to check if a strict dress code is being enforced the night you go.

✪ **Nell's.** 246 W. 14th St. (btw. Seventh and Eighth aves.). ☎ **212/675-1567.** Subway: 1, 2, 3, 9, A, C, E to 14th St.

Nell's was the first to establish a loungelike atmosphere years ago. It has been endlessly copied by restaurateurs and nightclub owners, who have since realized that if people wanted to stay home, why not make "out" just as comfy as "in"? Nell's attracts everyone from homies to Wall Streeters. Most of the parties have a soulful edge. Look for the hugely popular laid-back Voices, sort of a sophisticated weekly *Star Search* that's a showcase for a surprising number of new talents.

Polly Esther's. 1487 First Ave. (btw. 77th and 78th sts.). ☎ **212/628-4477.** www.pollyesthers.com. Subway: 6 to 77th St. Also at 186 W. 4th St. (btw. Sixth and Seventh aves.). ☎ **212/924-5707.** Subway: 1, 9 to Christopher St.–Sheridan Square.

Here's the ultimate '70s theme bar and club, where you can groove to the sounds of K.C., the Bee Gees, Abba, and every other band you loved when you still listened to AM radio and turned the dial on the TV set. Decor runs along Brady Bunch and Partridge Family lines, with tons of Me-decade pop memorabilia throughout. This place is really targeted to tourists, but who cares? Dig out those

It Might As Well Be Swing

It may have taken some time for the swing thing to make its way to the right coast, but New York has taken to it with a vengeance. It's a zoot suit riot, man.

Swing is a nightly affair at **Swing 46,** a jazz and supper club at 349 W. 46th St. (☎ **212/262-9554**). There's live swing every night at 10pm from big bands with names like the Flipped Fedoras and the Crescent City Maulers, as well as the club's own 15-piece Make-Believe Ballroom Orchestra. The young, enthusiastic crowd dresses to the nines, '40s style, and really knows the moves. Even if you're a first-timer, you can join in, too: Just come early for free swing lessons at 7 and 9pm.

On weekends, probably the best place to get jiggy is the **Supper Club,** 240 W. 47th St., between Broadway and Eighth Avenue (☎ **212/921-1940**), an ultra-plush dance hall that's been dressed and waiting for the swing trend to come along for a few years now. The 16-piece house band plays old-school swing every Friday and Saturday night early on for an older supper crowd. Later in the evening, around 11pm, the tables are cleared and the neo-swingers show up to strut their stuff to an ultra-hot visiting jump band like Zoot Suit Revue or Harlem's Yallopin' Hounds.

Another terrific spot for swing is **The Greatest Bar on Earth,** high atop 1 World Trade Center on the 107th floor (☎ **212/ 524-7000**). The live jive from circuit bands like the Camaros and the Blue Saracens starts Friday and Saturdays at 9pm; Thursdays are usually good for a little Latin-flavored swing. The dance floor is big enough for everybody to enjoy but small enough that you don't feel like you're on display—a blessing for those of us who don't exactly have our moves down pat. And no dance floor has more spectacular views.

bellbottoms, tie on those platform shoes, and hustle on over to Polly Esther's for a nostalgic good time.

If you're more of a Karma Chameleon than a Dancing Queen, then head to **Culture Club,** 179 Varick St., between King and Charlton streets (☎ **212/243-1999**), where the big '80s come to life in similarly silly fashion.

Roxy. 515 W. 18th St. (at Tenth Ave.). ☎ **212/645-5156.** Subway: 1, 9 to 18th St.

Getting Beyond the Velvet Rope

If your heart's set on getting into an exclusive club or lounge, here are a few pointers that may help to tip the scale in your favor:

- **Dress well and fashionably.** Like it or not, the doorman is sizing you up. If you want to get in, you have to play along.
- **Arrive early.** The bouncers are just not as vigilant at 9pm, when the place is half empty, as they are at 11pm—and once you're inside, you're in for the night if you wish. Weeknights are also a better bet.
- **Be polite.** No matter how obnoxious the doorman may be, giving attitude back won't help. And who knows? You might just charm him with your winning personality.
- **Don't try to talk your way in.** These guys have heard it all. If you're not wanted, why bother? Take your business to a friendlier establishment, where you'll be happier in the long run.

This could be the single best place to see the Manhattan night mix. You'll find fashion models, city club kids, wide-eyed kids from the 'burbs, straights and gays of every color, plus lights, sound, and action. Glamour is in the air, the space is monumental, and the beehive wigs reach for the stars. There's in-line roller disco on Tuesday (predominantly gay) and Wednesday (mixed). Friday nights draw a big Hispanic crowd with salsa and merengue, while Saturdays bring in a committed mixed gay/straight crowd in love with DJ Victor Calderone's tribal house mix. There's also a martini lounge, a cigar bar, and two VIP rooms.

Twilo. 530 W. 27th St. (btw. Tenth and Eleventh aves.). ☎ **212/268-1600.** Subway: C, E to to 23rd St.

Go west—way west—to this mega-size dance factory, on the site of the legendary Sound Factory. Superstar DJ Junior Vasquez still spins pulsating dance music marathons, called Juniorverse, for an adoring, mostly gay crowd on Saturdays. Fridays draw an energized straight crowd with imported international DJs.

XIT. 511 Lexington Ave. (btw. 47th and 48th sts.). ☎ **212/371-1600.** Subway: 4, 5, 6, 7 to Grand Central.

The former home of urban hoedown Denim & Diamonds has been transformed into a baby-boomer hangout spinning a mainstream mix of tunes ranging from the '60s to the top hits of today. Wednesday is salsa night, with a live band providing the beat. The club owners have issued a "no attitude" promise to the press, so everyone should feel comfortable here. There's a pool room in back.

7   The Gay & Lesbian Scene

For an up-to-date take on what's happening in gay and lesbian nightlife, pick up a free copy of *Homo Xtra (HX)* or *HX for Her,* available for free in bars and clubs or at the Lesbian and Gay Community Center (see "Tips for Travelers with Special Needs" in chapter 2), or go online at **www.hx.com**. *Time Out New York* also boasts a terrific gay and lesbian section.

These days, many bars, clubs and cocktail lounges are neither gay nor straight but a bit of both. Most of the clubs listed under "Dance Clubs & Party Scenes" above cater to a gay crowd, some predominately so.

Barracuda. 275 W. 22nd St. (btw. Seventh and Eighth aves.). ☎ **212/ 645-8613.** Subway: 1, 9 or C, E to 23rd St.

Chelsea is now central to gay life—and gay bars. This trendy, loungy place was voted "Best Bar" by *HX* and *New York Press* magazines, while *Paper* singles out the hunky bartenders. Look for the regular drag shows.

Henrietta Hudson. 438 Hudson St. (at Morton St.). ☎ **212/924-3347.** Subway: 1, 9 to Houston St.

This friendly and extremely popular women's bar is known for drawing in an attractive crowd that comes for the great jukebox and videos as well as the pleasingly low-key atmosphere.

✪ **Meow Mix.** 269 E. Houston St. (btw. avenues A and B) ☎ **212/ 254-0688.** Subway: F to Second Ave.

This funky two-level East Villager is the city's best, and probably its most popular, lesbian hangout. It draws in a young, attractive, arty crowd with nightly diversions like groovy DJs and the hugely popular Xena Night. Meow Mix is also booking an increasing number of good local bands, with most nights dedicated to the girls but one night set aside for all-boy bands.

Stonewall. 53 Christopher St. (just east of Seventh Ave. South). ☎ **212/ 463-0950.** Subway: 1, 9 to Christopher St.–Sheridan Square.

A new bar at the spot where it all started. A mixed male crowd—old and young, beautiful and great personalities—makes this an easy place to begin.

✪ **Wonder Bar.** 505 E. 6th St. (btw. avenues A and B). ☎ **212/777-9105.**
Subway: 6 to Astor Place.

The "sofa look" has lent a loungier, more stylish tone to this packed-
on-weekends East Village hangout. There's some male cruising, but
fun and friendly Wonder Bar gets points for making staights feel
welcome, too. DJs now spin a listener-friendly mix from the re-
vamped back room.

Index

See also separate Accommodations and Restaurants indexes, below.
Page numbers in *italics* refer to maps.

FROMMER'S® COMPLETE TRAVEL GUIDES

Alaska
Amsterdam
Arizona
Atlanta
Australia
Austria
Bahamas
Barcelona, Madrid & Seville
Beijing
Belgium, Holland & Luxembourg
Bermuda
Boston
Budapest & the Best of Hungary
California
Canada
Cancún, Cozumel &
  the Yucatán
Cape Cod, Nantucket & Martha's Vineyard
Caribbean
Caribbean Cruises & Ports of Call
Caribbean Ports of Call
Carolinas & Georgia
Chicago
China
Colorado
Costa Rica
Denmark
Denver, Boulder & Colorado Springs
England
Europe
Florida
France
Germany
Greece
Greek Islands
Hawaii
Hong Kong
Honolulu, Waikiki & Oahu
Ireland
Israel
Italy
Jamaica & Barbados
Japan
Las Vegas
London
Los Angeles
Maryland & Delaware
Maui
Mexico
Miami & the Keys

Montana & Wyoming
Montréal & Québec City
Munich & the Bavarian Alps
Nashville & Memphis
Nepal
New England
New Mexico
New Orleans
New York City
Nova Scotia, New Brunswick &
  Prince Edward Island
Oregon
Paris
Philadelphia & the
  Amish Country
Portugal
Prague & the Best of the Czech Republic
Provence & the Riviera
Puerto Rico
Rome
San Antonio & Austin
San Diego
San Francisco
Santa Fe, Taos &
  Albuquerque
Scandinavia
Scotland
Seattle & Portland
Singapore & Malaysia
South Africa
Southeast Asia
South Pacific
Spain
Sweden
Switzerland
Thailand
Tokyo
Toronto
Tuscany & Umbria
USA
Utah
Vancouver & Victoria
Vermont, New Hampshire
  & Maine
Vienna & the Danube Valley
Virgin Islands
Virginia
Walt Disney World & Orlando
Washington, D.C.
Washington State

FROMMER'S® DOLLAR-A-DAY GUIDES

Australia from $50 a Day
California from $60 a Day
Caribbean from $70 a Day
England from $70 a Day
Europe from $60 a Day
Florida from $60 a Day

Hawaii from $70 a Day
Ireland from $50 a Day
Israel from $45 a Day
Italy from $70 a Day
London from $85 a Day
New York from $80 a Day

New Zealand from $50 a Day
Paris from $85 a Day
San Francisco from $60 a Day
Washington, D.C.,
  from $60 a Day

FROMMER'S® PORTABLE GUIDES

Acapulco, Ixtapa &
  Zihuatanejo
Alaska Cruises & Ports of Call
Bahamas
Baja & Los Cabos
Berlin
California Wine Country
Charleston & Savannah
Chicago

Dublin
Hawaii: The Big Island
Las Vegas
London
Maine Coast
Maui
New Orleans
New York City
Paris

Puerto Vallarta, Manzanillo
  & Guadalajara
San Diego
San Francisco
Sydney
Tampa & St. Petersburg
Venice
Washington, D.C.

FROMMER'S® NATIONAL PARK GUIDES

Family Vacations in the
  National Parks
Grand Canyon

National Parks of the
  American West
Rocky Mountain

Yellowstone & Grand Teton
Yosemite & Sequoia/
  Kings Canyon
Zion & Bryce Canyon

FROMMER'S® GREAT OUTDOOR GUIDES

New England
Northern California

Southern California & Baja
Washington & Oregon

FROMMER'S® MEMORABLE WALKS

Chicago
London

New York
Paris

San Francisco
Washington D.C.

FROMMER'S® IRREVERENT GUIDES

Amsterdam
Boston
Chicago
Las Vegas

London
Los Angeles
Manhattan

New Orleans
Paris
San Francisco

Seattle & Portland
Vancouver
Walt Disney World
Washington, D.C.

FROMMER'S® BEST-LOVED DRIVING TOURS

America
Britain
California

Florida
France
Germany

Ireland
Italy
New England

Scotland
Spain
Western Europe

THE UNOFFICIAL GUIDES®

Bed & Breakfast in
New England
Bed & Breakfast in
the Northwest
Beyond Disney
Branson, Missouri
California with Kids
Chicago

Cruises
Florida with Kids
The Great Smoky &
Blue Ridge
Mountains
Inside Disney
Las Vegas

London
Miami & the Keys
Mini Las Vegas
Mini-Mickey
New Orleans
New York City
Paris

San Francisco
Skiing in the West
Walt Disney World
Walt Disney World
for Grown-ups
Walt Disney World
for Kids
Washington, D.C.

SPECIAL-INTEREST TITLES

Born to Shop: France
Born to Shop: Hong Kong
Born to Shop: Italy
Born to Shop: New York
Born to Shop: Paris
Frommer's Britain's Best Bike Rides
The Civil War Trust's Official Guide
to the Civil War Discovery Trail
Frommer's Caribbean Hideaways
Frommer's Europe's Greatest Driving Tours
Frommer's Food Lover's Companion to France
Frommer's Food Lover's Companion to Italy
Frommer's Gay & Lesbian Europe
Israel Past & Present
Monks' Guide to California

Monks' Guide to New York City
The Moon
New York City with Kids
Unforgettable Weekends
Outside Magazine's Guide
to Family Vacations
Places Rated Almanac
Retirement Places Rated
Road Atlas Britain
Road Atlas Europe
Washington, D.C., with Kids
Wonderful Weekends from Boston
Wonderful Weekends from New York City
Wonderful Weekends from San Francisco
Wonderful Weekends from Los Angeles